SUBVERSIVE CITIZENS

Power, agency and resistance in
public services

Edited by Marian Barnes and David Prior

D0967194

This edition published in Great Britain in 2009 by

The Policy Press
University of Bristol
Fourth Floor
Beacon House
Queen's Road
Bristol BS8 1QU
UK

Tel +44 (0)117 331 4054
Fax +44 (0)117 331 4093
e-mail tpp-info@bristol.ac.uk
www.policypress.org.uk

North American office:
The Policy Press
c/o International Specialized Books Services (ISBS)
920 NE 58th Avenue, Suite 300
Portland, OR 97213-3786, USA
Tel +1 503 287 3093
Fax +1 503 280 8832
e-mail info@isbs.com

© The Policy Press 2009

British Library Cataloguing in Publication Data
A catalogue record for this book is available from the British Library.

Library of Congress Cataloging-in-Publication Data
A catalog record for this book has been requested.

ISBN 978 1 84742 207 1 paperback
ISBN 978 1 84742 208 8 hardcover

The right of Marian Barnes and David Prior to be identified as editors of this work
has been asserted by them in accordance with the 1988 Copyright, Designs and
Patents Act.

The statements and opinions contained within this publication are solely those of
the editors and contributors and not of The University of Bristol or The Policy
Press. The University of Bristol and The Policy Press disclaim responsibility for
any injury to persons or property resulting from any material published in this
publication.

The Policy Press works to counter discrimination on grounds of gender, race,
disability, age and sexuality.

Cover design by Qube Design Associates, Bristol.
Front cover: image kindly supplied by www.alamy.com
Printed and bound in Great Britain by MPG Book Group.

In memory of Edna Prior

1920–2008

A gently subversive citizen

Contents

List of figures and tables

Figures

Table

Notes on contributors

Marian Barnes is Professor of Social Policy and Director of the Social Science Policy and Research Centre at the University of Brighton. She researches user involvement, public participation and new forms of democratic practice.

Gale Burford is Professor of Social Work and Director of the State/University Child Welfare Training Partnership at the University of Vermont. His research interests are in family engagement and decision processes in child welfare and youth justice services.

John Clarke is a Professor of Social Policy at the Open University. His work focuses on the politics of remaking welfare, states and nations, in which formations of citizenship occupy a central place.

John Flint is Professor of Housing and Urban Governance in the Centre for Regional Economic and Social Research at Sheffield Hallam University. His research interests include housing policy, housing management, crime and antisocial behaviour, neighbourhood renewal and community cohesion.

Nathan Hughes is Lecturer in Social Policy and Social Work in the School of Social Policy, University of Birmingham. His main research interests are in young people and social exclusion, and the experiences of young people in the youth justice system.

Shona Hunter is RCUK Academic Fellow in the School of Sociology and Social Policy at the University of Leeds. Her research addresses questions about the relationship between 'equalities' policies and the persistence of unequal social relations, including racism and sexism.

Kate Morris is Head of Social Work in the School of Social Policy, University of Birmingham. Her research centres on the involvement of children and families in planning and decision making, family support and prevention and partnership working.

Janet Newman is a Professor of Social Policy and Director of the Publics Research Programme within the Centre for Citizenship, Identities and Governance at The Open University. Her research addresses questions of new formations of governance, professional and organisational change, and the transformations of notions of publics and publicness.

Judy Nixon is Principal Lecturer in Housing Policy in the Centre for Regional Economic and Social Research, Sheffield Hallam University, working primarily in the fields of housing policy and sociolegal issues. She has particular research interests in antisocial behaviour policy and practice.

Sadie Parr is a Research Fellow in the Centre for Regional Economic and Social Research, Sheffield Hallam University. Her research interests lie broadly within the fields of urban governance, crime control and community safety.

David Prior is a Senior Research Fellow in the School of Social Policy, University of Birmingham. He researches policies and practices of local crime control and the governance of antisocial behaviour.

Helen Sullivan is Palmer Professor at the Centre for Public Service Partnerships, University of Birmingham. She has researched and written widely on collaboration, governance, public participation and neighbourhoods.

Louise Westmarland is Senior Lecturer in Criminology and a member of the International Centre for Comparative Criminological Research at The Open University. Her research interests include gender, the body and police culture, corruption and ethics.

Part One
Introduction

ONE

Examining the idea of 'subversion' in public services

Marian Barnes and David Prior

The central question addressed by this book is how front-line staff in public services and the citizens who use those services act in ways that modify, disrupt or negate the intended processes and outcomes of public policy. This is not a new issue. In 1980 Michael Lipsky coined the term 'street-level bureaucrats' to describe the way in which front-line workers could effectively determine policy through their actions, and to explore the way in which workers developed strategies to resist management control of their work. However, the world of public services and public policy has changed substantially since then and some of the most significant changes that have taken place – for example, the introduction of managerialist practices across the public sector – can be considered as responses to the resistance of workers and the need to very precisely counteract aspects of worker agency that undermined the achievement of policy objectives. A second set of changes, and one of the key developments in public policy during the closing years of the twentieth century, stems from the expectation that citizens as well as workers have responsibilities for delivering policy outcomes defined by government. Citizens have themselves become key actors in the delivery of policy at street level. Thus Lipsky's analysis, which locates workers and their clients within different spheres of interest and which views clients solely from the perspective of the workers' strategies for manipulating them, is clearly inadequate to an understanding of the way in which public policy objectives may be subverted within the current context.

The subversive citizens we are interested in here include both workers and citizens – or clients, consumers, users, customers. In this book we focus on workers and citizens and on the relationships between them as they interpret and reinterpret policy; negotiate their own values, identities and commitments in relation to the way in which they are encouraged and exhorted to act; determine what they consider is the right thing to do in particular circumstances; and challenge or resist the identities that are offered to or imposed on them by government.

In the chapters that follow the contributors draw on research in a number of policy areas to reflect on questions such as:

• How do policies seek to fulfil the objective of creating 'responsible citizens' – what does this form of citizenship entail and why does it remain elusive?
• Why does policy implementation sometimes fail, or at least deliver outcomes different from those intended?
• How do front-line public service workers and people who use public services subvert the aims of public policy and why?
• What forms does this subversion take and what are the sources of such alternative expressions of agency?
• What does this tell us about social theories of power and agency and their usefulness in analysing the contemporary governance and policy process?

In this introduction we map the broad landscape within which these detailed case studies are presented. We start by considering those changes in the configuration of public services and in the roles of public service workers that provide the context in which service users and citizens have been 'recruited' to the project of delivering public policy.

Transforming public services: management, governance and modernisation

Few would take issue with the assertion that since the election of Margaret Thatcher in 1979 there have been major transformations in the institutional structures and organisational practices of British public services, and that these have had substantial implications both for staff at the front line of public service delivery and for their users. Since the advent of New Labour in 1997, these processes of transformation have taken the distinctive programmatic form, and ideological justification, of 'modernisation' (Newman, 2001).

In brief, two broad trends can be identified in the shift away from the paternalistic administration that characterised the way the post-1948 welfare state was run. The first, signalling belief in the superiority of the market as a model for organising service provision and in the greater efficiency of the private sector, was the introduction of 'managerialism' to public services (Clarke and Newman, 1997). This involved:

• an emphasis on centrally defined strategy and policy objectives, with service goals expressed in quantifiable targets and outcomes;

- new regimes of accountability, in which processes of audit, inspection and performance management were to replace the professional regulation of services;
- the introduction of economic criteria for assessing service quality, such as 'efficiency' and 'value for money';
- the introduction of 'market mechanisms' such as competitive tendering, the separation of purchasers and providers and the redefinition of the service user as a 'customer' equipped and authorised to exercise 'choice'.

The second trend, stemming from crises in the fiscal viability and political authority of national welfare states, from the challenges of globalisation, and from the pressures of increasingly complex and diverse societies, was the emphasis on 'governance' as both an analytic description of and normative model for a new approach to public services (Rhodes, 2000; Kooiman, 2003). Governance gives prominence to 'networks' as a distinctive means of coordinating economic and social activity, alongside the established forms of 'hierarchies' and 'markets'. The delivery of services is no longer the prerogative of the state and this necessitates a devolution or decentralisation of power and resources away from the central state to a range of public agencies, private sector interests, voluntary organisations and community groups. 'Partnership' between agencies and across sectors becomes the key vehicle for planning and delivering services and thus new policy actors from the business sector, the voluntary sector and from 'communities' become participants in the policy process. In particular, in the context of the analysis we pursue in this book, communities and service users themselves become subjects in, objects of and resources for the policy process.

Both these sets of changes had the effects of transforming the terrain in which public officials work, reducing or constraining the power of some roles (professionals) but significantly enhancing that of others (managers); and of creating new identities for citizen–users – identities which frequently combined an apparent increase in power (as partner, as customer) with increasing responsibilities (to participate in policy making or service delivery, to make informed choices). They also altered the terrain by extending the range of institutional actors with responsibilities and powers for delivering public policy, particularly those in the third sector and in the business world. In New Labour's mission to modernise public services, these changes amount to an attempt to construct a new set of relationships between government, communities and citizens.

Transforming citizenship: private lives and public policy

We have previously argued – as have others – that a major shift within public policy during the second half of the twentieth century was from a conceptualisation of an active state that accepted responsibility for ensuring the welfare of its citizens, to the repositioning of citizens as bearers of duties and responsibilities to others in society (Barnes and Prior, 2000). In this new imagining of the welfare state, 'ordinary citizens, through the choices and actions which make up their everyday private lives, are themselves the primary resources for delivering public policy objectives' (ibid: 6). This shift has had important consequences for people throughout their lives as they interact with different arms of the welfare state, as the following examples illustrate:

- In education, parents have become consumers, responsible for choosing the 'best' school for their child (and sometimes going to great lengths to position themselves geographically and culturally to enable this), but also producers – becoming involved in running schools and having much closer working relationships with teachers and greater responsibilities for ensuring their children's learning. Children themselves have been expected both to take part in citizenship education and to practise citizenship through involvement in school councils and voluntary activities.

- Social security and labour market policies have become dominated by the work ethic. Work is seen as *the* route out of social exclusion and 'hard-working families' have become symbolic of the expectation of personal responsibility for ensuring welfare through work. This personal responsibility extends beyond an obligation to seek and obtain work, into the requirement that 'job seekers' adapt their personal conduct in ways that increase their value in the labour market.

- Responsibilities in relation to health and health services have been seen to reside not only in behaviours that will sustain health and limit demand on services, but also in relation to the responsible use of services: notifying an inability to make an appointment; managing the consumption of medications; taking appropriate measures to assist infection control in hospitals; commenting on services to help improve them, for example. An acceptance of the reality of health inequalities led to a dual strategy of state action and encouragement of healthy behaviours, what has subsequently been explicitly described as 'Choosing Health' (Department of Health, 2004).

- Previously implicit assumptions about family responsibilities for care giving have become an explicit 'cornerstone' of policy regarding social care for adults, and parental responsibilities for children are embodied in legislation. More recently, earlier reticence about the appropriateness of consumerism to social care has been swept aside, and with the introduction of individual or personal budgets service users are expected to take on responsibilities for planning and monitoring their own support services, at the same time ensuring that government-defined outcomes are achieved.

- Social housing provision has also become a site of action to influence and control behaviour. Tenants are required to enter into contractual obligations to conduct themselves in certain ways and to take responsibility for the conduct of other household members, and there is also an explicit expectation that tenants will take on collective responsibilities for aspects of the management of their estate or neighbourhood.

- Finally, the regulation of crime and disorder has become an activity in which 'local communities' are expected to play their part. There is a strong policy emphasis on local communities being 'empowered' to take responsibility for safety and security within their neighbourhood; parents can be subject to legal sanctions for failure to control the behaviour of their children; and behaviours that are not illegal can nonetheless be deemed 'antisocial' and subjected to legal controls (see chapters by Prior and Flint in this collection).

As these examples suggest, the emphasis on citizens being identified as responsible for acting in their private lives in ways that will contribute to the delivery of public policy objectives has been accompanied by an increasing emphasis on citizens and service users as contributors to the process of policy making and service delivery by taking on more public responsibilities. User involvement, community engagement, public participation – whatever the language used, across all areas of public policy it is now official policy that citizens should be actively involved in policy making and implementation (eg DCLG, 2007; Andersson et al, 2008; Barnes et al, 2008).

Subverting public policy

The transformations outlined above in the organisation and purpose of public services and in the relations of citizenship have not always proceeded smoothly or with the effects intended by government. One reason for this is that both public service workers and the citizen-users of services can and do act in ways that obstruct, deflect or subvert desired policy outcomes.

Thus, New Labour politicians have sometimes identified front-line workers as the 'enemy' standing in the way of 'modernisation' (Barton, 2008). Notoriously, in a speech to the British Venture Capitalists Association in 1999 Tony Blair referred to having 'scars on my back' after two years of seeking public service reform. In response Mooney and Law (2007) point to resistance and opposition within the workplace that has been focused on protecting public services. Thus, they discuss industrial action focused not on pay and conditions, but on the way in which public services are being delivered: for example, among social workers in Liverpool resisting the deskilling of social work (Lavalette, 2007) and among Department for Work and Pensions employees concerned not only about their jobs but about the deterioration in services available to disadvantaged people (McCafferty and Mooney, 2007). But in addition to collective resistance through trade union action, we can see more individualised responses to changes that are experienced as personally stressful and as undermining the values and commitments that brought people into front-line welfare work. This can include 'exit', for example nurses deciding to leave the NHS and join a nurse bank or leaving the profession altogether (Kennedy and Kennedy, 2007); the adoption of a 'reflective practice' which may challenge or conflict with dominant managerialist cultures (Issitt, 2000); or simply ignoring or bending the 'rules', as illustrated in the stories of teachers, police officers and counsellors in the US told by Maynard–Moody and Musheno (2003).

Certain groups of citizens have also been identified by government, explicitly or implicitly, as barriers to, if not potential saboteurs of, the mission to create a modernised, inclusive society by their reluctance to accept the 'responsibilities' on which citizenship status has become increasingly conditional (Dwyer, 2004; Flint, this volume). Such reluctance is countered with forms of official stigmatisation, exhortation and coercion (Barnes and Prior, 2000; Hewitt, 2000). Thus, people who resist the lure of the labour market because of childcare commitments or because of long-term ill-health or disability have been cast as 'work shy', subjected to increasing investigation of their capacity for work and 'encouraged' through possible withdrawal of social security benefits. Parents who do not ensure their child attends school or do not provide adequate support for the child's learning are stigmatised as irresponsible and, where persistent absence from school is involved, have been imprisoned. People described as antisocial are labelled as 'neighbours from hell', accused of destroying the quality of life of the 'decent majority' and wrecking communities, and subject to a range of legal sanctions (see Prior, Flint, and Parr and Nixon, this volume). Minority ethnic groups who maintain their own beliefs, customs and social networks have been viewed as excluding themselves from mainstream British society and put under growing pressure to 'integrate' (see Flint, this volume). These instances can be seen as different kinds of exception – as limiting cases – to the overall policy aim of creating responsible citizens who, in their everyday private activities, engage in and contribute to the productive social and economic life of the nation.

The opening up of opportunities for citizen participation in the policy process brings with it other possibilities for unintended policy outcomes. The diversity of context, approach and purpose that is evident within participation initiatives reflects different ideological influences and different discourses through which such practices are constructed. Barnes et al (2007) highlight four different discourses that are relevant to our discussion here: the 'empowered public', the 'stakeholder public', the 'consuming public' and the 'responsible public'. In each case it is possible to identify not only ways in which it is intended that different publics might contribute to policy objectives: relating to service provision, social order and cohesion, institutional and democratic process objectives, and outcomes relating to social inclusion and better health, for example; but also how participation might impact on those publics themselves, such as by increasing individual and collective capacity, and the development of civic virtues. What goes on in the spaces created for participative policy making is thus vital to understanding the potential for citizens to contribute to or subvert policy.

At the same time as citizens have been invited (Cornwall and Coelho, 2004) or encouraged to take part in official processes of policy making, they have also been offering challenges to policies and to the power of those delivering public services, through autonomous action among user groups, community groups and social movements (eg Campbell and Oliver, 1996; Barnes and Bowl, 2001; Wainwright, 2003). In terms of tactics, members of such groups have often had to make decisions about whether to 'take advantage of' the opportunities opened up by more participative approaches to policy making, or to remain autonomous and exert pressure from outside. In practice many do both and experience suggests that it is too simplistic to associate subversion solely with action outside the official sphere of participation (Taylor, 2003; Barnes et al, 2007). Another site within which we need to explore the dynamics of subversive citizenship is thus in those spaces where social movement, user and community group activists come together with public officials to seek change within the system.

We can, then, in very schematic form, identify a dual process in the contemporary governance of public services that generates contrasting possibilities of policy subversion. There is, on the one hand, a sense of a closing down of the 'space' for worker discretion and professional autonomy resulting from processes of managerialism and modernisation, and of the growing constraints on the private lives of citizens who are increasingly recruited to the project of delivering public policy objectives. Both workers and citizens are likely to react against such restriction and regulation in ways that subvert government intentions (as case study chapters in this volume attest – see Part Three). On the other hand, new spaces of decision making are being created through the recruitment of citizens as active and reflexive agents in the process of delivering public policies, supported and facilitated by public service workers who are encouraged to view such relationships as ones of partnership or co-production (see chapters by Barnes and Sullivan, this volume). These new spaces of dialogue and deliberation can then become sites for the generation and realisation of 'subversive' action. Workers and citizens are being encouraged to forge new and different types of relationship with each other at a time when modernisation is calling into question the values and assumptions that each hold about their relationship to public services. One of the objectives of this book is to explore the consequences of this: do officials and citizens become allies in delivering public policy objectives, do they develop alliances to subvert/resist, or does the new context simply provide a rather different environment in which relationships are negotiated and tensions worked out – or not?

Theorising subversion

This book does not propose a single theoretical approach to understanding the subversion of public policy outcomes. All of the chapters that follow are, however, theoretically informed and seek to analyse specific empirical contexts or processes through explicit conceptual frameworks. A number of theoretical concepts recur

– governance, power, discourse, culture, agency, identity – and certain theories or modes of analysis are explicitly referenced: for example, governmentality, discourse analysis, psycho–social analysis, social movement theory, activity theory. Such theoretical perspectives have differing aims and offer different insights into aspects of how policy works and the kinds of consequences it has.

We believe that this conceptual pluralism is healthy and helpful in opening up the study of issues that have to date been relatively unexplored. However, this is not a pluralism without limits: the book is grounded in a social constructionist or interpretivist approach to understanding social reality, and more specifically to understanding the public policy process – an approach that Frank Fischer gives the broad title 'post–empiricism'. This is an important demarcation from well-established positivist conceptual trends in the analysis of policy, marking 'a turn from the dominant emphasis on rigorous empirical proof and verification to a discursive, contextual understanding of social knowledge and the interpretive methods basic to acquiring it' (Fischer, 2003b: 211). Certainly, we do not consider that the dynamics of policy development and implementation, and particularly the dynamics of 'subversion' that the contributions to this book are concerned with, are capable of being adequately understood through neo–positivist theories of 'rational choice' or analytical approaches that regard the policy process as one of rational planning and linear implementation.

Here, our position is informed by experiences of policy evaluation in the context of another key characteristic of public policy under New Labour: that of 'evidence–based/informed policy making' which has given rise to multiple national and local evaluation projects. For example, one conclusion from the national evaluation of Health Action Zones (HAZs) (Barnes et al, 2005) was that the nature of HAZs was fluid, dynamic and subject to multiple interpretations. Local practitioners' understandings of HAZs changed over time, partly in response to local circumstances and partly as a response to what might be considered as subversion by government of the original intentions and aspirations of HAZs. The programme was initially viewed as a radical departure from Tory preoccupations with health service organisation and management through its focus on health inequalities and the root causes of poor health, but, as government priorities changed, became instead a vehicle for the delivery of targets such as cancer survival rates. One conclusion of the evaluators was that HAZs could not be understood as *a* programme, but that their achievements and limitations needed to be related to the different narratives constructed by practitioners to make sense of a constantly changing configuration of projects and governance arrangements. Hence the search for 'evidence' of 'what works' was inadequate, and more interpretive understandings of how and why HAZs evolved in the way they did was an important dimension of the learning contributed by this evaluation (Barnes et al, 2003). Reflecting on this experience from a perspective of 'subversion', one way of interpreting the very different characteristics of HAZs at different times and in different places is to see this as a consequence of workers using the opportunity offered by the programme to shape it in ways that made sense to them – including through resisting government attempts to limit its perceived radical potential.

In our conclusion we revisit questions of theory in the light of the analysis offered in the substantive chapters.

Analysing subversion

We have divided contributions to this collection into two broad parts. In Part Two we have included five chapters that address the issue of subversion from different perspectives. The opening chapter, by David Prior, offers a conceptual analysis of the processes at work in encounters at the front line between workers and service users and a way of understanding the potential for subversion that might exist in these spaces. Similarly, Marian Barnes (Chapter Three) is interested in the potential of participative spaces in which alliances may be built (or not) and the 'citizen–official' binary may be undermined. Helen Sullivan (Chapter Four) sees government itself as engaged in processes of subverting or unsettling institutionalised governance processes by its emphasis on neighbourhood governance. Each of these contributions highlights the way in which competing and multiple meanings that coexist within governance and service delivery processes may produce different possibilities in terms of the consequences of action and interaction. We cannot 'read off' the likelihood of subversion from a particular configuration of variables. Janet Newman and John Clarke's stories of subversion in action (Chapter Five) similarly emphasise the way in which things may come together and also come apart – adopting the concept of 'assemblages' to reflect on the way in which multiple resources and capabilities may be mobilised and brought into new alignments. The final chapter in Part Two is rather different but offers not only an important perspective in its own right, but also an important reference point for other chapters. John Flint (Chapter Six) explores the way in which citizenship itself is constructed and, in so doing, how some citizens who do not and cannot reflect these norms become de facto problematic or potentially subversive citizens.

The invited contributions to this collection were selected to offer perspectives on the processes of subversion across a range of different policy and service areas. In Part Three of the book we present case studies that emphasise the way in which workers and service users negotiate roles and identities and consciously or unconsciously resist or undermine government policy objectives. In many cases these case studies illustrate the contradictory potential of policy and the spaces this opens up for reinterpretation. They also demonstrate that subversion cannot be regarded as inevitably or automatically either progressive or defensive. Two chapters focus on new forms of practice for working with families which, in different ways, have been constructed by policy makers as 'problematic'. Sadie Parr and Judy Nixon (Chapter Seven) look at the way in which front-line workers have reinterpreted government strategies for intervening in the lives of families exhibiting 'antisocial behaviour'; while Kate Morris and Gale Burford (Chapter Eight) consider worker resistance and family counter-resistance to practices intended to enable families to come up with solutions to childcare problems. Shona Hunter (Chapter Nine) takes a detailed look at the way in which one healthcare professional resists and negotiates his personal and professional identity in the context of a modernisation discourse that creates dilemmas for him through its categorical assumptions concerning 'older, male Asian GPs'. And finally, Nathan Hughes (Chapter Ten) and Louise Westmarland and John Clarke (Chapter Eleven) take us into the world of criminal justice to offer two very different insights into the subversion of managerialism: in Hughes' study of a Bail Support and Supervision scheme, and consumerism in Westmarland and Clarke's study of responses to the consumer orientation in policing.

In the final chapter of the collection, Chapter Twelve in Part Four, we reflect more precisely on what these studies have to say about 'what' is being subverted, 'where' subversive practices take place and 'how' subversion happens. We also offer some conclusions about what the different perspectives adopted by the contributors to this collection can offer to an understanding of this aspect of the policy process.

Part Two
Perspectives on subversive citizenship

TWO

Policy, power and the potential for counter-agency

David Prior

Introduction

In one of his tantalisingly undeveloped remarks, Michel Foucault suggested that

> there are no relations of power without resistances; the latter are all the more real and effective because they are formed right at the point where relations of power are exercised ... [resistance] exists all the more by being in the same place as power; hence, like power, resistance is multiple. (Foucault, 1980: 142)

My aim in this chapter is to try to explore how the relationship between power and resistance might be understood in the specific context of the delivery of public services and, more particularly, to examine the conditions in which resistance to public service policies and practices can take the form of an oppositional or *counter*-agency on the part of both public officials and citizens.

The conceptual starting point for the chapter is 'governmentality', the analysis of the rationales and techniques of governing that, inspired by Foucault's historical investigations (Foucault, 1991), has been developed in the work of Nikolas Rose and others (for example, Rose, 1996, 1999; Dean, 1999; Miller and Rose, 2008). The crucial insight of governmentality is that contemporary processes of governing operate through a myriad of mundane, everyday techniques and routines of discipline and control that are exercised by individual citizens and which enable them to function as self-regulating members of the polity. In this approach, public policies and services are to be understood as principally concerned with the creation and maintenance of citizens who possess both the will and the capacity to conduct themselves in accordance with governmental objectives. However, it is a central theme of this chapter that this account is in itself insufficient in seeking to understand what happens in the delivery of public services, particularly 'at the point where relations of power are exercised' in encounters between officials and citizens. More specifically, it does not enable us to explain how and why public policies and services can be disrupted or subverted in their pursuit of defined objectives, and what the active role of both public officials and public service users might be in those processes of disruption and subversion. To attempt to develop such an explanation, I draw on both cultural analysis (for example, Bevir and Trentmann, 2007) and deliberative policy analysis (for example, Fischer, 2003a, 2003b) to provide a theory of agency to supplement the governmentality thesis. I also draw on examples from a range of research studies to provide some empirical illustrations of the processes I seek to explain.

Policy and practice in the governing of public services

The aim in this section is to develop an analysis of the process of governing through public services, and particularly of the role of policy and practice in that process. It is helpful to begin with the familiar service domains of the British welfare state: education, health, housing, criminal justice, social security and so on. In analytical terms we can characterise these domains as *forms of governing*: as broad clusters of policies, services, institutions, organisational structures and professional practices that are held together in some kind of discursive unity by their orientation around a common understanding of a fundamental social need or problem associated with particular social groups. Despite some profound internal changes to the different clusters, for instance as a result of market-led initiatives or new forms of management, these forms of governing have been of fairly long duration; however, we should note the more recent emergence of new forms of governing, such as those constituted through discourses of 'social inclusion' and 'community', which indicate significant processes of 're-clustering' within and across public policy domains (Rose, 1996).

The role of discourses, or, in the language of governmentality, of 'rationalities' of government (Dean, 1999: 211), is to provide narratives of ideas, values, beliefs and explanations that shape and organise collective thinking, both consciously and unconsciously, about needs and problems in society and the ways in which such issues should be addressed (Fischer, 2003a). However, the notion of 're-clustering' indicates that discourses of government are neither monolithic nor permanent but are 'relatively unstable and contradictory configurations' (ibid: 79) and, as such, are open to challenge from competing values or alternative explanations, both from within the existing dominant formations and from without. This is inevitable, given that governmental discourses are constituted through political processes characterised by compromise between competing rationales and temporary and uneasy alignments between different political projects. Thus, in discussing a specific instance of reclustering in New Labour's prioritisation of social inclusion as a primary goal of government, Levitas (2005) describes the coexistence of and struggles for influence between distinctive discourses of exclusion, each of which generates and sustains sets of policies, resource allocations, organisational forms and practices and defines particular kinds of citizens. It is, for example, evident that despite the neoliberal assault on social democratic 'welfare state' solutions to social problems, discourses and strategies of welfarism continue to be influential in shaping the values and practices of staff engaged in the delivery of public services and the experiences of public service users (O'Malley, 2004).

'Policy' is of particular significance because of its role as a principal means for the transmission of discourse. Policies represent a formalisation of discourse through which governments seek to stabilise the meanings associated with specific social needs or problems and to secure acceptance of these meanings among both those engaged in the delivery of policy objectives and those at whom the policies are targeted (Newman, 2007). Such needs and problems are to be understood not as somehow pre-existing or 'triggering' forms of governance; rather, both needs and problems and the social groups associated with them are themselves constituted in the process of governing. Through policies, as expressions of discursive power, meanings are attached to individuals and social groups and to different kinds of behaviour or activity, associating them with virtue or danger, with rewards or sanctions, with encouragement or discouragement; social groups are constructed through policies as making either positive or negative contributions to the social collective, and issues are identified either as problems warranting governmental intervention or as unproblematic and outside the scope of governmental concern (Fischer, 2003a: 66; Ball, 2008: 18). However, because policies are practical instruments for the administration of governance, they are not just discursive in their effects: they have material consequences for citizens in their everyday lives. This focuses our attention on the ways in which the material consequences of policies are produced; on the actions of practitioners in implementing policies; on *practice* as a component of governing.

Policy and practice should not be seen as separate and disconnected components of the process of governing; rather, they are different but dialectically related moments in the governmental process, and each is implicated in the other. Thus, at the moment of policy formulation the possibilities of specific forms of practice are both enabled and constrained by the meanings that the policy discourse seeks to secure, while at the moment of implementation the actions of the practitioner generate effects that simultaneously give expression to and test the viability of the objectives of policy. We can explore this internal relationship of policy and practice analytically by distinguishing between 'strategies' and 'technologies' as distinct categories of governmental action (Prior, 2007).

Strategies are concerned with action to achieve outcomes defined within a particular form of governing, for example within health, or education, or social security. They are strategic to the extent that they connect specific purposes with particular means, mobilising – and at the same time rationalising – sets of material and symbolic resources in order to meet defined objectives. This mobilisation is achieved through a range of technologies. Technologies of governing are focused on the question of means, defining *how* the outcomes and objectives of various forms of governing and their associated strategies are to be achieved. Crucially, all these technologies, although they cover a wide range of different methods of delivery, have the behaviour of individuals and social groups as their principal object. Strategies and technologies reflect particular social values and behavioural norms, which in turn are legitimised by policy discourses that seek to justify them in the context of people's actual life experiences. Thus, 'consumerism as a strategy for improving public service responsiveness to the demands of service users is located within a policy discourse that prioritises market mechanisms such as choice, which both reflect and reinforce the dominant individualist and aspirational culture that shapes people's identities and expectations as citizens' (Prior, 2007: 4; see also Flint, 2003). Similarly, policy discourse links technologies to broader strategies by enabling specific technologies to appear as 'natural' or 'commonsense' means of achieving desired outcomes (Ball, 2008). The use by schools of 'contractual' agreements with parents to secure the active involvement of the latter in meeting outcomes relating to the behavioural or educational performance of their children can be presented as a 'natural' development by a discourse that constructs parents and schools as partners with shared responsibilities for the child's success. Technologies that use publicity to 'name and shame' individuals who infringe social and legal norms (not paying television licence fees; engaging in antisocial behaviour) come to be seen as common-sense responses when policy discourse emphasises law enforcement as the principal strategy for securing social order. In these and other examples, discourse works by defining strategies and technologies as rational, consensual responses to commonly acknowledged problems (Atkinson, 2003; Fischer, 2003a).

The account given so far of processes of governing can appear overly deterministic, as if governmental processes always and necessarily operate as intended and are successful in meeting their objectives; and this is one source of criticism of the governmentality analysis. It is thus important to recognise that the links between strategies, technologies and discourses may not always be effective, that the justifications they provide may be ambiguous or even contradictory and that the connections they make may contain gaps or inconsistencies. It is evident, for instance, that strategies and technologies are, in practice, frequently underpinned by several different discourses that offer varying rationalisations for action (Atkinson, 2003; Barnes et al, 2007). For example, a consumerist strategy deploying technologies of 'choice' may be justified by discourses concerned with improving service quality, with reducing costs, with increasing the range of providers, with meeting the aspirations of citizens and with reducing the power of professionals. While some of these rationales may complement each other, others will be in uneasy relationship or simply incompatible: better quality may require higher expenditure; citizens may want professionals whom they can trust to be able to do what is required; a wider range of providers may merely result in confusion (Barnes and Prior, 1995). The uncertainties generated by such conflicts or inconsistencies open up the possibility for alternative forms of action to be developed, as will be explored further below.

Moreover, while the practice of officials is made possible, directed and shaped by the range of available technologies and by the policy discourse that rationalises those technologies, it is not wholly determined by them. Officials are human actors and as such bring their own agency to bear on the policy/practice dynamic when faced with the myriad choices involved in deciding what to do and how to do it in any particular situation (Wagenaar and Cook, 2003: 165). There is an interaction between the formal strategies and technologies and practitioners' own informal interpretations of the situation – interpretations based on their past experience, on their tacit or local knowledge of the particular circumstances they are faced with and on their subjective, emotional response to the issue they are required to act upon – resulting in *situated judgements* about the action to take (ibid: 167–8;Yanow, 2003; Bevir, 2007).What practitioners do, therefore, is not simply the application of an objectively considered selection from the repertoire of approved strategies and technologies; rather, it is the result of an engagement between, on the one hand, the practitioner's knowledge of, and skills in using, the various formal interventions and understanding of the expected policy outcomes, and on the other hand their individual, context-specific and emotionally and morally charged evaluation of particular needs and problems and assessment of the likely impact of different courses of action (such evaluations will of course themselves be shaped by the practitioner's exposure to different discursive frameworks) (Mayo et al, 2007).

Practitioners' awareness of the emotional and moral dimensions of their decision making is likely to be enhanced when their practice involves direct encounters with those citizens who are the intended recipients of policy outcomes. Here, the 'context specificity' of practice takes on additional significance as individual citizens bring their own agency to the 'moment' of policy delivery. Policy discourse seeks to create citizens as defined subjects of the policy process and constructs distinct subject identities for citizens within particular forms of governance (citizens as service users, consumers, customers, patients, clients, victims, tax payers, 'hard-working families', benefit cheats, 'neighbours from hell', etc).These identities embody particular ways of acting or forms of agency in response to government policies, including identities that construct the citizen as active participant in and co-producer of governance outcomes, as in current strategies of community engagement or service partnership (Newman 2007). But citizens are not 'empty vessels' waiting to be filled with the attributes and potentialities prescribed for them by dominant discourses (Yanow, 2003: 245). They respond to policies and engage with practitioners with their own understandings of the situation, their own sense of what would constitute a just or unjust outcome and their own capacities for action, including alternative sources of knowledge. Such understandings and capacities on behalf of the intended subjects of policy introduce a destabilising or unsettling dynamic into citizen and practitioner encounters, which thus involve a negotiation of meanings and a sense of openness about potential outcomes (Bevir, 2007). Of course, the extent of this uncertainty, of the scope for policy outcomes to be mediated through practitioner–citizen deliberation, varies greatly between different forms of governance, and there are situations in which the authority of the practitioner (whether legitimated by legal powers or by specialist professional knowledge) places strict limits on how far outcomes might stray from those prescribed in formal strategies of intervention – although there is plenty of sociological evidence to show that even in these situations professional norms can be adjusted, legal or bureaucratic rules can be bent and alternative outcomes can be achieved (Lipsky, 1980; Maynard-Moody and Musheno, 2003; Field, 2007; Sadler, 2008).

In summary, then, forms of governing, orientated around discursive constructions of particular problems or needs, give rise to distinctive clusters of policies and practices; these are realised materially through strategies and technologies which shape and constrain the formal context in which practitioner and citizen encounters occur. However, both practitioners and citizens are active agents in these encounters, bringing their agency to bear in their subjective interpretations of context-specific meanings and in their situated judgements about what action to take. The outcomes of practitioner–citizen encounters are therefore not pre-ordained, no matter how robust or definitive specific strategies or technologies may be. The ways in which practitioners draw on the strategies and technologies relevant to the form of governance in which they are operating is mediated through their agency, and the responses of citizens in their encounters with practitioners are, in turn, mediated by *their* agency. What actually happens is *contingent* on the interaction of structural elements (strategies and technologies) and cultural elements (the agency of practitioners and citizens) (Bevir, 2007).

Governmental strategies and the possibilities for subversion

Building on the analysis developed so far, in this section I want to suggest three broad and interrelated explanations for why the outcomes of governance are unpredictable and sometimes seem to subvert the intentions of policy. These three explanations are:

- the coexistence of and struggles for dominance between alternative strategies and technologies;
- the role of agency and the contingency of practitioner–citizen encounters;
- the effects of the material social context in which policies are implemented.

In examining each of these explanations more fully, I will draw principally on research into policy and practice relating to antisocial behaviour, although reference will also be made to other examples of contemporary public policy.

Competing strategies and technologies

Antisocial behaviour provides an interesting choice of topic to illustrate my argument, for several reasons. First, within the political discourse of the first New Labour government, antisocial behaviour (ASB) was very strongly identified as a major problem confronting British society and as one that demanded a clear and emphatic response based on the enforcement of new legal powers (Squires, P., 2006). This tended to be presented in ways that suggested that 'everyone' recognised the problem of ASB and, apart from the minority who engaged in it, would welcome tough measures to deal with it. Second, however, ASB policy has been developed and implemented on the basis of very little systematic knowledge of the nature and extent of the problem and a very vague definition of it; compared with other policy priorities, little or no empirical evidence about ASB and those who perpetrate it or about the effects of ASB interventions has been available to shape and evaluate policy (Millie, 2007; Prior, 2009). Third, and in part as a result of the first two factors, 'tackling antisocial behaviour' has become a priority within various forms of governing (for example, policing, housing, education, youth, community, urban regeneration) but with different understandings of the 'problem' and different kinds of strategies and technologies developed to address it (Jacobs et al, 2003; Parr and Nixon, 2008).

'Enforcement' can be identified as the dominant strategy for responding to ASB (Burney, 2005; Squires, P., 2006). This refers to the active use of a range of legal technologies such as ASBOs, Parenting Orders, Dispersal Orders, Child Safety Orders, Child Curfews and other measures, and also to interventions that are not themselves the result of court orders but which are backed up by the threat of legal action, such as Acceptable Behaviour Contracts, Parenting Contracts and Family Intervention Projects. Thus, breach of a 'voluntary' Acceptable Behaviour Contract can be cited in court as evidence in support of a subsequent ASBO application; failure to agree to engage fully in a Family Intervention Project can be penalised by legal sanctions (Respect Task Force, 2006). The enforcement approach is 'shaped by a discourse of "law and order", in which antisocial behavior is analogous to crime and is constructed as a problem of crime control' (Prior, 2007: 25), to be dealt with through the investigation of specific incidents and the imposition of sanctions against individual perpetrators in order to prevent further incidents. We can understand enforcement as a particular configuration of power, a distinctive combination of discourse, strategy and technologies that is evident in a variety of different policy contexts (Flint, 2006).

Such configurations are not, however, either necessary or permanent, rather they are contingent and always susceptible to possibilities for transformation. Change and development exists as a continuing dynamic within forms of governing and this is obvious from the many studies of the changing configurations of specific forms (for examples, see Flint, 2003 on housing; Ball, 2008 on education; Greener, 2009 on health). This is evident within the comparatively recent policy domain of antisocial behaviour itself, where the original crime-control orientation has come to be supplemented, altered and sometimes supplanted by discourses, strategies and technologies deriving from other policy domains. The interaction between different configurations can be observed, sometimes with confusing results, both in national policy initiatives (such as the 'National Strategy for Neighbourhood Renewal' (2001), 'Every Child Matters' (2004) and the 'Youth Task Force' (2007), each of which reflects the attempt at 'joining up' government) and in local initiatives based on multi-agency and multidisciplinary partnerships where different ways of defining problems and different ways of addressing them influence and impact on one another (Burnett and Appleton, 2004; Mason and Prior, 2008).

Change within established power configurations occurs because they are always open to influence or challenge from other discursive formations or from the interaction of their component parts. This can take the form of explicit conflict or struggle between alternative strategies and technologies, and it is here that possibilities for types of policy subversion can be identified. Thus, Flint notes the tensions within policy on social housing, which promote conflicting strategies that seek to construct tenants as both 'active, entrepreneurial consumers and also responsible, duty-owing members of communities', thereby generating potential sites of resistance (Flint, 2003: 625). The outcome of such conflict can be, of course, that a previously dominant discursive formation is replaced by another one, which then becomes the new orthodoxy. But that process of policy change at the macro level is not the focus of this chapter; rather, my interest is in the possible consequences of the uncertainty generated by the competition between contrasting strategies and technologies for the actions of service delivery staff and service users.

Agency and contingency

The changing relations of domination within processes of governing, discussed above, render the outcomes of such processes as necessarily contingent: it is always possible, if not likely, that official strategies will not be implemented in prescribed ways and that their effects will be different from those anticipated in policy discourse. Drawing on studies of urban regeneration strategies, Atkinson has observed that 'domination is only ever partial [and] programmes of government and their associated technologies are rarely realised as they were intended' (2003: 105). The agency of practitioners is crucial here in the choices they make about their context-specific interpretation and use of available strategies and technologies.

Research on local antisocial behaviour initiatives illustrates this in a number of ways in relation to the discursively dominant strategy of enforcement. For instance, alternative strategies may coexist in specific operational contexts, albeit in sometimes uneasy relationships. Thus, the championing of an informal preventative strategy within an ASB unit explicitly sets out to mitigate and pre-empt the official priority of enforcement, while acknowledging the importance of legal enforcement as a 'last resort' and, indeed, having to meet performance targets in relation to the latter (Prior et al, 2006a). Where staff from different agencies are brought together in 'partnership' structures with apparently shared objectives, advocates of markedly different strategies and technologies can find themselves in conflict, for example, in deciding how to plan a response to troublesome young people (Prior et al, 2006a). Research on the prevention of ASB within local Children's Fund programmes revealed initiatives that were clearly shaped by discourses and strategies concerned with prevention through child, family and community development, in which 'enforcement' had minimal presence (Mason and Prior, 2008). Gordon Hughes' suggestion that local community safety strategies are shaped by processes of 'compromise, contestation, even resistance' (Hughes, 2007: 114) seems highly apposite here.

The agency of those at whom policy and practice outcomes are targeted, the citizens and public service users, is a further factor in generating conditions of compromise, contestation and resistance to dominant modes of governing. Power flows in multiple directions and is not solely the property of those who govern or of the processes of government. Indeed, many contemporary governmental strategies rely on precisely that point for their effectiveness: the empowered consumers of public services, the active citizens engaged in their community, are key actors in the achievement of certain governmental aims. But even those who are less obviously 'empowered', the public service users and other citizens who lack overt political or economic power (Cruikshank, 1999), possess the capacity to contest and resist official strategies and technologies and thereby subvert planned policy outcomes. They may do this negatively by declining to undertake the role expected of them as service users or as citizens in specific policy contexts, or they may act more positively in generating alternative strategies and outcomes, as with those communities targeted by regeneration programmes who 'exploit gaps in the programmes and technologies of government to their own advantage, and develop forms of government and action that reflect their needs' (Atkinson, 2003: 102).

Thus, strategies and technologies can encounter resistance from citizens and their purposes be undermined and/or redefined as a result. This was evident in a project with social housing tenants who were at risk of eviction because of persistent antisocial behaviour: the strategy pursued by the project was one of behavioural change and a range of technologies aimed at improving self-discipline and developing personal and social skills were deployed (Prior, 2007: 10–14). Many of the tenants chose not to accept the 'offer' made by the project. In declining to become engaged they thereby avoided being subjected to the fairly rigorous demands that the project would make on them in terms of required changes to and restrictions upon their everyday life-style. Significantly, this choice was made in the knowledge of its wider implications: that the risk of the family losing their home was much more likely to be realised. A similar sense of resistance to governmental initiatives that seek to encourage citizens to act in accordance with official norms could also be observed in projects operating at a community level (Prior et al, 2006b). Residents of an area of substantial deprivation had, through local surveys and consultation meetings, identified ASB as a priority concern. However, the attempt by local agencies to encourage residents to address the problem themselves through a strategy of community engagement met with great difficulty in gaining active support. A collective lack of belief that anything could really be done, fears of reprisals against anyone who did cooperate with the authorities, and a pervasive sense that daily life was already too demanding meant that the great majority of residents opted not to participate. Moreover, when the police and local authority targeted certain neighbourhoods with intensive enforcement of the ASB powers, this generated a counter-reaction from residents who were concerned both about the impact on the reputation of their area and the effects on young people who were the principal targets of enforcement. While at the time of the research this reaction had not begun to identify an alternative strategy, it had started to open up dialogue with the police and local authority about the need for a different form of response.

The material context of social life

The research reported by Prior et al (2006b) on antisocial behaviour initiatives in an area of serious multiple deprivation, discussed above, suggests that strategies and technologies may fail in their objectives because they are employed in material social contexts in which they are rendered ineffective or irrelevant. The attempt to engage local people in the development of responses to ASB seemed to be undermined by the reality that this was just one of the many forms of deprivation and exclusion that residents of the area experienced. The possibility that their agency could be harnessed and directed toward socially constructive ends, which was the aim of the strategy of community engagement, was in part defeated by the fact that many were just too ground down by the experiences of daily life to have any capacity for such involvement. For some, the possibility of a more active agency was apparent in their determination not to put their energies into attempting to improve conditions in their local area but to move away from it as soon as possible: choice expressed in the very literal form of an 'exit' strategy. The research concluded that without effective intervention to address the overall causes and effects of deprivation it seemed unlikely that lasting reductions in levels of antisocial behaviour would be achieved; but this, because of the scale of resources implied, was not a strategy available to the local partnership body charged with leading the governance of the area.

The project of attempting to work to change the patterns of behaviour of tenants threatened with eviction frequently faced the entrenched complexity and difficulty of those tenants' lives, which seemed to create a barrier that was, within the terms of the project's remit, insurmountable. Case records of the families and households studied for the research revealed frequent issues of family breakdown, unemployment, drug and alcohol misuse, mental health problems, unauthorised school absences and poor educational performance, previous criminal convictions and civil sanctions, including ASBOs (see Matthews et al, 2007 for similar evidence). 'All of this suggested a paradox for the project, in that the technology of the contract typically required a level of discipline and organization on the part of tenants and family members that was precisely what these individuals and families evidently lacked' (Prior, 2007: 12). In situations where remembering to keep an appointment with project staff – a core requirement of the contract – was beyond the capacity of many tenants, the possibility of learning and using new skills of parenting or budgeting, or developing the self-discipline to avoid excessive alcohol consumption, and thereby of successfully completing the programme, was only ever likely to be achieved by a few.

There is, perhaps, in these examples a sense of the potential for governmental processes to be deflected or blocked in their encounter with empirical social contexts that simply to do not provide the conditions for the 'successful' constitution of self-regulating citizens, contexts that mean that the kind of agency that policy and practice requires is frequently unrealisable.

The potential for counter-agency – revision, resistance and refusal

These three explanations each point to 'contingency' as a necessary characteristic of policy implementation, of the inherent unpredictability of strategies and technologies of governing. It is this contingency that establishes the possibilities for outcomes that subvert the intentions of government. Such outcomes can be viewed as being shaped, in part, by 'counter-agency', that is, the agency of official practitioners and/or of citizens that is other than that implied, advocated, prescribed or predicted by policy and which generates effects that undermine the objectives of policy. Using the analytical framework developed above and again drawing on relevant research literature, it is possible to identify three forms of counter-agency, which I will refer to as revision, resistance and refusal.

Revision occurs when the objectives or intended outcomes of policies are modified in the course of implementation by service delivery staff adopting strategies and technologies other than or in addition to those prescribed in official strategies. Such modification, leading to the production of outcomes that differ in significant ways from those anticipated by the official strategy, may occur as the result of interaction, including dialogue, between worker and user, or may be a consequence of the worker or workers taking a decision to operate in a particular way in response to their assessment of the situation they are faced with. Revision – the reappraisal of what actions are required to produce the outcomes the worker believes are appropriate – can result from the worker's decision making being influenced by specific local or individual needs and circumstances, or by local political or professional values that may be at variance with the values embedded in the official strategy.

Examples of counter-agency in the form of 'revision' are provided by various research studies of public service staff. It was evident in the actions of officers in Antisocial Behaviour Teams – established with an explicit enforcement remit – seeking to develop and use informal interventions with young people aimed at prevention and support rather than coercive and potentially criminalising technologies such as ASBOs (Prior et al, 2006a); and in the reinterpretation of legislation and policy discourse on ASB in the light of local contextual factors so as to justify more 'appropriate' responses (Sadler, 2008). It was apparent among the staff of Family Intervention Projects in deliberately adopting approaches to their client families that deviated from official policy discourse by seeking to reduce the stigmatising assumptions that these were 'problem families' deserving of punitive sanctions (Parr and Nixon, 2008). A study of the staff of various Youth Offending teams (YOTs) showed them engaged in practice that was shaped by their concern to minimise the impact of political pressure to deal with young people in a more punitive style, including the adoption of strategies explicitly addressing young people's welfare needs and persuading magistrates not to issue Parenting Orders when parents had not voluntarily agreed to them (Field, 2007).

Resistance refers to action by citizens to develop alternative strategies or technologies in response to specific situations, in order to achieve outcomes other than those prescribed in official policies. This can occur when citizens recognise that 'something needs to be done' but reject the solutions offered by official policy. Resistance thus implies citizens' conscious engagement with specific needs or problems and the deliberate pursuit of courses of action. Again, this process of constructing alternative actions and outcomes may be achieved through dialogue with service workers, who may be complicit in the process either by tacitly allowing it to proceed or by actively facilitating it; or it may be the result of citizens acting wholly independently.

Resistance can take the form of either individual or collective citizen action. The main focus in this chapter has been on public service contexts in which counter-agency is more likely to be on an individual level; for example, when single mothers contest court decisions in relation to Parenting Orders and achieve outcomes different from those anticipated (Holt, 2008), or when parents of a child with special educational needs resist the school allocation policy of their local education authority and seek alternative educational provision for their child (Morgan, 2005). A very specific example of a form of individual resistance is described in Crewe's study of prisoners who subvert the dominant power relations of the prison regime, not by overt acts of disruption or rebellion but by seeming to accept the subject roles constructed for them by the regime while privately rejecting them and developing covert personal strategies for survival and eventual release (Crewe, 2007). But resistance can also be a collective activity, as in the case of private landlords resisting co-option into official strategies for managing antisocial behaviour and developing alternative approaches to dealing with tenant conduct (Cowan and Hunter, 2007), or of local authority housing tenants voting to reject a heavily promoted governmental strategy of large-scale transfer of tenancies to new social housing agencies and opting instead to remain under existing local authority control (Flint, 2003).

In contrast to the 'active' sense of agency implied by the notion of resistance, *refusal* signifies a more passive mode of response to problematic situations. It occurs when potential users decline to become engaged in official strategies and their associated technologies that have been designed to generate specific forms of citizenship practice; this can include refusing involvement as a client or user of a service or initiative, even when this might have negative consequences for the individual in the form of legal or administrative sanctions. Such refusal, even though it might involve the citizen in apparently 'doing nothing', is still a form of agency, since it requires an explicit choice between alternative courses of action. Here, service workers are less likely to be complicit in the citizen's decision, although they may well have had an important role in explaining to the citizen the potential consequences of a decision not to accept the service on offer. Examples already referred to include the tenants, at risk of eviction from social housing because of their alleged ASB, refusing to engage in the project which offered a possible way of avoiding eviction (Prior, 2007), and residents of a neighbourhood experiencing high levels of crime and ASB declining to engage with a project aimed at crime reduction (Prior et al, 2006b). There are also instances of public service staff refusing to comply with official strategies, such as nurses choosing to leave the NHS rather than accept increasing workload pressures and changes to nursing practice (Kennedy and Kennedy, 2007).

Conclusion

The introduction to this book referred to the ways in which contemporary governmental processes have the effect of reducing the space for discretion and autonomy on the part of public service workers and of putting increasing pressure on users to behave in ways that conform to policy requirements, to become 'partners' in the process of policy delivery. These pressures and constraints are real, but this chapter has tried to show that they do not – indeed, cannot – tell the whole story. Workers and users retain the capacity to act in ways that counter the dominant power of officially approved policy and practice and that subvert the intended service outcomes. The counter-agency of workers and users in revising, resisting or refusing policy imperatives is thus critical to an understanding of why policy sometimes fails at the point of front-line or street-level delivery and why and how alternative outcomes are (sometimes) achieved.

However, if it is the major thesis of this chapter that the outcomes of governmental processes are necessarily uncertain, the same is true of the outcomes of forms of counter-agency – of revisions, resistances and refusals. The research studies cited above seem to indicate that the consequences of subversion are profoundly ambiguous. Holt suggests that the mothers who successfully resisted the imposition of Parenting Orders may simply have created other routes through which they came to occupy subject positions that met the requirements of dominant policy discourse (Holt, 2008). The YOT workers in Field's (2007) study and the ASB team members in Prior et al's (2006a) study may have developed strategies that were more successful in controlling youth crime and ASB (the ultimate aim of government policy) than close adherence to the prescribed strategy would have been. In some circumstances, the consequences of a refusal to become engaged with public services – for example, eviction – could clearly be seriously damaging to individuals and their families. The identification of counter-agency may help to explain why official policy and practice does not always deliver the results as intended; but it does not necessarily imply the presence of radically progressive alternative outcomes.

It is therefore important that the notion of counter-agency that I have developed in this chapter is not seen as some form of romantic expression of underdog defiance or of revolutionary solidarity between workers and citizens – this is not intended as a 'heroic' account of policy subversion. Rather, I have tried to show that the conditions for counter-agency are to be found in the internal inconsistencies and ambiguities of the process of governing itself, and that the forms that counter-agency may take are themselves shaped by the particular and differing contexts of public service delivery.

THREE

Alliances, contention and oppositional consciousness: can public participation generate subversion?

Marian Barnes

Introduction

The development of new spaces within which citizens and officials meet together to deliberate, make and review policy has become a major focus for research within the UK and internationally. Such research has considered, for example, which citizens or service users take part in such initiatives, the deliberative dynamics of participation forums, the disputed issue of representation and representativeness, the capacity of such forums to lead to policy or practice change, the design principles on which they are or might be constructed, and the experiences of citizens and service users within them and the impact this has on them.

Much of this research questions the capacity of such spaces to offer fundamental challenges to the status quo. The ways in which institutional rules and norms act to constrain the potential for change was a key theme of my earlier work with colleagues and we have also considered the power of discursive norms to delimit what are considered acceptable ways of speaking and thus of deliberating policy issues (Barnes et al, 2007). Others have drawn similar conclusions from case studies of user involvement (Church, 1996; Hodge, 2005) and have pointed to a failure to secure major change in service delivery or policy outcomes as a result of sustained user involvement and public participation over many years. One conclusion that has been drawn is that, far from public participation providing opportunities for service users and citizens to become 'empowered' through offering major challenge to dominant policy discourses and service delivery practices, the participatory turn within public policy represents one way in which citizens learn to be self-governing subjects (Forbes and Sashidharan, 1997; Rose, 1998; Cruikshank, 1999).

This somewhat pessimistic view of the transformative potential (within the UK and elsewhere) contained within deliberative forums and other participatory spaces is countered by at least some evidence that they can be 'Spaces for Change' (Cornwall and Coelho, 2007). If this is the case, might we understand them in any way as spaces in which the resistance and subversion that we are exploring in this book might be both generated and expressed? In this chapter I address one aspect of this: the way in which participatory forums can enable the construction and reconstruction of individual and collective identities of both citizens and officials and thus hold the potential for undermining or subverting assumptions about both identity and expertise.

Most policy and research analysis focuses on those citizens, users, and publics who are to be engaged, coerced, empowered and made responsible through participatory initiatives. There has been little research that has been designed to explore the way in which public officials negotiate their roles and identities within participatory forums (but see Mayo et al, 2007), although the work that I undertook with Andrew Knops, Janet Newman and Helen Sullivan did include considerations of this (Barnes et al, 2006, 2007). In this chapter I draw from that work and other relevant research to explore the ways in which both citizens and officials negotiate individual and collective identities within participatory forums, and consider what this may say about the fluidity and permeability of the concepts of 'official' and 'citizen', and how both might seek to use such forums to achieve their own objectives and thus subvert official objectives or expectations which drive the expansion of the participatory sphere. I will interrogate the notions of expertise and of 'responsible citizens' in this context and offer a perspective on the exercise of power and agency within forums that are increasingly seen to be central to the delivery of public policy objectives.

Extending the front line

A key theme of Lipsky's study of 'street-level bureaucrats' is the response of these front-line workers to the clients they are employed to help, support or control. Lipsky (1980) argues that street-level bureaucrats are both dependent on clients – because they need to obtain client compliance when they are evaluated in terms of clients' behaviour or performance – and able to discount them because they have nothing to lose if they do not satisfy them. There is no motivation to learn from complaints received, and street-level bureaucrats are resistant to the exercise of influence by client groups.

This classic study of worker resistance to management control of their work thus clearly locates workers and clients in different spheres of interest. The relationship is one of 'unidirectional power', determined primarily by the priorities and preferences of street-level bureaucrats whose work routines are directed towards rationing services, controlling clients and reducing the consequences of uncertainty, husbanding worker resources and managing the consequences of routine practice.

The turn to consumerism in public services can be understood precisely as an attempt to counteract the effects of this form of worker agency. In one of consumerism's most recent incarnations – the introduction of individual or personal budgets in social care – advocates have explicitly claimed that this is intended to turn traditional service delivery upside down by enabling users to plan and control the services they need (Leadbetter at al, 2008). At the same time 'client groups' have developed their own forms of resistance to the impacts of worker control over their lives (for example, Campbell and Oliver, 1996; Baggott et al, 2005) and these have contributed to the overall acceptance of participatory governance across much of the public sector. Lipsky concludes his discussion of the future of street-level bureaucracy by arguing the need for front-line workers to be accountable to the client, rather than held to account to managers via standardised systems of performance management. One way of accounting for the tensions experienced by many front-line workers in contemporary public services is that they are being asked to do both. Hupe and Hill (2007) consider the effects of the multiplicity of accountabilities street-level actors are subject to in a consideration of street-level bureaucracy in the context of contemporary systems of governance. They conclude that a key feature of the contemporary situation is that street-level bureaucrats are constantly involved in a process of weighing up how to act and that the evaluation of these decisions is a matter of political judgement. One context in which such decisions take place is that created by the increase in spaces for deliberative policy making.

The proliferation of forums in which officials, citizens and service users meet to deliberate on matters of policy and service delivery has thus created a new front line. Here both citizens and officials are often constructed as 'partners' in a shared project of improving the quality and responsiveness of public services, and of delivering public policy outcomes. In practice these are often spaces where citizen aspirations confront institutional rules and norms, and power remains unequally exercised. They are also sites in which both citizens and officials negotiate identities and in which, at least in some cases, social movement activists engage with public officials, ostensibly with similar objectives of policy influence (Barnes et al, 2007; Castello et al, 2007). Thus, while official discourses refer to partnerships with users and in the delivery of public policies, we know that if they are partnerships they are usually unequal partnerships and the elasticity of the concept highlights its ideological rather than analytical usefulness. Many participation forums may be better understood as 'contested spaces' in which the contentious and often passionate politics of social movement activism, the aspirations of community organisation, or the hurt and pain of health and social care service users encounters the rational deliberative aspirations of participatory governance (Barnes, 2008). They are also created and creative spaces, in which both official and citizen participants can exercise agency and give meaning to the process of participation and deliberation. This implies a potential for subversion and it is this potential that I am examining here. In order to do so I draw from theories of both social movements and deliberative or discursive policy making.

Social movements and deliberative policy making

It is easy to relate ideas of resistance or subversion to social movements. The characterisation of social movement activism as 'contentious politics' (Tarrow, 1998) and of the psychological processes associated with such activism as the development of an 'oppositional consciousness' (Mansbridge and Morris, 2001) emphasises the radical and challenging nature of movement activism. It is less obviously the case that deliberative governance, involving, as Fischer has argued, a process of 'collaborative consensus-building inherent to participatory discourse [which] makes possible the identification and development of new shared ideas for coordinating the actions of otherwise competing agents' (2003a: 206) might be understood as subversive. Yet there is more overlap in the contemporary theorisation of both such processes than might initially appear likely.

As the Fischer quote indicates, deliberative policy making often takes place in the context of competing interests, values and opinions. Gutmann and Thompson (1996) very directly take as their starting point for the analysis of deliberation the centrality of 'moral disagreement' to policy decision making and question whether consensus is possible and desirable. In spite of the consensual objectives of deliberative policy making, therefore, contention is an empirical reality in this context as well as in the more obviously conflictual activities associated with social movement activism. Thus the processes by which differences are expressed, examined and vie for influence are central to both theoretical and empirical analysis in both contexts. There are differences among theorists of deliberative democracy concerning the extent to which it is possible to design deliberative spaces and processes in a way that will bracket unequal power relations (for example, Young, 2000), but central to an understanding of such practices is the importance of transcending a purely aggregative approach to decision making by enabling reflection on and transformation of positions held.

The question of the way in which policy issues are 'framed' through a process of discursive deliberation reflects the significance of processes by which contention is 'framed' in the process of social movement formation. From a perspective within deliberative policy analysis Fischer (2003a) argues that the process of policy making is both a narrative and an argumentative process, while Hajer (2003) discusses the interrelationship between vocabularies, story lines and generative metaphors, the formation of discourse coalitions around these and the specific practices within which discourses are produced. Tarrow (1998) and other social movement scholars have addressed the way in which movements construct meanings for action through the generation of collective action frames which often draw on the symbols and narratives of previous struggles (for example, Snow and Benford, 1992). As Crossley (2002) argues, frames themselves can be a site of struggle – contention over who has the power and authority to define the nature of the 'problem' is evident in such diverse contexts as environmental campaigning, the growth of the disability and mental health user movements, and AIDS activism.

One aspect of this is the significance of disputes over legitimate knowledge. Both bodies of theory recognise the importance of different and sometimes disputed types of knowledge and reject normative assumptions of expert knowledge as a basis for policy making. For example, Fischer (2000) develops this analysis in the context of environmental decision making, highlighting the tension between professional expertise and democratic governance as a key political issue of our time. Barnes et al (2008) employ the concept of 'local knowledge' to distinguish this from 'local representation' as a fundamental design principle within participatory governance. Designs based on the principle of local knowledge confer legitimacy on participants on the basis of the knowledge they bring, rather than the accountability they offer to a constituency. From a social movement perspective Seidman (1998) argues that the 'making of new social knowledges' was a central outcome of the emergence of identity-based social movements during the 1960s and 1970s. The influence of feminist thinking and of the social model of disability on social and public policy illustrate the impact of this.

Context is another factor that necessitates understanding the connections between social movements and officially sponsored participation. The identification of the significance of political opportunity structures to social movement growth (Tarrow, 1998) draws our attention to the political and policy environment in which they operate, of which an important element is the openness of political systems to potentially subversive influences. As Melucci has claimed, 'political institutions create room for the expression of social demands' (1996:215). Empirical studies have indicated that participation in officially sanctioned deliberative forums is more effective where participants are also engaged in autonomous action (Barnes et al, 2007) and 'deepening democracy' is seen to require both action within civil society and state sponsored initiatives (Gaventa, 2004). Effective social movement action is thus linked to effective participative governance, and an analysis that simply considers the way in which the official sphere may co-opt social movement or community activists is inadequate to an understanding of the relationship between them.

Collective identity building through processes of ongoing exchange and action has been recognised as important to enabling the sustained action and commitment necessary for social movements (Melucci, 1996). This might be understood as having similarities with the process that Fischer describes as the creation of an interpretative community in the context of deliberative policy making: 'Bringing together professional knowledge and lived experience, citizens and experts form an interpretative community. Through mutual discourse this community seeks a persuasive understanding of the issues under investigation. This occurs through changes – sometimes even transformations – of individual beliefs, including social values. In this process, the inquirer, as part of a community, is an agent in the social context rather than an isolated, passive observer' (2003a:222). In previous work colleagues and I considered whether participative forums could be considered spaces in which both citizens and officials built a collective identity and we concluded that there was some evidence of this, even in contexts where the participants had little or no previous experience of activism:

> Our results do not support a clear distinction between officially sponsored forums and those in which there is a dialogue between SMOs [social movement organisations]

and officials in terms of outcomes relating to collective identity formation. What appears rather more important than the 'category' of participative action is the way in which their purposes and methods are negotiated amongst participants, and the capacity of participants to create arenas in which communicative acts can create new meanings capable of transforming the discourses within which policies are made and implemented. (Barnes et al, 2006: 205-6)

The final point here concerns membership of social movement organisations. Activists are likely to be well networked and are rarely isolated or alienated. For example, Della Porta and Diani (1999) report that environmental activists come from 'the new middle classes employed in intellectual professions and social services, from the traditional middle class and the rural and urban bourgeoisie, and from the working class' (p 25). Thus, the social profile of movement activists indicates that we might expect to find public officials among their membership. If this is the case, then understanding how those who are both officials and movement activists might operate within and take advantage of new participatory forums becomes important in understanding their potential for subversion.

If many of the processes associated with the development and maintenance of action within social movements can be related to similar processes within participatory governance forums, then this suggests that such forums should be considered to contain the potential for subversion. Alliances may be struck between officials and citizens, deliberation may generate contention as well as consensus, and collective action within forums may generate an oppositional consciousness among participants from different backgrounds. In the contemporary context it is certainly not helpful to ignore the connections between social movements and participative governance. With colleagues I argued elsewhere:

> the existence of groups which organise outside the 'invited spaces' (Cornwall, 2004) of participative governance increases the potential that both the agenda for and the rules of deliberation will be constructed jointly, rather than imposed by officials. In this context social movements play a key role in seeking to keep open the boundaries, they 'push participation beyond the limits laid down by the political system, and they force it to change' (Melucci, 1996: 214). Thus the importance of social movements in

the contemporary system of complex and apparently open processes of governance is to constantly question the way in which the rules of the game are being determined and defined, in particular in relation to the rules governing the way in which those who are least powerful, or whose communication styles do not match official norms, are represented within such systems. (Barnes et al, 2007: 50)

The implication of this analysis is that the ways in which citizens and officials negotiate and work out their relationships with each other and with the official sphere are a major factor influencing the subversive potential of public participation. One aspect of this is a potential subversion of constructions of 'citizen' and 'official'.

Who's who? Subverting the citizen/official binary

The front cover of what is known as the 'Empowerment White Paper', *Communities in Control* (DCLG, 2008a), contains two photographs. On the left is a young woman wearing jeans and T-shirt and standing in an anonymous street. She is holding a card that reads 'Real People'. On the right a man in a suit stands on Westminster Bridge with Big Ben in the background. He holds a card reading 'Real Power'. Since the professed objective of the White Paper is to propose ways of enabling communities to take control, a first reading of these images might be to suggest that real people like the young woman can wield real power. But looking again, the images reinforce the distinction between 'the suits' who wield real power in places like Westminster and real people in other places who don't. They are different people. Rather than challenging the disempowerment of 'real people' these images reinforce the separation between power holders and others.

The contested issue of who (that is, which citizens) takes part in public participation is a key theme across initiatives designed to increase public participation in policy making and service delivery. Officially constituted participation forums constitute publics in particular ways, reflecting assumptions about legitimate membership, competence to participate and, above all, the significance of 'representation' (Barnes et al, 2003). Usually these processes of constitution are based on assumptions of the necessity to distinguish 'publics' from 'officials'. This is well demonstrated in Martin's study (2007) of the contortions into which the Department of Health and the Commission for Public Participation in Health got themselves in trying to describe the 'ordinary people' they want to take part in patient participation forums. Martin points to the 'strange mix of representativeness, diversity, ordinariness, knowledge and expertise' (p 12) required of these participants who need to know their community and thus, in the words of one recruitment leaflet, 'experts need not apply'. Similar conclusions were drawn by Contandriopoulos and his colleagues in Canada. While they identified many different ways in which concepts of 'the public' were constructed in the context of participation in health service decision making: 'during public hearings on the reorganization of health services delivery, hospital executive directors are not perceived as expressing "the public's" point of view. There is an apparent unanimity in discourses that, in this situation, these individuals are "insiders". They may be talking in the "the public's interest" (or they may not), but they do not talk as, or in the name of, "the public"' (Contandriopoulos et al, 2004: 1589).

Here and in other contexts the precise ways in which publics are constituted for the purpose of public participation reflects official assumptions about role, purpose and principles underlying participation initiatives – which are often implicit, may be contradictory and are rarely negotiated. But there is a clear distinction between insiders – public officials and politicians – and 'the public.'

Control over who takes part has been and continues to be a site for dispute between the official sponsors and those targeted for participation (Barnes, 2002). But it can also be a site of negotiation and dispute among publics themselves. In one of the case studies colleagues and I studied we encountered an interesting discussion about who was 'allowed' to become a member of the forum (Barnes et al, 2007, ch 5). The forum was a long-standing social services user group established to give a voice to service users in the planning and design of services. It was unusual in bringing together different 'client groups' (people with learning disabilities, other disabled people, older people) and carers, as well as anyone who was interested in community care and did not work for the council. Thus some voluntary sector workers were involved. This particular discussion was prompted by recognition that it would be possible, for example, for someone to work for the city council and also to be a carer of an older or disabled person. Should such people be allowed membership of a forum that explicitly excluded council employees? I am not sure that this was entirely resolved during the research period, but an interesting aspect of the debate was that it was veering towards an acceptance that front-line workers who were also carers (such as home helps or gardeners) might be allowed membership, but council workers in management positions would not be.

This is a good illustration of the problems associated with assuming one-dimensional identities and assigning people to categories on this basis. The initial constitution of the group had drawn a typical dividing line between 'service users' and 'council employees'. Only later did members recognise that the same person could be both. But it was easier for this group to recognise front-line workers as sharing the identity of carer than it was for them to recognise managers also having this identity, presumably because they considered that such workers also shared the experience of comparative powerlessness in decision making. This example also illustrates the importance of processes by which situated agents give meaning to the rules governing the practices of participation. What participation means in practice cannot be read off from the formal constitution of such processes. Participants themselves create different possibilities that affect the extent to which such practices might subvert official policy or constructions of citizens and officials. In this case, although the forum had a constitution that was agreed with the city council, deliberation among participants generated a process of reflection that questioned a basic principle on which this was built.

We cannot assume that participative or deliberative forums conform to a particular 'type' that determines the way in which they operate, nor that official rules which define their constitution prescribe relationships among participants and between participants, the institutions they seek to influence and others with an interest in their deliberations. Rather, we need to understand how internal negotiations, as well as particular local contexts, construct different potentials. One way in which this operates is via citizens' and officials' negotiations of their identities and positions in this context. The way in which both citizens and officials make meaning of these processes includes working out who they think *should* be members, and thus who they think they are. And this can subvert both official definitions of the publics they want to engage and distinctions between citizens and officials.

Identity and relational dynamics in deliberative forums

In our analysis of case study data from the Power, Participation and Political Renewal project we identified different ways in which workers who facilitated or engaged in dialogue with citizens negotiated their own positions – both as 'officials' and as people who shared social identities or values with the citizen participants (see Barnes et al, 2006, 2007). And we also identified citizens who in other contexts could be considered 'officials' and identified different ways in which this affected the positions they took within these forums. I will discuss examples of this in order to reflect on the dynamics that might contribute to the potential for subversion.

One case study was of a Minority Ethnic Group Council (MEGC) established by a health service trust in order to improve the accessibility and appropriateness of health services to a large minority ethnic population. The trust employee who facilitated this was a Hindu woman who spoke of her involvement in voluntary and community activity, located this in her faith, but who drew a very clear line between her identity as a 'member of an ethnic minority community' and her identity as trust employee – and came down on the side of the latter in the way in which she responded to issues in the forum:

> "I'm biased. I'm the XXX Trust, I'm not a community member and that has to be very clear in my head. And that's the only way I can do this kind of work or the boundaries will get fudged, and I can't let that fudge my thinking process because then I'd become judgemental as well in how I work with the communities and so a line has got to go up."

An Indian doctor, ostensibly involved in the MEGC as a community representative, drew on research knowledge to make contributions to forum discussions that focused on evidence of different health needs and circumstances among different minority ethnic communities. He questioned the authority of other 'community representatives' to contribute effectively because they did not have such 'expert' knowledge and somewhat dismissively referred to positions taken by community members representing other black groups who adopted more overtly political stances. While the trust officer sought to bracket her 'community' identity in her interpretation of what was required for her official role, the doctor effectively subverted his assumed identity as community representative to use the forum to promote his 'expert' views.

There was very little evidence in this forum of community representatives engaging in contentious politics, nor of oppositional consciousness based in ethnic identity being forged across the citizen/official divide, or indeed among community representatives. A more obvious dynamic was the tendency on the part of all community members to craft their input in ways that they considered to be 'reasonable' and unlikely to provoke difficulties for trust managers. The generation of a culture of reasonable and good-humoured debate among a group of primarily professional 'community representatives', plus the explicit reference to expert knowledge on the part of the Indian doctor, tended to blur the distinction between citizens and officials – in spite of the concerns of the trust's facilitator that she should not 'cross the line' and identify with community representatives. If what was being sought was the input of 'ordinary people' as community representatives, then it is perhaps this idea that was 'subverted' in the way in which the forum operated.

A rather similar outcome can be seen to have emerged from a very different set of dynamics evident in a community health forum. This had grown out of campaigning for improved health facilities in an area of substantial deprivation and at the time of the research forum members were involved in developing proposals for a community-led healthy living centre. Among the membership of this forum was a woman who worked as a public official in the area (she was the manager of a Sure Start project) but whose membership did not derive from her official status – rather, from her interest in and commitment to the area. She was uncertain how to play her role in the group, but had decided that she should curtail the extent to which she drew on 'insider knowledge' in order not to 'skew' the deliberations of the group. She recognised the significance of this as a 'community-led' initiative and did not want to undermine this. She also talked of not wanting to 'go native', which, when asked, she defined as: 'Become a member of the community and lose my skill.' Her uncertainty and ambivalence about her identity in this group was accompanied by a perceived necessity on the part of other key community members to get to grips with the official rules and procedures necessary to construct a funding bid, and to negotiate with health service officials about facilities for GPs in the new centre. This squeezed out the potential for more radical and innovative ways of thinking about what a healthy living centre might be. Arguably, some (though not all) of the community members felt they had to act like officials in order to succeed in their objective of securing funding for the centre and this effectively undermined any subversive potential that the forum might offer. This suggests a further subversion of the idea that 'ordinary people' will be able to use participatory spaces to promote their community identities rather than developing identities as 'experts.'

We can see rather different possibilities in a Sustainability Forum facilitated by a local authority officer who was herself a committed environmental activist. She was very conscious of the tensions between her role as an employee of the city council and as a citizen who shared many of the beliefs and objectives of other forum members. Because of this, she had made a conscious decision not to take part in neighbourhood forums in order to pursue her environmental commitments:

> "Who am I? What's my role here? They say just come as a resident. Well I am, but they won't know where my views are coming from, one moment I'll be Ms Council and the next Ms Resident."

But her formal role as facilitator of the Sustainability Forum gave her the opportunity to use this position to pursue issues within the city council that she both supported and felt had some chance of success. For her,

> the forum constituted an 'internal pressure group' that enabled her to "put weight behind some of the issues that we were already trying to push". She acknowledged that her role in the agenda setting group enabled her to influence the agenda and her role in writing up and presenting the results of forum discussions gave her some power over the issues to be highlighted. (Barnes et al, 2007: 178)

Arguably, this enabled her to subvert or at least selectively amend aspects of the positions adopted within forum discussions. But she also described examples of using her understanding of the way the council worked and of spotting opportunities to pursue forum objectives that were unlikely to be achieved through official channels.

Other examples of alliances between sympathetic officials and citizen/user participants were found in a social services user group, a Sure Start participation initiative and in relationships between the Women's Advice Centre and council officers. In each case insider knowledge was used to support citizens and service users to pursue their objectives when these were not in line with official policies or priorities. Others have reported similar dynamics elsewhere. Innes and Booher (2003) describe one consequence of a collaborative approach to policy making in relation to the management of the water supply in northern California. A group of 'contentious stakeholders', representing business, agriculture, local government and environmental interests, met over a period of time during which one businessman was accused of going over to the environmental side and 'becoming one of them' (p 33). In a very different context Rodgers (2007) identifies the way in which a participatory forum in Argentina became capable of 'subverting the subversion' of politicisation by political parties through the development of personal relationships within and across a number of local associations who were able to come together in a participatory budgeting process.

From a different perspective we also observed a number of cases in which citizens who might have used deliberative forums to oppose official policy or positions effectively constructed their interventions by reference to what they considered officials would find 'reasonable', or at least unthreatening. As well as in the case of the MEGC referred to above, this was, for example, very evident in a Patients' Participation Group linked to a GP surgery, and in dialogue between Muslim community representatives and health officials over the availability of religious circumcision within the NHS. Here there was an interesting dynamic. Not only did the lead community representative seek to offer the key NHS official input that would help him achieve an official policy objective (reducing the incidence of heart disease among the Asian population) which was not the objective that had motivated the current deliberations, the NHS official also recognised the high profile of the representative within his community and thus sought to ensure that he was not undermined by coming away completely empty handed. The official's position was also influenced by a broad commitment to social justice that he sought to reflect within his official role. Thus, each recognised the contextual nature of the other's stance and identity and endeavoured to use this understanding within the dialogic process to achieve mutually acceptable outcomes. Although the different positions each occupied clearly influenced the substance of the dialogue, the way in which each framed the issue under discussion built on their insights into these differences in order to avoid overt moral disagreement.

Other case studies offer evidence of the significance of the situated agency of participants (both citizens and officials) in shaping both deliberative dynamics and policy influence. We can conclude from this that the dynamics of participation are neither predictable nor obvious and the likelihood that such spaces might generate subversion is a matter of why people take part and how they use the opportunity this provides, rather than being determined by the formal design or constitution of such spaces. Identities are multiple and constructed rather than singular and ascribed, and participation forums become another context in which identity work can be undertaken. Because the location of these spaces, bridging as they do the official and the public spheres, is different from that of social movements or the spaces in which what Fraser (1997) has described as 'counter publics' pursue alternative strategies, the identity work that takes place is different from the process of collective identity building that Melucci discusses as being necessary to building and sustaining motivations to act in the context of social movements. Any sense of 'oppositional consciousness' that might be considered to arise is constrained by the different positions of citizens and officials – although this is not unidirectional. Citizens constrain their oppositional stances, as well as officials using these forums to offer challenges they might otherwise not have been able to make. But the dialogue-based practices of these participation forums do contain the potential to undermine presumed oppositions between officials and citizens, as well as to develop both shared understandings and shared meanings of the issues being deliberated. At least some of these forums generate a sense of a 'community of ideas' (which was a term used to describe the Sustainability Forum) – that is, they are spaces in which both officials and citizens may, if not developing the collective identities of social movements, at least move towards a shared framing of issues. Within such forums it is possible to generate new discursive constructions of policy issues and new repertoires of action to achieve change. It is perhaps this that creates the positive potential of such forums that cannot be achieved solely by either state or oppositional action.

One important aspect of this is the acceptance that knowledge and expertise are not the sole preserve of officials. This is also evident in other locations in which assumed or established social relations of production/consumption, service delivery/service use or policy maker/welfare subject are being unsettled. When a woman who uses mental health services takes part in the education and training of mental health workers, she becomes the expert and they are the users; when residents of a deprived neighbourhood undertake their own research into health needs and use of health services in the area, they are generating the evidence on which policy can be made.

Conclusion

One of the consequences of the participatory turn within governance and service delivery is that both the relationships between street-level bureaucrats and their clients, and the spaces within which they might meet them, have changed since 1980 when Lipsky published his book. One consequence of this is that the orderly separation of worker and client, officials and citizens, is itself being subverted. Citizens are learning the institutional rules they need in order to operate within public bureaucracies, they are entering different spaces as experts rather than as clients and they are building alliances with as well as challenging and opposing public officials. Officials recognise and draw on personal identities and ideological commitments in working out how they should respond to those who can no longer be identified as 'their clients'. Although power remains very unequal, the notion of unidirectional power does not work in this context. The policy objective of the 'empowerment' of citizens is too simplistic but nor is it useful to understand these forums simply as another place in which officials exercise power over citizens/users.

This analysis also suggests that we need to interrogate the notion that 'responsible citizens' are service users and community members who are expected to share responsibility for delivering public policy objectives, and not public officials who are employed to make and deliver public policy. Do officials evidence a sense that they should behave as responsible citizens in the way in which they negotiate their positions within participation forums? If so, what constitutes such an understanding? For some it is evident that they see their primary responsibility as being to the agencies for which they work. Others seek to demonstrate their commitments to specific publics, or to values such as social justice or environmental sustainability, through the way in which they exploit the opportunities opened up by the expansion of spaces for participation. But behaving responsibly in this way may be construed as being subversive of their identities as public officials.

What is very clear is that it is not possible to characterise public participation per se as a process either of creating self-governing subjects, or as generating oppositional consciousness. Such spaces contain both conservative and subversive potentials.

FOUR

Subversive spheres: neighbourhoods, citizens and the 'new governance'

Helen Sullivan

Introduction

Changes to governance institutions and practices in western democracies have created the conditions for multilevel governance and supported the development of new forms of political agency and organisation (Lowndes and Sullivan, 2008). These developments have enabled the emergence of the neighbourhood as an important component of this multilevel environment, and evidence from a number of European countries suggests that both the idea and the practice of neighbourhood governance are now embedded in public policy (Atkinson and Carmichael, 2007). Considerable attention has been focused on whether or not neighbourhood arrangements 'work', that is, whether they deliver desired outcomes more efficiently and/ or effectively (see, for example, Smith et al, 2007). The focus of this chapter is rather different. It is concerned with examining why UK neighbourhood governance initiatives purposely designed to engage more directly and productively with citizens as users of services, voters, workers and local representatives often fail to do so, instead generating frustration and antipathy expressed through attempts at subversion or, ultimately, withdrawal.

The chapter argues that the roots of this apparent disconnect between purpose and outcomes in neighbourhood governance are located in the differences between the values and practices of 'big' versus 'small' local governments and the tensions that arise when attempts are made to combine them (Dahl and Tufte, 1973; Newton, 1982). These tensions mean that, among and between politicians, the public and professionals, there may be different and competing views about the appropriateness and contribution of neighbourhood governance, views informed by the legacy of policy makers' fluctuating fascination with 'the neighbourhood' in the post-war period. Importantly, these tensions permit powerful actors, for example central government, to use neighbourhood governance initiatives as instruments of 'subversion', unsettling institutionalised governance arrangements in pursuit of policy goals.

The chapter then considers the variety of neighbourhood governance initiatives and argues that underpinning them are specific and potentially conflicting interpretations, each of which has more or less appeal to local citizens as politicians, professionals and the public. Drawing on the work of Lowndes and Sullivan (2008), it describes the four dominant interpretations of neighbourhood governance, identifies the implications of each for citizens as politicians, professionals and the public and highlights points of complementarity and conflict between them. It argues that in practice these multiple interpretations will coexist, undermining attempts to promote a single, shared meaning of neighbourhood governance. The chapter uses research evidence from an ESRC study of public participation to illustrate how the coexistence of these different interpretations generates conflict over the design and implementation of neighbourhood governance initiatives and creates opportunities for local citizens (as politicians, the public or professionals) to subvert formal policy goals via strategies of reshaping, disruption and even sabotage.

When 'big' and 'small' governments collide: tensions in neighbourhood policy

The values and practices of 'big' and 'small' local governments differ in a number of important ways (Dahl and Tufte, 1973; Newton, 1982). 'Big' local government is associated with efficiency, economies of scale and equity. It is an expression of representative democracy. The body of councillors is 'representative' in that it tends to reflect the diverse wishes and the make-up of the local population, party systems are well developed and local interests are also represented through a wide range of community and other organisations (Newton, 1982). 'Big' government is more likely to be pluralistic, accepting of multiple loyalties to different interests and accommodating the dissent and conflict that results when conflicting interests collide (Dahl and Tufte, 1973; Newton, 1982). 'Big' governments operate through professional bureaucracies, and decision making is informed by the disinterested application of professional values and rationalities.

By contrast, 'small' local government is associated with participation, responsiveness and economies of scope. It emphasises the values of participatory democracy and seeks to engage the public directly in decision making, service design and delivery. Party systems are likely to be less well developed locally and possibly even considered less important in the selection of representatives. Local councillors are more likely to be known to the public and their interactions with them are likely to be more frequent and more intense (Dahl and Tufte, 1973). 'Small' governments tend to reflect the homogeneity of their local community and to sponsor the development of common identities. Citizens' emotional attachment to these identities means that civic relationships are affective relationships with political debates emotional rather than rational affairs (Dahl and Tufte, 1973). The relatively small number of professionals working in 'small' government, the greater proximity of officials to community members and service users and the emphasis on responsiveness brings different values and rationalities to decision making.

UK government – both central and local – has reflected the values and practices of 'big' government, although regular attempts have been made to accommodate the values of 'small' government. This is most evident in local government's promotion of decentralisation initiatives, but it could also be argued to underpin central government's repeated 'neighbourhood-based' policy initiatives in the post-war period (Lepine and Sullivan, 2007; Lepine et al, 2007). Three important tensions surface for politicians, the public and professionals when attempts are made to combine the values and practices of 'big' and 'small' governments and these manifest themselves differently, depending on the shape and nature of particular neighbourhood initiatives.

The first tension concerns the primacy of local politicians and how they navigate the different emphasis placed on their role in representative and participative democracy. Neighbourhood governance initiatives aim to realise democratic renewal by bringing decision making processes closer to the neighbourhood and opening them up to influence by the public, usually through some form of decentralisation. In the UK local government has considerable experience of experimenting with decentralisation schemes for a variety of purposes, usually including enhanced public participation in local decision making (Burns et al, 1994; Sullivan et al, 2001). In these 'top-down' schemes the demand for decentralisation was an expression of a desire to bolster the legitimacy of representative government through improved public participation that was channelled through and mediated by the local councillor.

Grass-roots organisations have also made use of neighbourhood-based approaches. For example, the Neighbourhood Councils movement of the 1960s and 1970s sought to establish urban parish councils in metropolitan areas as a means of bringing government closer to communities (Cockburn, 1977). In these 'bottom-up' initiatives the demand for decentralisation was linked to a desire either for an alternative form of representation or for a new kind of participative democracy, both of which denied the primacy of the local councillor.

In practice these different demands for decentralisation often coexisted, resulting in politicians being challenged in their claims both to be 'the' local representative and to develop different, more interactive ways of governing with, rather than on behalf of, the public. This tension between representative and participative democracy was one which New Labour appeared intent on exacerbating, first in its National Strategy for Neighbourhood Renewal and later in policy proposals for neighbourhood governance aimed at giving individuals and communities greater 'choice and voice' over services (ODPM/HO, 2005; ODPM/DfT, 2006).

The second tension focuses on the agency of the public and how its expression is constructed in different contexts. In 'small' government the public are valorised as potential 'co-governors', strongly identified with the values and practices of the neighbourhood. By contrast, 'big' government considers the public as one of a number of interests whose views and potential opposition need to be mediated in pursuit of the wider public interest. The active involvement of local communities is often considered key to the success of neighbourhood initiatives. Two assumptions are at work here: that the empowerment of neighbourhood communities enables the lay expertise and energy contained within those communities to be released; and that neighbourhood initiatives provide community members with appropriate opportunities for them to contribute to the good governance of their communities.

Evident in the Community Development Programmes (CDP) of the 1970s and the Conservative government's Single Regeneration Budget programme of the 1990s, this community orientation found, arguably, its strongest expression in New Labour's neighbourhood renewal strategy, which identified the neighbourhood as the source of local intelligence, community motivation and momentum for renewal (SEU, 1998). Here, communities were potential 'co-governors', strongly identified and aligned with government goals. What this New Labour discourse did not allow for was either the release of community energy in opposition to the agenda of the state as represented by different neighbourhood initiatives (and which occurred in the CDP projects), or the development and application of community capacity in pursuit of 'good (neighbourhood) governance' outside the state sphere, for example in civil society.

The third tension highlights the role of professionals, conceived as disinterested agents of the wider public interest in 'big' government, but as responsive and accountable to the local constituency in 'small' government. Targeting resources and activities into specific neighbourhoods to alleviate poverty and stimulate regeneration has been popular with policy makers since the 1960s, despite being criticised for failing to take sufficient account of the fact that the root causes of disadvantage may lie in the dynamics of economic and social change operating beyond the neighbourhood (Bradford and Robson, 1995). Neighbourhood targeting also ran counter to the universalist principles held by many professionals as the most appropriate way to deliver welfare, and they too voiced criticisms of this approach (Dale, 1987).

Despite this, governments continued to promote neighbourhood regeneration activity partly because of awareness that persistent inequality and poverty in neighbourhoods might not be explained by individual and collective pathology, but instead might be the result of the actions of unresponsive and uncoordinated public service organisations (Sullivan and Skelcher, 2002). The policies and programmes of the 1990s reflected this emphasis, with initiatives like City Challenge and the Single Regeneration Budget covering a range of policy areas and involving representatives from the public, private, voluntary and community sectors in the delivery of programmes. Differences between the 'special forces' working in and identified with the regeneration initiative (for example, community development workers, project managers, technical advisers) and mainstream professionals working for much bigger organisations (for example, social workers, teachers, housing officials) remained, however. These provided an important context for New Labour's neighbourhood renewal programmes, which aimed to transform the mainstream through successful neighbourhood interventions and to make mainstream the employment of 'neighbourhood managers', individuals whose job it would be to coordinate the activities of local professionals and increase their responsiveness to the needs of the neighbourhood (Sullivan, 2002).

UK neighbourhood policy in the post-war period has surfaced important tensions for local politicians, the public and professionals because it brings together the competing values and practices of 'big' and 'small' government. New Labour has made use of these tensions in its neighbourhood policies to deliberately unsettle particular groups – for example, local councillors who were perceived to be unrepresentative of their local communities and professionals who were considered to be unresponsive to users – and to encourage a particular kind of public participation strongly identified with the values and goals of the state rather than constructed in opposition to it.

However, there is more going on in neighbourhood governance than the subversion of established institutions and interests by central government. Closer examination of neighbourhood initiatives reveals multiple and potentially conflicting interpretations of neighbourhood governance, each of which has more or less appeal to local citizens as politicians, professionals and the public, and each of which has specific implications for how neighbourhood governance is practised.

Neighbourhood governance models and the roots of subversion

Lowndes and Sullivan (2008) have argued that there are four 'ideal types' of neighbourhood governance – neighbourhood empowerment, partnership, government and management. These 'ideal types' reflect the dominant rationales for devolved approaches in contemporary public policy. Each is underpinned by a particular rationale and contains prescriptions for institutional arrangements and the roles of key actors. These are described below and summarised in Table 4.1.

Neighbourhood empowerment embodies the civic rationale which draws on the work of political theorists such as Mill, Rousseau and de Tocqueville to emphasise opportunities for direct citizen involvement. The small size of neighbourhood units and the fact that many public services are consumed at the neighbourhood level makes them more accessible and makes direct communication more feasible. This provides a platform for empowerment, which aims to increase the citizen 'voice' by developing forms of participatory democracy (Hirschman, 1970). The key leadership role is to enable the public to participate and specifically to involve traditionally marginalised or excluded groups. It is not clear who would take this leadership role – politicians, professionals or other local leaders – and relatively little attention is paid to their contribution. However, it is clear that the performance of the leadership role would require very different skills and styles – facilitating rather than directing – to those used by politicians and professionals in their existing roles.

Table 4.1: Forms of neighbourhood governance: four ideal types

	Neighbourhood empowerment	Neighbourhood partnership	Neighbourhood government	Neighbourhood management
Primary rationale	Civic	Social	Political	Economic
Key objectives	Active citizens and cohesive communities	Citizen well-being and regeneration	Responsive and accountable decision making	More effective local service delivery
Democratic device	Participatory democracy	Stakeholder democracy	Representative democracy	Market democracy
Citizen role	Citizen: voice	Partner: loyalty	Elector: vote	Consumer: choice
Leadership role	Animateur, enabler	Broker, chair	Councillor, mini-mayor	Entrepreneur, director
Institutional forms	Forums, co-production	Service board, mini-LSP	Town councils, area committees	Contracts, charters

Source: Lowndes and Sullivan, 2008: 62

The focus of neighbourhood empowerment is very much on the public and, in the 'new governance', the neighbourhood may be more than the most appropriate space within which to exercise 'voice and choice'. It may also be a space within which members of the public 'co-produce' policy and services in and around existing political frameworks. This implies a much more active role for the public and has implications for the role of the professional, though this receives less attention. In relation to the public, Bang and Sørenson (1999) call for the recognition of a new kind of citizen – the 'everyday maker', someone working for community well-being but doing so outside of established political constructions of citizenship. This insight is important, as it offers an alternative perspective on the contribution of the public in 'small' government. 'Everyday makers' may strongly identify with the neighbourhood, but this identification is not subject to or managed by ideas that the state may communicate about what it is to be 'empowered'. This alternative expression is possible partly because of the 'new' politics which has developed alongside the emerging multilevel governance and which operates through alternative forms of political agency and organisation, challenging the authority and legitimacy of national and local governments (Newman, 2005).

Neighbourhood partnership expresses the social rationale which points to the possibility of a public-centred (rather than politician or professional) approach to governance, building on the work of Fabians such as G.D.H. Cole. Neighbourhood partnerships offer the best prospect for 'joining up' local action to provide a more integrated approach to well-being, as they bring together the key service providers and decision makers to pool resources, risks and rewards in order to achieve improved delivery of each stakeholder's objectives and the creation of new opportunities. Professionals are important in neighbourhood partnership, as it is only through them that 'joined-up' local action can be achieved. Fulfilling this role requires professionals to be able to work collaboratively with others and to overcome any boundaries (such as professional, organisational) that may hinder their progress. While recent evidence does suggest that many public service professionals have become adept at working in partnership (Skelcher et al, 2005), the dynamics of neighbourhood partnership working, for example balancing universal standards with particular needs, may have less appeal.

Neighbourhood partnerships express a form of stakeholder democracy, but members have different kinds of mandate and legitimacy – a source of strength and conflict (Hirst, 1994; Lowndes and Sullivan, 2004). Within a neighbourhood partnership, the public is one of the partners, linked to the governance process through a relationship of 'loyalty' in which partners expect each other to conduct themselves reliably and honestly (Hirschman, 1970). The key leadership roles within a neighbourhood partnership are those of the broker, who brings partners together, and the chair, who facilitates collective decision making and arbitrates in the absence of consensus. This offers an important role for local politicians, though in practice it is not one they have always been keen to take up, as evidence of the relative absence of politicians from Local Strategic Partnerships (LSPs) and related arrangements testifies (Sullivan and Howard, 2005; ODPM/DfT, 2006).

Neighbourhood government expresses the political rationale which focuses on improvements in the accessibility, responsiveness and accountability of decision making, drawing on arguments made by Plato, and later by Robert Dahl. Neighbourhood government is part of an attempt to restore trust in government. It focuses on the representative role of councillors as local leaders. Leaders at neighbourhood level are more likely to be known to the public and to be responsive to them, as well as being more accountable because of the relative visibility of their decision making and its consequences. Neighbourhood government seeks to enhance the representative role by establishing an ongoing dialogue between councillors and constituents, and promoting councillors as community advocates and scrutineers of the work of the local authority and other service providers.

The public have considerable experience and knowledge of the key issues in the neighbourhood and so are able to make informed inputs into policy making. The public's role is to act as informed electors, with their key resource being their vote.

Neighbourhood government contains clear and unambiguous roles for politicians and the public, based on a replication of the system of representative democracy in operation locally. The role of professionals is not considered explicitly but it is reasonable to assume that it would be as changed or unchanged as those of politicians and the public.

Neighbourhood management emphasises the economic rationale of efficiency and effectiveness gains in local service delivery. The economic rationale identifies neighbourhood units as better placed to identify diverse citizen needs and provide appropriate services, as well as rooting out waste by exploiting economies of scope. This is contingent on the empowerment of front-line managers, who are required to possess an entrepreneurial skill set, including a customer focus and a capacity to innovate and take risks.

The prospects for neighbourhood management have been enhanced by new technologies that allow for backroom functions to be carried out at a central base and by externalisation, which can allow neighbourhood managers to commission services to suit local needs from providers who operate on a much larger scale. While most neighbourhoods are not able to take advantage of the operation of market democracy, in which consumers may choose to take their 'business' elsewhere, the development of neighbourhood charters and performance indicators is one attempt to mirror this relationship. Neighbourhood management privileges the role of the professional, identifying them as key to making sense of how services can be designed and delivered in such a way as to respond to the needs of informed consumers (which is how the role of the public is conceived). What remains unresolved in this model is an examination of the relationship between professionals and any generic 'neighbourhood managers' that may be appointed in a coordinating capacity. Politicians receive little direct attention in this model.

This brief summary of four 'ideal types' highlights the very different emphases placed on the contribution of local politicians, the public and professionals, depending on which type of neighbourhood governance is being pursued. Neighbourhood government is the most familiar type, replicating the values and practices of 'big' government at the neighbourhood level. However, each of the other 'ideal types' unsettles these values and practices and challenges local politicians, the public or professionals to adopt new roles and relationships. In some cases, such as neighbourhood partnership, significant roles are available to all. However, in others, for example, neighbourhood empowerment and neighbourhood management, the focus is on either the public (empowerment) or the professionals (management), with local politicians' contribution left rather ill defined.

Lowndes and Sullivan (2008) acknowledge that neighbourhood governance is more messy and multifaceted than the depiction of 'ideal types' would suggest, but argue that this depiction exposes the challenges inherent in designing new governance systems. They conclude that designers of neighbourhood governance schemes need to address questions about purposes, priorities and rationales, fully aware of the challenges that will arise and the trade-offs that will need to be made in the process. However, I want to argue here that satisfactory trade-offs may not result, either because the value bases underpinning competing manifestations of neighbourhood governance are fundamentally different (for example, compare 'neighbourhood empowerment' and 'neighbourhood government') or because they expose one or more of the core tensions identified above: the ability of local elected representatives to navigate participative democratic practices; the construction of public agency as that of 'responsible' rather than 'resistant'; and the capacity of 'disinterested' professionals to adapt to more intimate neighbourhood arenas.

Consequently, different actors will continue to bring to the design and practice of neighbourhood governance competing interpretations of what neighbourhood governance could or should be, regardless of the 'official' version. The dissonance generated by the coexistence of these interpretations creates opportunities for local citizens (as local politicians, professionals or the public) to subvert formal policy goals through strategies and practices of reshaping, disruption and even sabotage.

Subversive neighbourhoods: strategies and practices

Renewed enthusiasm for the neighbourhood has been evident among national and local governments in most parts of the UK. In England the National Strategy for Neighbourhood Renewal identified and sponsored initiatives within England's most deprived neighbourhoods: the New Deal for Communities programme supported community-led regeneration; the Neighbourhood Management scheme aimed to improve the coordination of local services; the Neighbourhood Renewal Fund offered a resource stream to local authorities and their partners; the Community Empowerment Network targeted the building and organising of local community capacity; and the Sure Start programme focused on improving the life-chances of children aged 0–4. Similar initiatives in Scotland and Wales included the development of Social Inclusion Partnerships (Scotland) and the Communities First programme (Wales). Local councils also explored the potential of neighbourhood governance through decentralisation schemes, neighbourhood projects and community participation programmes (Smith et al, 2007).

The ESRC Democracy and Participation Programme provided an opportunity to research some of these initiatives, and with colleagues Marian Barnes, Andrew Knops and Janet Newman I examined neighbourhood governance as part of our Power, Participation and Political Renewal study (Barnes et al, 2007). Through case studies we explored the impact of neighbourhood governance initiatives on local politicians, the public and professionals. We found that citizen actors drew on a range of strategies and practices in their interactions with neighbourhood initiatives, to support or resist them. The capacity of these different actors to effect change (or not) was contingent on a combination of factors, including: the context within which the initiative was introduced, the institutional robustness of the initiative, the availability of different sources of agency and counter-agency, and the ability of actors to draw upon them.

Context matters in a temporal as well as a material sense. As neighbourhood initiatives have been an almost constant feature of the policy landscape in the post-war period, 'new' initiatives are rarely experienced as such by those expected to implement or participate in them. Rather, each 'new' programme is imbued with the legacy of past initiatives, shaping the local appetite for engagement with it (Smith et al, 2007).

Context is also important as a physical expression of what a neighbourhood is at any given moment. Conventionally, local authorities and national governments have identified and described neighbourhoods by following political-administrative boundaries, or clusters of indices of deprivation. Despite their value to policy makers, they may not mean a great deal to residents in an area or professionals working a patch. Some local authorities, such as Birmingham, have experimented with 'natural neighbourhoods'. Here, residents and others describe what their neighbourhood looks like (with the offer of different definitions for different purposes), so as to generate more locally relevant 'maps'. The value of this kind of activity was supported by our research, which found that potential participants were much more likely to identify with the neighbourhood governance initiative if they were influential in its design, including determining the rules of engagement and conduct (Sullivan et al, 2003).

As neighbourhood initiatives are introduced into contexts imbued with the legacies of past experiences, the interaction between initiative and context will surface differing views about its potential and limits, which in turn may stimulate attempts at reshaping the design of the initiative. For example, one of our case studies was of a residents' group established as part of an estate-wide regeneration scheme (Barnes et al, 2007: ch 5). The introduction of the scheme onto the estate had been controversial, partly because it had replaced existing initiatives and partly because local residents were concerned that the scheme would have unequal benefits for tenants, leaseholders and owner-occupiers. The regeneration organisation was overseen by a partnership board with a range of representatives from different sectors, including representatives of the local residents. One of its objectives was to support and foster the development of resident participation in the regeneration programme through the establishment of residents' groups. Our research into one particular residents' group revealed how different interpretations of neighbourhood governance, combined with institutional flexibility and powerful resident agency, resulted in a reshaping and rebalancing of the relationship between the regeneration organisation and the residents' group.

The regeneration organisation was keen to promote a model of neighbourhood partnership in its relations with residents and it conceived of residents' groups as 'partners' in governance. This was exemplified by the availability of places for residents' representatives on the estate-wide partnership body. However, the residents' group that we studied held a different view of their role in neighbourhood governance, one in which they were participants in processes of governing but also had a clear and separate identity from the governing body, leaving them free to disagree with it when necessary. Consequently, the chair of the residents' group refused to stand for election onto the partnership board, as these were paid positions which, in his view, would place him in a position of weakness in his relationship with the regeneration body.

The residents' group was able to negotiate its relationship with the regeneration body even though it had little resource power of its own because of its credibility and legitimacy with its members. Central to its perceived strength was the fact that it had emerged 'bottom up' and was led by individuals with considerable experience of working with a range of interests in previous roles, and with confidence in their own capacity to act and influence. The chair, vice-chairs and secretary drew on their own experiences as trade union representatives, as committee members in voluntary organisations and on their work experiences to develop a set of rules that governed their activities in a way which they believed provided them with considerable legitimacy as a group and which maintained a clear separation between them and their sponsoring body.

Importantly, the resident leaders were aware that they had choices in developing their relationship with the regeneration organisation – they could work with the body and negotiate ways of working that suited both parties, or they could opt out of the negotiation and continue to press for change on the estate on their own terms. However, they were also helped in the negotiation process by the fact that the regeneration organisation was aware that its lifespan was limited and that part of its role was to foster participative processes that could be self-sustaining once the regeneration programme came to an end.

The above example illustrates how negotiation can help to support the design of 'good governance' in neighbourhood initiatives. However, it is not always the case that initiative designers are amenable to negotiation about rules and practices. Consequently, other strategies and practices are applied by citizen actors in attempts to disrupt, subvert or even sabotage the initiative. Again, evidence from our research suggests that the impetus for these practices stems from competing interpretations about the nature of the initiative, and their impact depends partly on the agency of those practising resistance and partly on the flexibility of the initiative.

One case study from our research – an area committee – illustrates how citizen actors used disruptive practices to express their discontent with the working of a neighbourhood governance initiative (Barnes et al, 2007: ch 5). Following a change in political control in the local authority of a large city, the new administration declared its ambition to develop a more participatory local democracy, partly through the introduction of area committees. The stated aim of these area committees was to give local people an opportunity to take part in the decision-making processes of the council and to hold local councillors to account for the performance of council services and of other public service bodies. The committee meetings tended to be very formal, not least because they were framed by the rules and practices governing council committees, a deliberate design decision by council officials. Each committee meeting followed a common format, which included a period of 'question time', the point in the meeting where local people could raise issues with and get a response directly from their local representatives.

Our research suggested that there was a mismatch between the public's expectations and those of local politicians in relation to the role of the area committee. This was illustrated by the difference in actors' interpretations of 'participation'. For example, for some local politicians enhancing public participation was about broadening and deepening the level of interaction between local politicians and the public, in order that local politicians were better able to represent the views of their local communities. For them the area committee was an example of neighbourhood government. By contrast, some members of the public interpreted public participation in the area committee as an expression of neighbourhood empowerment, having the opportunity to set the agenda and directly shape decisions. Other members of the public considered the area committee an opportunity to raise their concerns as consumers of council services and have these responded to (the neighbourhood management model).

This mismatch in expectations generated conflict between the public and local politicians and the local professionals assigned to support the area committee. This was compounded by the fact that the area committee had no power to take executive decisions but, rather, was advisory. Nonetheless, local people attended the meetings and populated 'question time' with demands for 'something to be done about' a range of small but significant unresolved local issues, including rats, rubbish and unlicensed taxi drivers.

The combination of competing interpretations about the purpose of the area committee and what was perceived as the repeated failure of the council to rectify the problems identified by the public reduced the public's commitment to the initiative, but also stimulated new forms of behaviour at the meetings by some members of the public. A key act was not to observe the rules of 'question time', which permitted asking a single question (usually writing it down in advance) and getting a response. Alternatives to this approach used by disgruntled members of the public included not asking a single question but using the time allocated to make a speech about an issue (not always related to the question), asking more than one question and/or drawing on the support of others to express disapproval over the council's failure to act on any given issue. These strategies and tactics were not popular with many of the participants at the area committee; one respondent described them dismissively as 'just shouting'. They also did not appear to have any positive effect in terms of achieving change on substantive issues, but it was not entirely clear that members of the public using these tactics had ambitions beyond disrupting what they perceived to be an inflexible and inappropriate means of engaging with them.

Among professionals, whose agency is rooted in their expert status and their resource power, non-compliance can be a powerful and subversive act. Neighbourhood management programmes in which a neighbourhood manager is appointed to improve service coordination and responsiveness rely heavily on the cooperation of local service professionals: for information about service use and capacity, for participation in reviewing services and possibly reallocating resources, and for endorsement about the value of the endeavour. However this cooperation may not be forthcoming, and even where agreement to the initiative is formally given by the head of the respective department or organisation, this may not be supported by practical action.

Our research demonstrated the power of professional non-compliance in a neighbourhood-based Sure Start programme (Barnes et al, 2007: ch 5). This particular Sure Start programme was attached to a large local voluntary-sector provider and the Sure Start organisation included staff with backgrounds in voluntary and community sector work as well as professionals employed by social services and other public service providers.

The Sure Start programme manager had a background in community development and was strongly committed to the idea of empowering parents through the application of community development principles and techniques in Sure Start activities. She was supported in this view by those staff with experience of working in the voluntary and community sector. However, she felt herself to be fighting against other members of her staff team (who were social workers), who she believed were engaged in 'calculated manipulation' to undermine her, principally by not adopting a community development approach to their work.

From their perspective the staff team members considered that the Sure Start programme was an opportunity to make more effective and coordinated interventions in the lives of children, with the aim of improving their life-chances. Sure Start enabled professionals to work in partnership to deliver better support to parents and their children. However, the professionals were clear that this partnership approach should not result in the dilution of important aspects of good social work practice, for example, visiting service users in pairs. The agency the social workers were able to draw on, imbued with the values of professional norms and codes and combined with the risk of what could happen if these norms were not observed, presented a significant challenge to the Sure Start manager and her ambitions for a more community development-oriented initiative.

Acts of sabotage were rare in our research but, paradoxically, it was local politicians who came closest to this, through their conduct in their own neighbourhood governance initiative (the area committee), described above. Our research showed that, despite setting up the area committees, many local politicians appeared unable or unwilling to engage in the activities that were designed to improve the effectiveness of the committee meetings, such as agenda-setting sessions with senior officials (who also rarely attended) and development sessions with other local representatives from different sectors (Barnes et al, 2007: ch 5). Once at the area committee meetings it was not uncommon for councillors to use the meetings to make speeches or to appear uninterested in proceedings by doing paperwork, fiddling with keys, talking to colleagues and leaving the meeting early.

Even those instrumental in driving the area committee initiative seemed unable to change their behaviour in the meetings, often engaging in arguments with those whom they perceived to be their political opponents or dismissing the interventions of members of the public who breached the rules in an effort to make their voices heard. On one occasion a councillor turned on the committee chair (a party colleague), accusing her of conducting meetings in such as way as to inhibit real debate and declaring that 'the agenda should be ripped up'. The effect of this was to alienate councillors from the public, intensify the divisions between them and highlight the limitations of the initiative.

Elsewhere we have described initiatives like this as 'institutional prisons' where none of the participants are able to operate in the way they profess they would like to (Barnes et al, 2007: ch 5). Why this might be so may be explained by the different interpretations that politicians and the public had in relation to the purpose of the area committee, which generated immediate dissonance between them; the lack of flexibility in the design of the initiative, which replicated the operation of 'the council' within the neighbourhood and consequently alienated many potential citizen participants (public, professional and politicians); and the lack of awareness, willingness or ability on the part of local politicians to navigate the tension in the relationship between representative and participative democratic practices.

Conclusion

Policies supporting neighbourhood governance of one form or another have been popular with successive national and local governments in the post-war era. They have been of particular fascination for New Labour because ideas about the neighbourhood seem to embody a coincidence of state and civil society interests, a coming together of 'top-down' with 'bottom-up' desires and demands. However, there are important tensions in the theory and practice of neighbourhood governance which confound its easy acceptance by politicians, the public and professionals. These tensions are important illustrations of inherent differences in the virtues of 'big' rather than 'small' governments. Any attempt to introduce neighbourhood governance (small government) into wider local or national systems (big government) activates these tensions and creates the potential for subversion. Consequently it can be argued that neighbourhood governance policies are themselves subversive acts, designed with the express purpose of unsettling the established relationships of politicians, the public and professionals in the pursuit of new ones. New Labour's National Strategy for Neighbourhood Renewal can be understood in this way, as can many local authority initiatives in neighbourhood governance.

Examination of neighbourhood initiatives reveals multiple and potentially conflicting interpretations of neighbourhood governance (neighbourhood empowerment, partnership, government and management), each of which has more or less appeal to local citizens as politicians, professionals and the public, and which exposes one or more of the core tensions identified above: the ability of local elected representatives to navigate participative democratic practices; the construction of public agency as 'responsible' rather than 'resistant'; and the capacity of 'disinterested' professionals to adapt to more intimate neighbourhood arenas. The dissonance generated by the coexistence of these different interpretations helps to create the conditions in which politicians, the public and/or professionals engage in subversive acts, acts whose impact is conditioned by a combination of agency and institutional context.

Recent developments in governance and politics suggest that the interplay of interpretations, tensions and agency in the theory and practice of neighbourhood governance may be operating in rather different ways and with rather different effects. For example, Bang and Sørenson's (1999) characterisation of the 'everyday maker' offers the possibility of a new kind of public citizen, one that exists outside the traditional prescriptions of 'big' and 'small' government. Similarly, the institutionalisation of collaboration between professionals, coupled with the growth in the number of public services delivered by private companies, has reshaped the idea of what it is to be a public service professional. Finally, the repeated challenges to the legitimacy and relevance of the local politician suggest that finding a way to successfully navigate the representative/participative boundary at the neighbourhood level may be key to their survival in the future, where party politics itself becomes increasingly fragmented and 'issue'-specific movements gain greater influence. These developments have implications beyond the operation of neighbourhood governance, but the neighbourhood will continue to provide an important space for politicians, the public and professionals to interact and reshape or subvert their futures.

FIVE

Narrating subversion, assembling citizenship

Janet Newman and John Clarke

In this chapter we use two stories – one about citizens and one about non-citizens – to explore some of the issues that are brought into view by the phrase 'subversive citizens'. These stories generate three such issues for us: first, what is it that is being subverted through the active engagement of people as workers in or users of public services or public institutions? Second, what does it mean to call these actors 'citizens'; in what ways is this identity significant (and how does it differ from other terms such as 'worker', 'user' or 'resident')? Third, how do we understand the field of relationships in which such actors act? That is, how is the practice of subversion located, framed and understood? The stories have been told to us by friends and colleagues: they are drawn from their work and experience, rather than from our own. But both of the stories, when we heard them for the first time, provoked puzzled reflections on what was at stake when citizens (and non-citizens) acted in these particular settings.

We begin, however, with some thoughts about the field of relationships in which these actions take place. Subversion, like related conceptions of transgression or resistance, tends to be framed in binary terms. Sometimes these binaries appear as topological metaphors (the distinction between top-down and bottom-up approaches, or between centre and periphery, for example). Elsewhere they are temporal metaphors: the opening phase of policy formulation succeeded by implementation, when the objectives of policy may be subverted or inflected in practice (by 'street-level bureaucrats' or by innovative users). More generally, several perspectives share a view of social life organised in power-structured dyadic relationships (even though they may disagree about much else). For example, Marxism's distinction between dominant and subordinated classes has echoes of the Hegelian conception of the master–slave dyad that has proved influential in psychoanalytic and literary approaches (Jenks, 2003). Meanwhile, Foucault's understanding of power stresses that it is intrinsically and intimately involved in the incitement of its other: resistance. In what follows we want to step away somewhat from these binary distinctions and dyadic models of power relations and towards an engagement with the multiple forms of power and lines of force that are in play in particular situations, the heterogeneity of which has to be negotiated and mobilised by actors in those situations.

In trying to formulate alternative ways of understanding the field we have drawn from current work on rethinking the formation of publics and publicness (Newman and Clarke, 2009). Here we view policy instruments and other governing technologies as part of *assemblages* rather than as temporally separated elements of a cycle of actions and effects. The concept of assemblage is usually associated with the actor network theories of Latour, Callon and others (for example, Callon, 1986; Latour, 2005); but it has also been taken up and developed within anthropology (for example, Ong and Collier, 2005; Ong, 2006; Li, 2007; Sharma, 2008). Assemblages bring together, align and condense multiple projects, discourses, acts and identities. For example, writing about empowerment as a vital assemblage in the attempted reconfiguration of relations between government and people in India, Sharma insists on viewing it as 'an evolving formation and flexible technology of government rather than a singularly coherent discourse and method' (2008: 2). She argues that dominant ideas and hierarchies are contested; that maintaining them requires work, and that such work entails assembling elements of both hegemonic and counter-hegemonic discourses and practices into new ensembles. Assemblage, then, provides some conceptual leverage for understanding both the work of assembling (the building of assemblages in and through which governing is enacted) and the vulnerability of assemblages to coming apart (under the strain of maintaining their internal connectedness or apparent coherence). In developing this view of assemblage we want to emphasise how particular forms of power and authority are mobilised and made productive (Allen, 2003). In the following examples we will make visible the different sorts of authorisation to which 'subversive citizens' lay claim.

The landscape of contemporary governance is littered with sites where multiple resources and capacities are mobilised and brought into new alignments: the partnership initiative, the community empowerment project, the public participation exercise, the political campaign or the development programme. Viewing these as assemblages helps to highlight the complex flows of power and resources, the enrolment of different ideas, interests and agents, the potential instabilities embedded in the apparent coherence, and the ways in which contestation is masked, reworked, silenced or accommodated. However, the concept of assemblage risks flattening the spatial and temporal dimensions and thus making it difficult to capture the dynamics that are at stake in the alignment of objects and actors, and indeed in their coming apart. In what follows we explore two narrative framings of the issues and dynamics at stake in specific sites of contestation. Such narratives tend to be organised around temporal framings – the succession of events, the ebb and flow of action and reaction. We have chosen in each case to focus on local struggles. However, rather than seeing the local as a distinct level of analysis, what each of these stories reveals is how particular local struggles condense and mobilise different contestations, different levels and different fields of relationships (Massey, 2004). The local – like other spaces – is the focus of contested claims making, not least about who 'owns' the local. In each of our cases the story is constructed, translated and woven into a whole by a researcher relating her experience of studying a specific struggle over a relatively long period. Of course, researchers never simply report the 'facts of the matter', but bring their own orientations and commitments into the process of research and reportage; for example, the commitment to bring a particular issue or set of voices and experiences into the public domain. In this chapter, we subject these stories to a further process of selection and translation, bending them to our interest in practices of assembling and reassembling forms of power. We owe a substantial debt to Anne Helset in Norway and Kathy Coll in the United States for the time they have spent with us recounting and explaining the stories, and for allowing us to mobilise their stories in new ways.

Story 1: Subversive citizens

This story emerges from within a long-term study of 'senior centres' in Norway. Anne Helset's ethnographic work traces how plans to make cuts, reduce staff and close centres in one municipality were successfully resisted by citizens, and how citizens remained dissatisfied with the 'broken promises' that were made. Anne is pleased to recount the story, since problems about anonymising key actors meant that publication of the report was delayed, even though it is what she termed a 'good news' story.

Senior centres in Norway developed from the 1950s as a preventative movement on the part of those who shaped the early welfare state in Norway, including physicians. Elderly people – a third of whom are frail and in need of assistance – attend for meals, activities, advice and other services. Some 25% of participants, most commonly women, also work at centres as volunteers. The research took place in an affluent municipality with a tradition of active community organisations and women's groups. In the 1960s and 1970s, senior centres were based on co-production arrangements between community organisations and local authorities. However, in the 1990s changes in the financing of municipalities led to a search for financial savings, and the 2004 budget proposed to concentrate provision in 2 out of the 14 existing centres, with the remainder offering reduced services from a smaller and differently configured staffing base.

This led to what the researcher termed the 'big happening'. This was a huge protest of elderly people at the town hall, where the budget was being debated, with much booing of the speakers. The result was not only a partial (50%) restoration of the budget but also a proposal to set up a negotiation process in which three elected representatives of the users of senior centres would take part in discussions with the Radman (chief executive of the municipality) about the future of the centres. At the same time, however, the Radman established a separate project group charged with finding ways to reduce staff costs. This comprised the senior managers of the two largest centres, the head of the service and trade union representatives. The project group was also to produce a 'dossier' of facts about the senior centres, to be used to support the Radman in negotiations with centre representatives. But the significance of the citizen protests also led local politicians to set up a group that met with senior centre user representatives and a wider group of managers. That is, three different consultative processes were established: the first between a narrow group of 'representative' service users and the Radman; the second involving senior managers and trade union representatives; and the third a wider, politically led consultative process with service users and staff. These were uneasily aligned, producing further tensions and protests.

The narrowly defined and clearly bounded consultation between the Radman and the service user representatives led to significant concessions on the part of the municipality: all centres were to remain open and properly staffed. However, the costs of meals would be raised and users would be asked to 'voluntarily' pay for other activities. This agreement was confirmed by politicians and was widely viewed as a success. Anne showed a newspaper picture of a smiling group – three politicians, three user representatives and the Radman – with glasses in hand, smiling and toasting success. But service users felt cheated when it was discovered that service managers were cutting back on staff in the smaller centres. They felt that they had been part of a genuine process of negotiation, but that all the time managers – and the project team acting in secret – were producing a plan in line with the 'real' intentions of the Radman. More protests and negotiations followed. Staff frequently aligned themselves with service users, not only because of the projected job losses but also because of the impact of cuts on service users (especially those unable to pay the full cost of meals and to fund other activities). Some politicians attempted to distance themselves from plans that had been 'stitched up' between trade unionists and managers. At some points the Radman was a prominent actor, at others he decided to distance himself from the process. A letter of protest was written by the two senior managers of the largest centres, complaining about their treatment by the Radman's representative at a particular meeting and claiming that existing policy and rules on staffing were being undermined. Letters from service user representatives to the Radman carried both implicit and, sometimes, explicit threats to take complaints to politicians.

The resulting negotiations produced financial concessions that allowed some staff to be restored and some recompense for users who could not afford the new fees. This was, then, an example of the success of public protest and, at the same time, an example of the ways in which public protest may be channelled, accommodated and perhaps sidelined. The way in which the account was presented to us left little doubt but that the researcher had aligned herself with the expressions of 'good citizenship' and community activism on the part of service users and volunteers. But she took pains to recount the story fairly, without glossing its complexities and ambiguities. Her narration suggested that, despite the apparent success, there was no sense of closure around a positive outcome.

Comment

There are several ways in which this narrative might be interpreted. It could become a tale of micro-politics, with events hinging on the actions of key individuals. The story could be read in terms of the effectiveness – or not – of the general turn to participative governance; or in terms of the inevitable logic of neoliberal rule, in which small gains on the part of citizens can only provide a temporary stay to the cost-reduction imperative, and in which citizen power and agency are readily incorporated. But in the context of this chapter we want to suggest the value of viewing the senior centre service, in this place and this time, as a complex assemblage in which different forces, forms of power, technologies, resources and actors were entangled.

For example, we can see how long-standing notions of citizens as 'volunteers' were entangled with notions of citizens as 'service users', as 'consumers' paying to receive services, as 'participants' in a quasi-democratic consultative process, and as 'activists' engaging in public protest. These were not, then, simply 'subversive' citizens, adapting or resisting public policy, but actors who brought different identities and capacities to their relationships with senior centres, politicians, policy makers and municipal managers, and who were summoned to engage in producing changes in these relationships. The mobilisation of these different conceptions of citizenship within a single service produced instabilities, as is evident from the continued upheaval as apparent resolutions came unstuck. But instabilities also resulted from the uneven assemblage of political, managerial, worker- and citizen-based forms of power and agency. These different forms of power were combined with multiple techniques – the project group, the letters of protest, the dossier of 'facts', the consultative forum, the public protest – through which the meaning of 'policy' was negotiated, reassessed and contested.

While the dominant actor – the Radman – could deploy significant organisational resources, we can see how citizens mobilised different forms of organisational power and deployed not inconsiderable symbolic capital. We can see the ways in which temporary alignments and mobilisations of professional, managerial, trade union, political and service user power were produced. But the story also demonstrates how such alignments can come apart. For example, resistance on the part of politicians to the proposals of the 'project group' comprising managers and trade unions was possible because right-wing politicians resisted the idea of 'being dictated to' by the trade unions. Nevertheless, the consensus between left and right was highly conditional, while the fragility of the alignment between the interests of service managers and service users was made evident when it became clear that managers were intending to implement cuts despite the negotiated agreement. 'Dossiers' and letters, project groups and consultative forums, were all deployed to try to stabilise events and align actors around a common view of the 'facts' of the matter or a consensus about future plans.

But these failed, in the end, to resolve the contradictions produced by the attempted modernisation of the service. Nor was there an apparent resolution between conflicting conceptions of active citizenship: that of protest and dissent on the one hand, and that involved in the day-to-day voluntary work on which the centres depended on the other. We may wonder about how the dynamics between these different versions will be played out, not only in terms of individual citizen identities and the performance of citizenly acts, but also in terms of their contribution to the future of this particular service.

Story 2: Subversive non-citizens

Between 1999 and 2005, the anthropologist Kathleen Coll studied the Immigrant Voting Rights campaign in Cambridge, Massachusetts. This campaign was an attempt gain the right to vote in local elections for non-naturalised residents of Cambridge. Citizenship and nationality are entangled in complex ways in different national contexts, but in the US, since the 1920s and 1930s, the voting rights of citizens have been increasingly closely tied to the condition of US nationality. As a result, residents who have not been naturalised have no right to vote in either local or national elections. The campaign observed by Coll contested the exclusion from the right to vote locally, arguing that, as residents who paid local taxes, contributed to the local community in many ways and used public services, they should be allowed to vote in local elections (for the city council and school board, for example).

The campaigners were involved in a programme of simultaneously trying to subvert the legal-national structuring of voting rights in the US, while borrowing from archetypal features and images of US political culture. Thus, the campaign laid great emphasis on the character and contribution of these 'non-citizens' who nevertheless behaved in citizenly ways: being law-abiding, hard-working, tax-paying residents. More dramatically, they borrowed the core concept that led to the War of Independence: 'no taxation without representation'. Although attempting to subvert and transform a specific legal and political condition, the campaign deliberately represented its cause as hyper-American – representing the best of Americanism, rather than a threat to the legal and political order. In a forthcoming article, Coll describes one of the key scenes in which the campaign was publicly dramatised:

> On May 5, 2003, the dark-oak-trimmed and heavy-curtained chambers of the Cambridge City Council were filled with dozens of city residents including immigrants from Africa, the Middle East, South Asia, Latin America, the Caribbean and Europe. School district employees, small business owners, taxi-drivers, stay-home mothers, immigrant advocates, tenant leaders, community lawyers, perpetual progressive activists, and one anthropologist had shown up on a Monday evening to testify on behalf of a proposal to grant all local residents the right to vote in local elections. Individual speakers represented the major immigrant groups in the city and their economic and racial diversity. Even

city councilors who disagreed with the measure listened attentively as speaker after speaker testified to the number of years they had been waiting to naturalize, what it felt like to be unable to vote for School Committee when their children were attending local public schools, and how they identified with Boston Tea Party activists in 1773 who first uttered the slogan of 'no taxation without representation.' In these testimonies, immigrant and non-immigrant city residents invoked the history of the practice of non-citizen voting. They also pointed to examples of the practice in other cities in the U.S. and overseas, arguing that universal local suffrage forms a new international norm of advanced democratic practice.

It was an elaborate, ritualized, and well-coordinated performance that discursively placed non-citizen community members at the heart of city life and politics. It also claimed the place for this locality in global debates over the boundaries of the state, the meaning of sovereignty and the reconfiguring of citizenship. At the end of the public testimony, there was discussion amongst the city councilors that mainly included declarations of admiration and personal identification with the contemporary immigrant community as virtuous contributors to the city, just like previous generations before them. While individual city councilors expressed concern that the measure was 'purely symbolic' or inappropriate for a local government, since immigration is the purview of the federal, they all voiced their 'deepest respect' for the immigrant Cantabridgians who presented the petition, and assured them that they always had their interests in mind, even though they were not formally part of the electorate. At the same time, opposing councilmen voiced various versions of the position that voting was a sacred right and obligation reserved for legal citizens. (Coll, forthcoming: MS pp 6–7)

The resistance to this campaign both claimed to defend the status quo and suggested that the campaign concealed a greater subversion than it claimed. This conception of the status quo explicitly aligned nationality status, citizenship and voting rights. This was the intention of earlier political decisions (at national level) and could not be put aside by local political choices. Moreover, despite the campaigners' insistence that their interest lay in connecting residence and local participation, their opponents saw any concession here as opening the door to a larger subversion. Once the non-naturalised resident could vote locally, what would prevent this being enlarged to the national level and thus unravelling the tightly knit connections between nationality, citizenship and political rights? In the process, opponents argued, citizenship would itself be 'cheapened' and the contributions, struggles and even waiting times of those who had been born to, or achieved, full citizenship would be undermined.

Coll talks about how very different sorts of resources were mobilised in building the campaign, trying to win support and constructing alliances. The campaigners both drew on and were emboldened by a variety of transnational connections (material and symbolic). These ranged from activist experiences that some members of the campaign brought with them from their places of departure, to the imagery of Dublin as a capital city that had established resident/non-citizen voting rights. The symbolic value of such Irish examples is strong in the Cambridge/Boston area, given the long history of Irish immigration and the power of the real and imagined connections (leading one city councillor to announce that 'If it's good enough for Dublin, it's good enough for Cambridge'). The campaigners also assembled historical resources (pointing to 18th- and 19th-century practices of resident/non-citizen voting throughout the US) and legal research and argumentation to support their case.

In her reflections on these processes, Coll draws out a series of puzzles: what the campaign reveals about the construction of citizens and citizenship; how resources and alliances are mobilised for a specific project of subversion; and how 'subversive' struggles are delicately and unstably balanced. She points out how the campaign carefully limited its demands and appeals – always working within a profoundly juridical and ethical discourse about residents as 'good citizens' – even when they were aware of the wider field of possibilities that might be at stake in disrupting the relationships between residency, citizenship and political rights. Equally, the opponents of the campaign feared subversion – seeing it as a movement that (intentionally or not) threatened a series of cherished distinctions (legal/illegal residents; residents/citizens) and the status of voters as members of a *political* community.

In this example subversion becomes not just a characteristic of an act or a movement. Rather, it is a practical concept that actors in the situation deploy, negotiate and try to manage. For the campaign's opponents, identifying the subversive possibilities behind the limited and legalistic claims making of the campaign was itself a tactic to undermine the claim. This should not surprise us, of course. Defenders of the status quo often raise the stakes around particular issues by pointing to how demands may put cherished values, institutions, practices or even ways of life 'at risk'. Equally, campaigners worked to manage the relationship between the specific claim (residents' voting) and the other destabilising possibilities that it brought into view (the supposed distinction between legal and illegal people; the relation between nation, nationality and citizenship; and even the promises of 'representation' itself).

Comment

We want to draw out three points here concerning the reach of subversion, the question of assemblage and the problematic politics of citizenship as seen by the researcher herself. First, then, demanding residents' voting rights for local elections may appear a small and not very subversive step in the long drawn-out saga of voting rights in the US (and elsewhere). Often such processes appear as legal or even technical matters. However, the Cambridge campaign and others like it indicate that subversion may not be a process of changing or challenging specific policies, regulations or statutory positions. Rather, it may be the process of bringing into view – rendering visible and uncomfortable – the network of assumptions that sustains and supports the existing field of distinctions, regulations and practices. For example, in engaging with the struggle to enhance immigrant voting rights, campaigners had to operate within a very state-centred legislative process in ways that partly reinforced, rather than challenged, nationalist conceptions of citizenship. As Coll comments, 'A vision of disentangling citizenship from the confines of the nation state in the context of transnational migration from the post colonial world was not going to move either the local elected officials or the state legislators empowered to allow such a measure to take effect' (Coll, forthcoming: MS pp 18–19).

Second, we can see how the idea of assemblage that we introduced earlier might illuminate dynamics of the situation Coll presents. We can see the campaign for immigrant voting rights as centred on tactics of *disassembling* an existing arrangement. It carefully and delicately attempted to unlock the ties, connections and articulations of the system of voting rights in the US and in Cambridge. In doing so, it enrolled a variety of resources into a project of change – legal knowledge, history, local and national popular cultural references and, not least, images of the resident (as hard working, familial, tax-paying, etc). This is a struggle not to subvert or transform the whole assemblage of voting rights, citizenship and nationality – but to rearrange its elements in a new configuration, to create new spaces, identities, points of access and possibility.

Third, both the example and the issue matter to the researcher in particular ways. The example is intrinsically important – and Coll has committed time and energy to tracking and reflecting on the processes, conflicts and negotiations that it involves. She is reluctant to treat it as 'merely' an example of larger structural forces or processes, instead trying to make visible the complex and contradictory dynamics of the campaign and what is/may be at stake within it. But it also links to a larger intellectual and political orientation towards the question of citizenship – and especially its relationship to nationality and migration. In that sense, this study connects with other work on migrants and citizenship in the US which foreground the ways in which people both make and make sense of citizenship in hard times. Anti-immigrant politics have been a powerful strand in US politics since the 1990s – and questions of citizenship and nationality mark a critical meeting point for Coll (see, for example, Coll, 2004, 2005).

Assembling power, subverting power

Our insistence that acts of subversion take place in a field of relationships points to difficult questions about the place of power in this sort of analysis. The first concerns the impossibility of treating subversion as part of a simple dynamic of domination and resistance, given the multiple forms of power and authority that are in play in any one situation. Both the stories presented above demonstrate some of this multiplicity. Both involve actions taken by subordinate social groups who occupy relatively powerless positions in the national and local social fields of which they are part (as retired older people; as non-national non-citizens). They engage with relatively powerful institutions of public authority and bureaucracy. But in their collective action, they mobilise a variety of resources, including considerable symbolic power (the dignity and deservingness of elders, their rights as respected citizens; US iconography and the 'good standing' of law-abiding, hard-working, family men and women). In the public settings, these symbolic resources disrupt the dominant assemblages, reworking their apparent coherence and solidity. More generally, we think this implies being attentive to the diverse forms of power and authority that are in play in particular situations, rather than assuming that such situations are merely examples of pre-given binary distinctions (whether of class or gender, or even state/citizens).

Our view is, then, closer to what Allen and Cochrane describe as power being 'negotiated in a tangle of interactions and capabilities' rather than the binary of domination and resistance (2007: 1171) But we also think it is important to explore how such negotiations produce situations that are tendentially 'structured in dominance'. How do certain sorts of actors become dominant, how do certain sorts of knowledge become privileged, how do certain sorts of outcomes come to be desired? In the stories, it is possible to see the traces of how these situations are structured in dominance: in Norway, the dominance of managerial calculation and authority forms a central point around which much of the story revolves (managerialism occupying a particular place in the processes of retrenchment and remaking of welfare states in Europe: Clarke and Newman, 1997; Newman and Clarke, 2009). But managerialism is itself assembled (not always comfortably) with other forms of authority: electoral and public politics; trade union negotiating rights; expectations of citizen entitlement and so on. Equally, the story of Immigrant Voting Rights is structured in dominance around national legal-political authority (the capacity to define the terms of citizenship). But it too is uncomfortably assembled with other sorts of authority: legal authority may itself be multiple and contested rather than singular; popular discourses of entitlement and desert coexist alongside the juridical specification of the citizen; and the iconography of a national political culture – 'no taxation without representation' – may be enrolled into new projects.

There is a danger that the concept of assemblage invokes images of horizontal fields of practice from which questions of power differentials and inequalities are bracketed away. However, we have tried to indicate how the different elements, actors, texts and resources may be structured in dominance. In the context of public service partnerships and other governmental projects the work of translating policy and creating and sustaining assemblages tends to be managerial work, or at least work that draws on managerial logics and rationalities as coordinating and framing devices. Such an approach may help to explain why those involved in public service work, translating multiple theories and conflicting policy prescriptions in specific sites, or doing the work of maintaining fragile assemblages, find themselves constantly faced with contradictions, dilemmas and paradoxes. Analysing governance as assemblage not only produces interesting academic puzzles about the relationship between theory, policy and practice; it suggests ways of making visible some of the material consequences for those implicated in the processes of governing. It also makes visible the moments at which users/citizens/residents refuse the places or roles they are allocated – or at least refuse to perform them according to dominant scripts (Clarke et al, 2007a).

Conclusion

In the introduction to this chapter we identified three questions to be explored through the stories: What is being subverted? Who gets to act as 'citizens'? What is the field of relationships in which 'subversion' is located? Turning to the first of these, the two stories suggest that the object being subverted is an existing official policy – a specific organisational decision (in the Norwegian case) or a set of legal–political definitions (in the US case). Neither of these stories is about subversion in any larger sense of subverting the social order, though both of them bring into question particular forms of established authority. Both have potential for the *possibility* of movement beyond the immediate situation (as identified by the opponents of the Immigrant Voting Rights campaign, for example, or the use of the modernisation of senior centres in one municipality as a model for others looking to introduce change). But our interest in these local situations does not mean that they are 'merely local'. These situations are configured by forces, processes and authorities that are also national and transnational. Such forces and processes *condense* in such local settings. For example, the managerialism at the centre of welfare service planning decisions in Norway is itself a transnational phenomenon (as are the fiscalising logics of welfare planning: see Prince, 2001, for example). The Immigrant Voting Rights story operates on deeply entangled local (Cambridge, the Boston area, the Commonwealth of Massachusetts), national (US citizenship rules, federalism, and political–cultural iconography), and transnational relationships (the processes of immigration, the experience of politicisation and political action elsewhere, and the US's anxiety about migrants). Answering the 'what is being subverted' question is difficult, not least because so many processes, relations and logics are condensed in particular situations. The concept of assemblage offers one way of thinking about this sort of condensed multiplicity. Through it, we can see that challenges to specific policies (whether funding/service changes or juridical statuses) have to work on and through assemblages, reconfiguring the alignments of different people, resources, discourses, and forms of authority.

Second, the two stories (intentionally) demonstrate important issues about who get to act as 'citizens'. At first glance, it is simple: Norwegian citizens act as citizens of good standing to contest official policy in the name of their entitlements as citizens. By contrast, non–citizen residents in Coll's account carefully avoid the status of citizenship in trying to link local residency and local voting rights. But questions of residence, nationality and citizenship are themselves so deeply entangled in both juridical and popular conceptions of citizenship that the US campaigners had to struggle to not 'talk citizenship' (Clarke, forthcoming). What both stories indicate is how bound up with other categories and identities citizenship is. The Norwegian citizens are also residents, voters, volunteers and service users – and they mobilise those different identities and affiliations in the conflict (they are not just abstract citizens, but embodied as older people, residents of a particular place and people who use and produce these particular services). They are already the 'active citizens' so desired by contemporary governments. In the US story, the subjects of the Voting Rights campaign position themselves as workers, taxpayers, parents and active members of a local community who wish to become (local) voters (as responsible residents). They have to manoeuvre around the question of citizenship, given its tightly drawn ties with nationality. But, in writing about the case, Coll suggests that they are performing 'citizenly acts', even if they are not citizens. This points to the capacious character of the concept of citizenship, which cannot be reduced to questions of formal legal-political status but also includes acts, relationships and (contested) identifications.

We have tried to indicate the importance of being attentive to the field of relationships in which subversive acts are located and seeing how subversion works within and on particular assemblages. This helps, we think, to unlock the problem of power with which we began. As Ewick and Silbey argue,

> Power – whether hegemonic or contested – is exercised by drawing on the symbols, practices, statuses and privileges that have become habitual in social structure. Although structures – what we construe to mean the schemas and resources that pattern social life – often confront us as external and coercive, they are more accurately understood as emergent features of social transactions ... Enacting and exercising power, actors draw from this pool of commonly available structures: symbolic, linguistic, organisational, and material phenomena (2003: 1334–5).

Both stories, we think, illustrate how subversion is enacted in and through different forms of power and how different resources are mobilised by politicians, civil servants, civil society actors, service users, 'volunteers', trade unions and protest organisations. We have tried to show how cultural and institutional resources, governing technologies and forms of 'symbolic capital' are enrolled and activated within specific assemblages. Power or, more accurately, the heterogeneous forms of power and authority are both the means of unlocking existing assemblages and the effects of practices of reassembling. Assemblages, as we have tried to show, organise forms of power and authority in particular alignments: they construct specific formations of domination and subordination, inclusion and exclusion, centrality and marginalisation, empowerment and refusal.

Finally, we have tried to suggest something of the power of storytelling itself. Here we confront a paradox: while analytically we might critique oppositional notions of domination and resistance, such notions, and the stories in which they are embedded, may well serve as powerful mobilising forces. As Ewick and Silbey argue, 'resistance is enabled and collectivised, in part, by the circulation of stories narrating moments when taken-for-granted social structure is exposed and the usual direction of constraint is upended, if only for a moment' (2003: 1329). Such stories often acquire their social and political weight from dramatising contentious issues as the struggle between dominant and subordinated or between the powerful and powerless. Heroic tales of opposition and subversion, of triumph of the powerless over the powerful, or of success in overcoming the entrenched orderings of governmental power are more potent than depictions of complex and entangled assemblages. They have a greater capacity to mobilise other forms of agency and to engender the hope that alternative social or political arrangements might be possible – to subvert, if you like, the taken-for-grantedness of hegemonic forms of rule.

But our two stories highlight two important points. First, that Ewick and Silbey's view of structural constraint and the taken-for-granted character of social order risks an overly static view of the status quo – in which being able to imagine and bring about change is associated with popular forces. However, the rise of New Right politics and policy has tended to disrupt the relationships between change, conservatism and power. Policies variously described as New Right, neoliberal or neoconservative (note the emphasis on the new) have been the forces demanding and insisting upon the necessity of change (Clarke and Newman, 1997, ch 3). Where our US story involved a politics of change (making a new assemblage of rights appear possible), our Norwegian story is different, since the struggles are about the preservation of existing rights, relationships and practices in the face of dominant demands for change. Blackwell and Seabrook (1993) have pointed to how new political forces and discourses dramatically reworked the relationship between change and radicalism at the end of the 20th century, producing a 'revolt against change'. Second, we want to stress how ethnographic research can offer more nuanced and fine-grained accounts of contestation, opening up ambivalences and uncertainties around what is 'really' at stake, the flow of events and what the eventual outcomes may be. We think that these two stories that we have borrowed illuminate the multiplicity of ways in which power and agency can be mobilised. Rather than distinguishing between domination and resistance, they show how subversive citizens (and non-citizens) are multiply located with fields of relationships, drawing on resources that are neither wholly hegemonic nor counter-hegemonic – what Judith Butler refers to as the 'difficult labor of forging a future from resources inevitably impure' (Butler, 1993: 241). But we think the stories also have something to say about the ways in which citizenship identities are mobilised both in emerging strategies of governing and in struggles for social justice.

SIX

Subversive subjects and conditional, earned and denied citizenship

John Flint

Introduction

> Everywhere the old order is passing, but the new
> order has not arrived. Everything is loose and free, but
> everything is problematic.
> (Harvey Warren Zorbaugh, 1929: xviii)

This chapter explores how citizenship and its alleged subversion are constructed and codified in contemporary governance discourse and public policy in the UK. Zorbaugh's words illustrate how a contemporary 'vertigo of late modernity' – a pervasive sense of insecurity, fluidity and transformation, as identified by Young (2007), is not new. Rather, governmental conceptualisations of subversion are inextricably linked to fluid definitions of citizenship and the norms and priorities underpinning them in particular historical periods. The chapter examines four selected categories of 'problematic' citizen (or non-citizen): the 'antisocial', the workless, immigrants (and migrant workers) and Muslims. These populations are often collectively identified as 'suspect communities' (Hillyard, 1993), but there are important differences in how their forms of 'subversion' are conceptualised and responded to within public policy.

Subversion in this sense represents a process whereby an individual or population is viewed as challenging, reinterpreting, realigning or redirecting the perceived 'original' purpose of social policy or the 'traditional' settlement between citizens and the state. As will be shown, subversion may be codified as actual inappropriate conduct or illegitimate physical acts. It may also be associated with the failure to act, as in the perceived passive dependency of welfare benefit claimants. Subversion extends to the alleged values and orientations perceived to underpin behaviour, such as the ambivalent loyalty of Muslims to the secular state, the lack of a work ethic among welfare benefit claimants or the selfishness of the antisocial. Underpinning these various definitions of subversion are two key ideas: that it represents a challenge to the authority of government and that it is a manifestation of individuals abdicating their responsibility to the state and to their fellow citizens. Discourses of subversion also conflate the subversion of individuals with their membership of a population and its collective identity as potentially subversive, as in the case of Muslims above. The chapter will examine the variety of allegiances, identities, institutions and social processes perceived as being subverted, and their porous boundaries and shifting classifications.

Two key trends in the contemporary governance of subversion in the UK are explored. First, the increasing use of conditional and 'earned' forms of citizenship to limit the social citizenship rights (Marshall, 1950) of immigrants, the workless and the antisocial. Second, the intensification and expansion of governance attempts to address the 'subversive' behaviour and values of individuals that go beyond merely excluding or marginalising the subversive subject.

Constructing and codifying citizenship and its subversion

There is a tendency in political and policy discourse in the UK to identify a contemporary 'crisis' in civility, citizenship and community cohesion in which 'society has retreated', there is a need to 'reclaim the streets' and new forms of ethno-religious tensions represent a particular crisis of the present (Respect Task Force, 2006; Smith, 2008; Sparrow, 2008). Likewise, academic commentary often classifies the punitive or intensified activities of governance as recent phenomena, arising in particular from the economic and population restructuring of neoliberal globalisation. However, Elias (2000: 68) identifies the very long history of civilising offensives enacted by elites and targeted at 'subversive' foreign populations and lower classes within Western nation states, such as the 18th-century legislation restricting the movement of 'aliens' around Britain and their intensive surveillance and, on occasion, deportation (Goldsmith, 2008: 10). Although parallels are drawn between contemporary Muslim populations and the previous experience of the Irish as suspect or subversive populations, there is actually a far longer history of religion and its institutions being viewed as a threat to the secular authority of the state (see Burleigh, 2005). Similarly, in contrast to the conceptualisation of incivility in public spaces as a contemporary manifestation, Marne (2001: 441) describes how the strict regulations governing public parks in Liverpool during the Victorian era were subverted by 'gentlemen who will insist on riding on the footways and let their dogs swim in the lake' and who responded to park keepers 'with ridicule'. This example highlights both the historical ubiquity of perceived subversion and its multifaceted definitions. In this case, the initial breaking of park rules and codes is accentuated by the lack of due reverence being given to official authority. Further historical examples are provided by Curry's (2007) account of disorder and incivility among football spectators in Sheffield in the same period, and Griffin's (2007) description of tree-maiming and the subverting of social codes of respectability in late 18th-century England.

Contemporary policy responses to subversion in the UK, including reducing the payment of welfare state benefits to individuals, or the use of Family Intervention Projects with core block residential accommodation to house 'antisocial' families, are often viewed as innovative, a reflection of a particularly intensive disciplinary contemporary apparatus for the 'regimentation of subordinate populations' (Schram et al, 2008: 30). However, they have their precedent in 19th-century industrial schools, labour colonies for the unemployed and residential 'recuperation centres' for 'unbilletable' and 'semi-problem' families in the 1950s and 1960s (Welshman, 1999, 2008; Walters and Woodward, 2008).

The construction of subversion and its subsequent codification and equation with social groups or behaviours within public policy discourse and practice is an act of government. Frameworks for governing subversion are shaped by the expectations, evaluations and imaginations *of government actors* about different groups of the population (see D'Arcus, 2004: 358). As Gilmour (2007) shows in his study of the Victorian Raj, it was civil servants' particular education, social codes and values, linked to a sense of 'Britishness' and specific forms of imperial duty that shaped how the civil service in India conceptualised subversion. These government-generated frameworks of understanding within contemporary policy development determine that inner-city neighbourhoods need to be 'civilised' (Clement, 2007) or define what constitutes 'poor parenting' (Walters and Woodward, 2008) in juxtaposition to 'normal' or 'mainstream' society as it is conceived to exist by senior policy makers. These frameworks and their classifications of subversion are therefore politically and socially defined categories within a construction of citizenship that is in itself a political and governmental project, enacted through contemporary attempts to resurrect civility, reduce antisocial behaviour or encourage the integration of immigrants (Clarke, 2005; Walters and Woodward, 2008). These governance frameworks of understanding link subversive citizens to their spatial manifestations in a normative geography of 'sink estates', 'ghettos' or 'enclaves' (see Flint, 2009, forthcoming). Their populations become subject to socio-spatial forms of exclusion or exceptional or conditional citizenship, such as Anti-social Behaviour Orders, dispersal orders, or restrictions on the call to prayer *(Adhan)* in predominantly Muslim neighbourhoods (see Cameron, 2007 for a fuller discussion and further examples from the US).

The subversive or suspect community (Hillyard, 1993) requires an imagined national community (Anderson, 1983) against which it may be contrasted and its contours defined. Indeed, the reintegration of subversives is only conceptually possible if the larger community is viewed as sharing a common normative universe, including, for example, attitudes to employment (Feely and Simon, 1992; Vaughan, 2000; Clarke, 2005). Thus the UK government, in perceiving a need to 'reinforce our shared values', argues that 'people should play by the rules' (Home Office Border and Immigration Agency, 2008a: 5), providing the narrative of there being a collective set of norms that are being subverted by particular groups. As D'Arcus (2004: 358) observes, the full citizen or subject does not exist apart from the subversive or conditional citizen. Rather, the population is subject to a categorisation of binary divisions of the active/working and passive/workless or responsible/antisocial and is differentiated and subject to different governmental practices (Clarke, 2005). This is not new, as Elias (2000) illustrates in his account of the civilising process and the formation of the modern nation-state. For example, the Victorian conceptualisation of urban 'civility' and attempts to address public drunkenness conceived it as subversive to the moral character of the imperial metropolis, the perceived requirements of the nation-state and the imagined community of (sober and industrious) citizens that constituted the shared normative universe of 'Britishness' (Kneale, 2001). The enactment of the welfare state in Britain and other nations during the 20th century was always partly about preventing insurrection, disorder or insecurity (Marshall, 1977).

Elias (2000) observed that the perceived need for elites and governing groups to reaffirm and codify desirable and undesirable conduct is often a symptom of societies experiencing significant economic and social transition. The quote from Zorbaugh's description of Chicago 80 years ago that opened this chapter could easily describe the contemporary policy narrative of receding past certainties (manifested in incivility and worklessness) and uncertain futures (as a result of immigration and migration) evident in the UK. The need to codify and classify required behaviour and allegiance is evidenced through the government's commissioning a *Review of Citizenship*, which concluded that there was a need to 'enhance our national narrative' (Goldsmith, 2008: 7). The allegiance of new citizens, and the prevention of citizenship being subverted, is to be ensured by aligning conduct to imagined national norms and 'plac[ing] the values of the British people at the heart of the journey newcomers take towards citizenship', based on the notion that: 'Integrating is not just about understanding British laws but also learning about everyday behaviours' (Home Office Border and Immigration Agency, 2008a: 14). The codifying of these everyday behaviours is evident in the growing use of migrant information packs which set out details of mundane conduct that is apparently synonymous with British values, such as queuing and punctuality, along with prohibitions of the anticipated conduct of migrants that may subvert codes of civility such as spitting, pushing into queues or inconsiderate parking (DCLG, 2008b; DCLG and I&DeA, 2008). The government is explicit that these migrant information packs should 'give a clear sense of national values, not just local amenities' (DCLG, 2008b: 1).

This codification of required conduct is not limited to new migrants. The growing use of 'good neighbour agreements' which prohibit or promote a set of behaviours in residential areas and the over 20,000 Acceptable Behaviour Contracts enacted with individuals engaged in antisocial behaviour are evidence of such official statements of behavioural standards, and similar trends are apparent in the US (Schram et al, 2008). In each case, an 'unwritten' code of civility is conceptualised as requiring to be reaffirmed and upheld against those who would subvert it, 'the deviant anti-citizen upsetting the organic balance ... of local place' (D'Arcus, 2004: 357).

Conditional, earned and denied citizenship

Clarke (2005) has identified how governmental processes generate different conceptualisations and categories of citizenship, such as the activated, empowered, responsibilised and abandoned citizen, premised around key motifs of employment, morality and self-direction. This section argues that, as a response to the perceived subversion (manifested in acts and value orientations) of 'traditional' notions of citizenship, government rationales and policies are reconstructing the legal and social rights of particular groups of citizens and realigning the routes into and out of forms of citizenship. The mid-20th-century notion of citizenship, albeit premised on the centrality of male employment, conferred lifelong citizen status automatically and universally on those meeting eligibility criteria. However, contemporary governance processes are generating forms of citizenship that are more conditional on individual conduct, with increasing attention being given to the idea that some rights of citizenship, such as access to social housing, should be proactively earned rather than being an automatic entitlement.

Conditional citizenship

The growing use of contractual forms of governing deviant citizens (Crawford, 2003), and the rewriting of the social contract for low-income households that this entails, has resulted in access to the social rights of citizenship being realigned so that eligibility for unemployment benefit or access to social housing has become conditional on working-age recipients' compliance with efforts towards behavioural modification and with work-related requirements (Schram et al, 2008). This is evident in the new framework for the management of the workless, which is explicitly linked to a sense of contract and a reinvigorated citizenship, to be enacted through addressing the subversion of the founding values of the welfare state: 'The third principle of the Beveridge Report is that social security must be achieved by co-operation between the state and the individual ... We need to return this principle to the centre of the welfare state and redress the erosion of the responsibility to work' (Department for Work and Pensions, 2008: 24).

Welfare benefit reforms are conceptualised as a means to 'explore how personalised conditionality can best be designed to influence behaviour ... the patterns and habits of work' (Department for Work and Pensions, 2008: 41–2). In order to 'improve the conditionality regime' a 'stronger sanctions regime' will be used (Department for Work and Pensions, 2008: 39–41). After three and then six months of claiming benefits, jobseekers will be expected to intensify their job search activity and comply with an action plan, including a skills health check and appropriate training, which may require daily attendance at a Jobcentre Plus office (Department for Work and Pensions (2008: 13). Benefit claimants will be required to 'do more' as the duration of their claim period increases, with the application of sanctions for those not meeting these requirements and the piloting of specific forms of conditionality for lone parents (see Schram et al, 2008 for an account of similar benefit sanctions regimes in the US).

In social housing, allocation policies and tenancy agreements have always made access to tenure conditional. However, the explicit deployment of conditionality as a mechanism of governing deviancy has been strengthened by the introduction of demoted tenancies, through which the subversion of tenancy conditions may result in the security of tenure being reduced. As a result of the Welfare Reform Act 2007, the government is also piloting a scheme in eight English local authority areas in which households evicted for antisocial behaviour and who make a subsequent claim for Housing Benefit may see their benefit payments reduced or halted if they refuse to engage with a programme of support to address their behaviour (see Flint et al, 2008). This use of Housing Benefit sanctions in relation to antisocial behaviour comprises a complex mix of coercion, exclusion and denial of forms of citizenship with an intensification of publicly funded interventions aimed at reintegrating individuals and households (see Deacon, 2004 for a thoughtful justification of the use of benefit sanctions). In common with a key theme in this volume, it should be noted that practitioners in local areas conceived the Housing Benefit sanction pilots in different ways and, one year after the legislation was enacted, no household had been subject to sanction (Flint et al, 2008). A similar attempt in France to link parental responsibility to benefit sanctions has also been scarcely used by local authorities.

Earned citizenship

Conditional citizenship is based on the idea of a pre-existing entitlement being rescinded as a result of inappropriate conduct. But recent policy discourse challenges this fundamental premise of existent universal entitlement through the argument that citizenship must be *earned* (Home Office Border and Immigration Agency, 2008a: 11). This is evident in immigration policy: 'Citizenship must be earned ... anyone who wants to live here long term must learn our language, obey the law and contribute to the community' (Home Office Border and Immigration Agency, 2008a: 5). In order to 'earn' this citizenship, 'newcomers' must demonstrate their 'commitment' to the UK, in part through volunteering, an activity that apparently reflects 'a British way of life' (Home Office Border and Immigration Agency, 2008a: 7). The concept of 'earned' citizenship thereby reconfigures the idea of a 'right' to citizenship, which is based on proactive endeavour rather than passive qualification and provides an additional mechanism of conditionality for classifying potential citizens.

The concept of earned rights of citizenship has also been prominent in social housing policy discourse. What appears new about the rationalities of earned citizenship is the connections made between disparate social rights of citizenship and the basis on which entitlement may be 'earned'. The Housing Minister identified a link between employment and access to a social housing tenancy. In common with the conditionality underpinning worklessness policy, contractual mechanisms are proposed to ensure the 'self-improvement', 'commitment' and 'activity' of tenants:

> A voluntary contract will set out the opportunities on offer, underscoring the commitment of the tenants to self-improvement ... could new tenants who can work sign commitment contracts when getting a tenancy, agreeing to actively seek work alongside better support? (Flint, 2008)

The minister challenged the traditional 'passivity' of both government and tenant, calling for 'a change of culture from when the council handed someone the keys and forgot about them for 30 years' (quoted in Wintour, 2008). The minister suggested that tenants moving to employment be given priority for a subsidised tenancy. Another government minister, apparently responding to a perceived subversion of social housing allocation processes by migrants, suggested that the 'legitimate sense of entitlement' felt by an 'indigenous family' should override the legitimate need of a migrant. Therefore access would be earned on the basis of the length of residency, rather than priority need (Hodge, 2007).

Denied citizenship

Vaughan (2000: 36) argues that governance mechanisms, including punishment, are now being used 'not upon those who are thought to be conditional citizens with a view to reintegration but against those who are thought to be non-citizens to disable or exclude them'. In other words, citizenship may be denied. This can be achieved most obviously by preventing access to the country in the first place, for example through tightening visa regimes. Such policy responses are premised on the belief that subversion may to some extent be classified and predictable between population groups, although this conflates assumed identities, value orientations and actual conduct. Across Europe immigrants are seen as a threat deserving of suspicion, neutralisation or exclusion (Muncie, 2008). Thus, visa regimes will be tightened for countries 'whose nationals pose significant risks to the UK', while there will be a visa waiver test for 'trusted foreign travellers' (Home Office Border and Immigration Agency, 2008b: 6–7). The intensification of governance is evident in the requirement for employers and colleges providing positions to migrants to obtain a licence and to undertake monitoring of these individuals (Home Office Border and Immigration Agency, 2008b).

The denied citizen is also subject to exceptional forms of government that in themselves appear to subvert the principles of citizenship applying to indigenous populations (see also Vaughan, 2000). Compulsory identity cards will be introduced for foreign nationals (Home Office Border and Immigration Agency, 2008b). The government also proposes that, in order to alleviate 'short term pressures resulting from migration', funds are to be raised through fees for immigration applications, with migrants 'who tend to consume more in public services – such as children and elderly relatives – paying more than others' (Home Office Border and Immigration Agency, 2008a: 35). Thus, for new migrants the traditional provision of the social rights of citizenship is reversed and inverted, with the attempted exclusion, rather than prioritisation, of the very young and the very old. Of course, government plans to 'ask newcomers to contribute extra in payments to the public purse' (Home Office Border and Immigration Agency, 2008a: 7) are themselves based on the idea that welfare has been subverted from its 'original' purpose of providing for the 'indigenous' population of the UK.

Such forms of pre-emptive exception and exclusion are not limited to non-citizens. The growing use of 'mosquito' devices to regulate public spaces illustrates this (see Welsh, 2008). These devices emit a high-pitched sound only audible to those under the age of 25, with the sole purpose of moving groups of young people away from the device-owner's property. Clearly, this denies access to public space to particular groups of citizens, who may not be engaged in any forms of antisocial behaviour. It is fitting, in a volume on subversion, to reflect on the fact that, as Welsh (2008: 132) describes, such technologies may be adapted and deployed by the populations they are aimed at subjugating. In a 'subversive display of teenage ingenuity' children have appropriated the mosquito buzz as a mobile phone ring tone, enabling the covert use of text-message alerts in school classrooms!

The corollary of conditional and earned citizenship or its denial is the explicit use of probationary periods for those deemed at risk of engaging in future forms of subversive conduct. The government's immigration proposals create a category of probationary citizen, a status that will apply for a minimum of two years, even for those individuals deemed as active and committed. These probationary citizens will 'not be entitled to access mainstream benefits or their local housing authority' (Home Office Border and Immigration Agency, 2008a: 29–34). In social housing probationary tenancies have also been introduced to reduce the security of tenure of those tenants documented as previously having been involved in antisocial behaviour or other breach of tenancy conditions.

Cultural dimensions of citizenship

It is evident that a growing focus on cultural dimensions of conduct and belonging characterises the concepts of earned and denied citizenship. This increases the (non-legal) duties and obligations of citizenship and extends the risk of subversion to include incivility or cultural difference: 'Responsibilities [of citizenship] also mean much more than just paying taxes and obeying the law, responsibilities include following the unwritten rules of behaviour and norms in each area' (DCLG, 2008: 1). For migrants these cultural dimensions of citizenship require them 'to demonstrate a more visible and substantial contribution to Britain' by 'joining in with, and integrating into, the British way of life' (Home Office Border and Immigration Service, 2008a: 7). There will therefore be a reduced period of probationary citizenship for those who have 'demonstrated their commitment to the UK by playing an active part in the community', for example by volunteering, running a playgroup, or being a school governor. In addition, the cultural assessment of potential or new citizens recasts integration, previously related to employment and education, as requiring an explicit and unambiguous loyalty to the nation-state (in the Netherlands this may include giving up dual nationality, see Roggeband and Verloo, 2007: 284). The construction of new cultural mechanisms for determining citizenship may also make 'stranger citizens' of some groups with legal citizenship status (Kundani, 2007). The controversy surrounding Islamic hijabs and niqabs as a form of incivility in public spaces in the UK, and proposals to ban them in public spaces in the Netherlands, provide one example (ironically, the wearing of hijabs and niqabs is, in part, subversion by young people of the habits of their parents' generation). The focus on cultural dimensions of citizenship leads to an equation of (legal) actions (not volunteering, wearing religious iconography) with subversive value orientations.

Intensifying responses to subversion

A key question is whether these emerging forms of citizenship are accompanied by, or are indicative of, a more intensive and punitive governance of subversion. Gilmour's (2007) study of the Victorian Raj showed how subversion could be enacted by civil service colleagues as well as by governed subject populations. Other chapters in this volume explore the subversion of those charged with delivering public policy. Just as Clarke (2005) points out that the envisaged citizens or subjects are not necessarily produced by governmental practice, so Muncie (2008: 118) makes the crucial point that policies and trends may be mediated by 'parochial' localised practitioner cultures and institutional constraints that may resist and deliver less punitive policies (see also Morgen, 2001). Similarly, research suggests that, in the US, welfare benefit case managers may vary in their willingness to issue sanctions, based on their assessment of the consequences for families (Schram et al, 2008; see also Fording et al, 2007).

Suffice it to say that we need to reflect on the complexity and nuance of the regimes of legitimacy that determine how an act, or the values thought to underpin an act, are defined as subversive. In his study of the policing of housing projects in Nashville, Tennessee, Websdale (2001) describes how officers dissuaded some female residents from officially reporting incidents to the police (the very act that official policy was desperately trying to promote), as the officers judged that making such a report would be detrimental to the individual residents' safety. The same study also highlighted how what constitutes subversion is differentiated by the priorities of particular professional codes – illustrated by the varying responses among his colleagues, from admiration and gratitude to social opprobrium, encountered by an officer reporting a fellow officer for planting drugs on a suspect.

Rather than being some form of policy aberration or resistance, these cases reflect the ambiguous and nuanced history and contemporary manifestation of how the state has responded to subversion. As Foucault (1978) identified, responses to subversion often seek to make visible and engage with subversive acts and individuals rather than seeking merely to silence, marginalise or punish them. One of the 'great animating pulses of modern punishment was to convert conditional citizens, through character transformation, into full citizens rather than excluding them' (Vaughan, 2000: 26). Therefore, Vaughan suggests, the historical development of modern punishment was always partly an inclusionary project, aimed at (re)incorporating offenders, and the same is true of the management of the workless or immigrants. The governance of subversive citizens is not exclusively the exercising of coercive authority, but rather may involve intensive attempts to actually transform human subjectivities and to change individuals' understandings and desires (Schram et al, 2008). In other words there is an ambitious attempt to govern subversive orientations and not just physical acts.

The former Home Secretary argued that the government 'has expanded our ambition to ensure that all live up to their responsibilities' (Smith, 2008) and suggested that the antisocial individual should:

> Themselves be harried and harassed ... that car of theirs, is the tax up to date? Is it insured? Let's find out. And have they a TV licence for their plasma screen? As the advert says, 'it's all in the database'. As for their council tax, it shouldn't be difficult to see if that's been paid. And what about benefit fraud? Can we run a check? (Smith, 2008).

This may be rhetoric, but it illustrates the growing propensity of government rationalities to seek to link subversions across different policy areas and to consider interventions at the various points where the individual citizen and government interact, as we have already seen with housing, worklessness and antisocial behaviour. In addition, the government proposes to follow policy in the United States by linking drug testing and treatment to benefit payments and job-search interviews and worklessness regimes (Department for Work and Pensions, 2008: 46–50).

There are many examples of local policy initiatives providing a more intensive response to subversive behaviour, from the 'taxi marshal' scheme in Leeds, providing for the policing of key taxi ranks in the city, to the pre-emptive questioning, by Telford and Wrekin Council officials, of single adults in public parks about their reasons and motives for being there. The government is explicit that its new action plan for tackling youth crime 'will radically extend the reach of the challenge and support we are offering to young people at risk of offending' (HM Government, 2008: 7) with a growing confidence that 'increasingly we know how to identify these young people [involved in offending] early on' (HM Government, 2008: 1). The Youth Crime Action Plan will make use of 'intensive family support', with families deemed to require these services 'encouraged and challenged by key workers, with non-negotiable elements of the support and sanctions for a failure to engage' (HM Government, 2008: 5). This mechanism of sanction for failure to engage with support services mirrors the worklessness regime and the Housing Benefit sanction pilot described above.

The use of intensive family support projects, which in some cases include residential 'core block' accommodation with strict rules and surveillance of families, crystallises the trends and ambiguities in the contemporary governance of subversive citizenship in the UK. For critics such as Garrett (2007) these 'sin bins' epitomise the coercive, domineering, disciplinary and exclusionary management of 'deviant' families, within a wider reduction in inclusionary motivations and techniques in social and criminal policy and practice (Vaughan, 2000; Muncie, 2008). However, these projects involve the deployment of considerable public resources and are explicitly about the reintegration (rather than permanent marginalisation) of families, so that children are reintegrated into education and adults are supported back into a mainstream tenancy in a local neighbourhood. These projects, like their predecessors in the 1950s and 1960s, continue to conceptualise problematic families in terms of the failings of the mother (see Welshman, 2008). But these earlier forms of governance provided their range of domestic management and citizenship classes within the rationale, noted by Beveridge after a trip to the Brentwood Centre, that housewives may need rehabilitation in the same way as an injured airman or worker, and many mothers were positive about their experiences there (Welshman, 2008).

It is apparent that there are increasingly intensive attempts by the state to police South Asian (and specifically Muslim) communities in order to counter subversion (Wilson, 2007). In addition to anti-terrorism legislation, these include the prominent regulation of mosques, with a wider conceptualisation of 'Islamic' urban space and its institutions and populations as denoting potential sites of insurrection (Phillips, 2006). Thus, the Centre for Social Cohesion undertakes research to 'discover the extent of Islamic radicalism at universities' (Thorne and Stuart, 2008). At the same time, the Department of Communities and Local Government commissions new research on the extent (rather than existence) of community support for terrorism in Muslim neighbourhoods. However exclusionary in their outcomes, these actions are located within a wider attempt at fostering community cohesion – an inclusionary as well as a marginalising project of government. These ambiguities are summed up by the government's statement that: 'We want to encourage people with the right qualifications and commitment to take up citizenship so that they can become fully integrated into our society' (Home Office Border and Immigration Agency, 2008a: 6). So, as Vaughan (2008) suggests, citizenship is conditional and built upon attempts to integrate, include and exclude. This explains why, simultaneously with the tightening of visa regimes and the increasing conditionality of access to citizenship for new subjects, the Goldsmith Review of Citizenship proposes associate citizenship status for those settling long term but unable to access dual nationality (Goldsmith, 2008: 6).

Passivity as subversion

A failure to act may also be interpreted as a form of subversion, with passivity viewed as symptomatic of problematic value orientations. The passivity of the poor has long been conceptualised as a moral subversion of national values (D'Arcus, 2004: 361). New conditionality and sanction mechanisms are located in 'a welfare system that enables people to become the authors of their own lives' (Department for Work and Pensions, 2008: 11), an 'active regime' requiring individuals to 'take responsibility for their skills needs' and 'demonstrate active citizenship' (Department for Work and Pensions, 2008: 5). This is conceptualised in terms of a 'work rather than welfare *culture*' (Department for Work and Pensions, 2008: 19, emphasis added).

Such rationales are also evident in new conceptualisations of the role and behaviour of victims of antisocial behaviour, in which their passivity or inappropriate response to deviant behaviour becomes conceptualised as subversive in its own right and in need of correction. The client book and programme of work used with witnesses and victims by North Lanarkshire Council states that it will:

> Help you deal with antisocial behaviour that is going on around you at present. As your case is nearing closure you will be given a copy of your workbook to keep and reflect on. It is hoped that in the future, if you are faced with stressful times you will be able to look back and use the techniques you have learned. (North Lanarkshire Council, 2008)

Here, the very status of victimhood becomes subject to scrutiny and attempted reform: 'Being assertive means being able to behave in a rational adult way. Above all being assertive means having self respect and respect for other people', and: 'You can learn to choose how to deal with frustrating situations – to respond rather than automatically react like a juke box' (North Lanarkshire Council, 2008). The examination and reflection of self, anger management, and promotion of assertiveness and self-esteem within the programme mirror those interventions with families in intensive support projects or with workless individuals.

Similarly, the passivity of some women within the context of South Asian marriages is portrayed as subversive: these women become victims without agency who need to be saved (Wilson, 2007: 30). The state is seen as protecting 'civilised' but insufficiently rational or proactive British South Asian women in particular against the coercion of non-British partners. In the UK, and in other states like the Netherlands, unequal gender relations are regarded in public policy discourse as problematic and demonstrative of the backward character of Islam and of immigrants (Roggeband and Verloo, 2007: 272). As the state seeks to intervene in the 'organisation of the sphere of intimacy within the migrant community', it generates a need for migrant Muslim women to adapt to Dutch norms through an 'extra change of culture' within a policy 'frame extension' that identifies migrant (or Muslim) women as a cultural as well as a socio-economic problem (Roggeband and Verloo, 2007: 277– 81). So Muslim and migrant women become the principal policy targets and principal agents of change to address subversive gender roles, codes of intimacy and labour market inactivity, and are required to take the steps of 'indigenous' women to become emancipated (Roggeband and Verloo, 2007: 282).

Conclusions

Forms of citizenship, and their subversion, are dynamic and contingent. They may be granted, extended or rescinded as conditional or probationary citizens are subject to normalisation, correction or segregation (Vaughan, 2000). These populations are 'located in the twilight space between inclusion and exclusion, normalcy and deviance, compliance and disruption' (Schram et al, 2008: 18). Citizenship becomes conditional, to be earned or denied, with cultural dimensions of behaviour and belonging constituting more important determinants of status, and passivity viewed as subversive. This conditionality is enacted through a strengthened and increasingly connected nexus of worklessness, benefit claim, social housing and antisocial behaviour. Although there is evidence of a more intensive and punitive governance of subversive citizens and non-citizens, this is still located within aspirations and mechanisms for the inclusion and reintegration of subjects ('no-one written off': Department for Work and Pensions, 2008), an inclusion that the allegedly subversive are often anxious to pursue (see *Sheffield Weekly Gazette*, 2008: 10).

Although new forms of conditionality, sanction and citizenship are conceived to be primarily a system for disciplining subordinate populations for their failure to integrate themselves into low-wage labour markets (Schram et al, 2008), their essence and their narrative power lies in a conceptualisation of subversive citizenship as responsibility abdicated (D'Arcus, 2004: 361). The government problematisation of the workless, the antisocial or the immigrant is not ultimately their perceived dependency, inactivity or incivility, but rather that their conduct is interpreted as a subversion of the values and purposes of the welfare state and, through this, the British nation-state. In response, and in the ultimate subversion, 'social security' is transformed from the social (or national) collective protecting the individual, to the social rights of citizenship becoming a further mechanism for providing the collective with security from the problematic individual.

Acknowledgements
I am grateful to Elizabeth Burney, who shared her knowledge of policy in France with me, and to Ken Gibb for his suggestion of a key reference.

Part Three
Subversive citizens in public service settings

SEVEN

Family intervention projects: sites of subversion and resilience

Sadie Parr and Judy Nixon

Introduction

Drawing on an analytical framework developed by Uitermark (2005), this chapter considers the processes of translation that characterise antisocial behaviour (ASB) policy enactment. Scrutiny of the contested development of intensive family support projects (IFSPs), which more recently have been subsumed under the title Family Intervention Projects (FIPs) (Respect Taskforce, 2006), serves to highlight the way in which technologies of governance devised at the centre are linked to and dependent on activities, organisations and individuals operating in a local context. Scrutiny of the process by which FIPs emerged in England over the period 2003–07 provides an interesting illustration of local–central interactions in policy-making processes and exemplifies how local actors can modify the intended outcomes of national policy.

First established in 2003, IFSPs were designed to provide families who were homeless or at risk of eviction as a result of ASB with support to address the 'root causes' of disruptive behaviour, with the overarching aim of breaking cycles of disruptive behaviour and bringing families back into mainstream housing. The model of provision offered an alternative to punitive enforcement action and was based on the work of the Dundee Families Project (Dillane, 2001), in which families are provided with a range of services, including some or all of the following types of intervention:

- floating outreach support to families in their existing homes;
- outreach support in dispersed tenancies managed by the project;
- support in core residential accommodation managed by the project, involving intensive daily contact and surveillance by project workers.

Initially, these projects were seen by local stakeholders to be a 'high risk' activity with the outcomes by no means certain. By 2004, only eight English local authorities, working closely with housing associations and charities, had set up FIPs, of which six agreed to participate in a three-year (2004–07) government-funded study to evaluate their effectiveness in terms of costs, benefits and lessons for wider dissemination (Nixon et al, 2006, 2008). The empirical basis for the discussion that follows arises out of this evaluation, together with PhD research by one of the authors, carried out in one of these six case study locations. In particular, the findings presented here are derived from repeat semi-structured interviews with key local actors who were pivotal in the instantiation of the projects: project managers and workers; referral agencies; and local strategic players such as police officers, community safety coordinators, housing managers, Youth Offending Team (YOT) and social services staff. Analysis of this rich case study data serves to illustrate the ways in which local actors reinterpret formal policy agendas in order to create alternative discourses which both challenge and, in turn, influence national strategies.

By way of context, the chapter starts with a brief outline of New Labour's ASB agenda, charting the way it has shifted in focus and emphasis since 1997, with increasing attention being paid to control measures involving 'whole family' approaches and parenting interventions. In the second part of the chapter we draw on an analytical framework developed by Uitermark (2005) to reflect on the processes of local–central exchange that characterise the genesis and evolution of ASB policy. Applying this framework to family-based ASB interventions reveals the extent to which policy transitions are always partial, provisional and characterised by counter-trends (Flint, 2002; Raco, 2003; Stenson, 2005; Hughes, 2007; Prior, 2007). Indeed, the empirical evidence suggests that while local actors may be able to subvert and divert the aims of public policy, it is also possible for the state to reclaim such subversive moments through selective appropriation and redistribution of local narratives.

The emergence of FIPs

Since coming to power in 1997, New Labour has placed tackling ASB at the forefront of its political programme, with ASB measures located within the wider policy agenda of revitalising disadvantaged neighbourhoods and stimulating civic renewal. From the outset, policy discourses constructed ASB in emotive terms, with the government's commitment to tackling this form of disorder driven by a moral imperative to regulate and control the behaviour of marginalised groups. Within this agenda, structural disadvantage resulting from poverty and inequality was reframed as individual deficiencies and personal failure (Gillies, 2005). Within political rhetoric, antisocial acts were described as 'blighting lives', 'destroying families' and 'ruining communities', with those responsible for such behaviour constructed as a dangerous minority who destroy the lives of the decent, law-abiding majority (Nixon and Parr, 2006). A distinctive feature of this characterisation of ASB was the way in which target populations were singled out, with young people variously referred to as 'feral', 'yobs' and 'louts' and a minority of 'problem families' as dysfunctional and anchored in 'bad' parenting. In reality, as Gillies (2005) points out, the focus on 'bad' parents thinly disguises the fact that it is predominantly mothers who undertake responsibility for childcare, and indeed the empirical evidence confirms that it is lone-parent women who are one of the main target groups for ASB interventions (Hunter and Nixon, 2001; Nixon and Hunter, 2009).

This partial and particular construction of the problem of ASB provided the rationale for the introduction of measures to control conduct, with a focus on self-regulation reinforced by the use of punitive sanctions (Squires and Stephen, 2005). Beginning with the flagship 1998 Crime and Disorder Act, a range of new control mechanisms was introduced by the New Labour government, including Dispersal Orders, Antisocial Behaviour Orders, Acceptable Behaviour Contracts, Parenting Contracts/Orders, Closure Orders, Fixed Penalty Notices and Antisocial Injunctions. At a local level, however, reactions to this armoury of new powers were mixed. While some authorities were initially zealous in their use of ASB interventions, others proved remarkably reluctant to embrace the new provisions, preferring to rely on case management interventions led by multi-agency partnerships (Burney, 2005). The government responded with action to promote its preferred approach. In early 2003 a special ASB Taskforce was established in the Home Office, heralding the start of an aggressive drive to promote the use of disciplining interventions to control the 'behaviour of a persistent minority'.

Despite the lack of empirical evidence on the efficacy of enforcement action, the language used by the government to exhort local authorities to increase their use of such measures was both confident and unequivocal. In 2005, for example, Hazel Blears, the then minister of state, issued over 10 press releases promoting the use of enforcement action to deal with the 'neighbours from hell':

ASB is a menace for many people and it needs to be dealt with swiftly and effectively. ASBOs make a real difference to people's lives by helping to rebuild confidence in communities and bringing the actions of a selfish minority to task. The statistics published today show that local authorities are responding enthusiastically to the powers available to them. (Blears, 2005b)

Such assertions regarding the efficacy of enforcement measures were not shared by many local practitioners. Indeed, independent research evidence suggests that there was a growing rift between the national push to prioritise punitive interventions and local concerns to develop early forms of intervention and diversionary activities. The National Community Safety Network, a practitioner-led organisation representing those involved in community safety work in local areas, for example, called for more emphasis and resources to be given to early intervention with families, schools and peers and for the national ASB strategy to be more closely integrated into the Every Child Matters agenda (NCSN, 2005). Millie et al (2005) confirmed that local practitioners were increasingly sceptical of the simplistic binary divides used by the Home Office 'Together' campaign to distinguish between the 'law-abiding' citizens and the 'antisocial' perpetrator. In comparison with national actors, local community safety professionals' definition of the nature of the problem was more nuanced and sophisticated; it recognised that ASB was not simply a problem of 'feral' youth or 'dysfunctional families', but rather reflected a set of complex problems emerging as a result of conflict within communities with limited capacity for self-regulation (Millie et al, 2005: ix).

Furthermore, telling criticisms of the UK government's approach to ASB were made by Gil-Robles, the European Human Rights Commissioner reporting on his visit to the UK in 2004. He noted that the government appeared to be in the grip of 'ASBO mania' and identified four principle concerns about ASBOs, focusing on, first, their scope in terms of the broad range of prohibited behaviour; second, the ease with which such orders could be obtained; third, the use of publicity strategies associated with orders; and fourth, the serious consequences of breaches (Gil-Robles, 2005). He concluded:

It is difficult to avoid the impression that the ASBO is being touted as a miracle cure for urban nuisance. The police, Local Authorities and other empowered actors are thus

placed under considerable pressure to apply for ASBOs.
(Gil-Robles, 2005: para 113)

In response to such criticisms, together with the apparent reluctance of
many local authorities to make use of the new enforcement measures
(Burney, 2005) increased attention began to be given, at a national level,
to the use of control measures involving 'whole family' and parenting
interventions. Perhaps the rhetoric was running out of steam, but while
a tough line remained, space opened up in the government discourse
for recognition that enforcement alone was not enough, and there
was increasing acknowledgement that some families require specialist,
intensive and long-term support tailored to their particular needs.
The Home Affairs Select Committee enquiry into the government's
strategy for combating ASB concluded that the development of
'intensive family-based interventions are essential if the deepest-rooted
ASB problems are not simply to be recycled from one area to another'
(Home Affairs Select Committee, 2005).

After winning the 2005 general election, the then Prime Minister, Tony
Blair, announced that dealing with ASB remained a key priority for the
government, which was committed to 'bring[ing] back a proper sense of
respect' (Blair, 2005). Symbolic of this renewed drive to tackle ASB, in
January 2006 the government launched the Respect Action Plan, which
featured the implementation of 'a new approach to the most challenging
families', involving a national rollout of 53 Family Intervention Projects
inspired by the Dundee Families Project (DFP) (Respect Task Force,
2006). Although endorsed as 'good practice' (SEU, 2000; Home Office,
2003) in policy position papers, until then this approach to tackling
ASB had never been highlighted as a policy priority, and enforcement
approaches, justified by an appeal to 'the protection of the community',
had dominated. Within a remarkably short period of time, however, FIPs
had been transformed from a high-risk activity piloted by a handful of
local authorities to a national flagship measure heralded as an effective
means of 'turning families round'. This policy shift raises a number of
interesting questions about the nature of central–local relations, and it is
to this issue that we now turn.

Local–central interplay and the genesis of FIPs

Critical analyses of community safety policy have frequently been
situated within one of two theoretical frameworks: neo-Marxist
or political economic accounts, and Foucauldian governmentality
approaches (Beckett and Herbert, 2007). The former attribute the rise

of new social control measures to the ascendance of a neoliberal global capitalism with the accompanying reconfiguration of political power, and draw particular attention to the central role of the state. Within this body of work approaches inspired by regulation theory (Jessop, 2002) have been particularly influential (Stenson, 2002, 2005; Helms et al, 2007; Coleman, 2004). Governmentality approaches also link the governance of ASB to broader changes in governance processes at a macro-level, characterised by technologies of the self and processes of responsibilisation, but direct analytical attention away from the actions of representatives of capital and the state, towards the localised settings in which power is exercised.

These approaches offer distinct ways of conceptualising power, and the genesis and evolution of policy. Both, however, have their drawbacks. Uitermark (2005) suggests that the structural analysis at the heart of regulation theory often renders accounts of policy processes incapable of accounting for variations between nations and cities. At the same time, he suggests that governmentality approaches often fail to take full account of the importance of the properties of materialised institutional structures in which the microphysics of power is located and operates, and which facilitate as well as constrain action. Uitermark suggests, however, that the conceptual tools these two approaches have developed are largely complementary and, when combined, can offer an analytical framework that overcomes the shortcomings inherent in each.

As a way of understanding the process of central–local exchange that characterises the development and implementation of ASB policy, we draw on the analytical framework Uitermark has developed to illuminate the processes of local–central exchange in the analysis of the process of policy formation. Using insights from both regulation and governmentality approaches, Uitermark's focus is on understanding the effects of the perpetual interaction between 'local' and 'central' actors in the emergence of policy:

> In sum, rather than privileging the local over the central level or vice versa, we need to study at least three aspects of central–local reciprocities in order to appreciate the multi-scalar origins of urban policies: the strategic interests of local actors, which are discursively formulated in relation to the institutional environment in which they are embedded and the entity over which they are supposed to exercise control (a neighbourhood, a housing block, etc.); the strategic interests of central actors and specifically the central state, which are determined by, for example, election results, party

politics and ideologies, the functioning of the economy, etc., and are always strategically and spatially selective; and the ways in which local and central actors communicate with each other, select each other and realign their interests in such a way that they become complementary. (Uitermark, 2005:159)

In this formulation, Uitermark draws attention to the local, which, he argues, is a neglected but decisive site informing the development of central government policy for a number of reasons. First, information collected at a local level directly informs and shapes national conceptualisations. Second, it is the local level which is a key site of innovation and experimentation. Third, situating his work within the general emergence of new forms of 'governance' (be they 'advanced liberalism' or 'neoliberalism'), Uitmermark argues that the central state increasingly has to tailor its policies in line with local interests, since it is dependent on informed local actors to instantiate policy developments. Thus, he claims that while the nation–state still plays a pivotal role, it is a role which is increasingly based on strategic partnerships with local actors. Actors at the local level are therefore conceptualised not only as responsible for executing central policies, but also as a political force that works to both constitute and subvert state policy.

Seven interrelated hypotheses form the core of his analytical framework, but in its application to concrete case study sites Uitermark warns against adopting a checklist approach. Rather, he advocates a more selective application of the principles outlined. In the remainder of this section, we use four of these hypotheses in order to illuminate the power and agency of local actors. Drawing on empirical material regarding the development of IFSPs, we explore both how local practitioners negotiate the aims of central policy and how the central state also draws on and appropriates these moments of subversion in the (re)formulation of national policy.

1. Institutions that identify, classify and govern disadvantaged neighbourhoods and populations generate knowledge to conceptualise the problem and the role of the state

Following Foucault, Uitermark suggests that institutional actors at a local level and with knowledge of a particular environment develop rationalities and technologies that are deemed useful and functional for the formulation of policy in those neighbourhoods and on the problems identified therein. The six FIPs included in our research were initially established as part of local governance regimes and did not represent the local implementation of a central policy. Across the six case study sites, one of the stimuli for the introduction of this new approach to dealing with those accused of ASB was a perceived lack of provision for families suffering from a range of welfare support needs and who were repeatedly presenting as homeless, due to the disruptive behaviour of family members or visitors to their property, and who were suffering associated deleterious consequences, such as family breakdown. Major gaps in the provision of support for this group were identified in all case study locations:

> "I think it was very much about addressing gaps ... support and intervention was the domain of social services, but often support and intervention would be missing because social service criteria for what they will accept and deal with is so high ... so yeah, I think there was a gap and this was partly about plugging that gap." (Housing manager)

Critically, the issue of ASB was placed within the broader context of social exclusion, and aligned with other policy agendas such as homelessness and child protection. At the heart of this problematisation, rather than construct the 'antisocial' pathologically as morally deficient or wilfully irresponsible, as was the case in 'official' government rhetoric at the time (Nixon and Parr, 2006), those responsible for establishing and managing the projects drew attention to the underlying causes of disruptive and damaging behaviour. A range of personal factors was seen as precipitating problematic behaviour and homelessness, including domestic violence, health, substance misuse and debt. Issues of powerlessness and lack of control which featured strongly in service users' accounts of why they had been referred to a project were also reflected in local actors' accounts of the damaging consequences of cycles of eviction and repeat homelessness:

> "You're talking about very needy families, and very, very often families who exhibit ASB are victims of ASB also. Often because they're vulnerable in some way or another, you know, single parents or families with special needs of some sort, or an alcohol, drug, whatever else issues." (Project manager)

Conceived at a local level, then, the projects developed an alternative conceptualisation of 'the problem' of ASB that, in part, contradicted the national, popular discourse dominant at the time. Furthermore, project workers actively challenged media stereotypes that referred to families as 'neighbours from hell' or 'yobs'.

> "We're not calling them, I wouldn't call them antisocial families, that kind of skews the meaning completely and I wouldn't call the kids yobs like the government like to do." (Project manager)

These alternative interpretations of the 'problem' of ASB, with a greater focus on the multifaceted nature of the underlying causes, had significant consequences for the delivery of a policy solution and the role of the state. It brought with it a need for professional dialogue between agencies. By bringing together different arms of the local state, including health, adult and children's services, housing, police and community safety, together with third sector organisations such as National Children's Homes (NCH) (who were responsible for managing five of the six projects included in the study), it was hoped that these organisations would act together to address the problem identified:

> "The Youth Offending Team may have a role, there may be a role for our colleagues in attendance and assessment, in children and families section which we used to know as Social Services. Education would definitely have a role to play if the young person is under 16. So if we're not working together complementary to each other we're not actually serving that family and giving them a choice and a menu of services that they can have access to." (YOT manager)

It is important to note, however, that although local actors in the six projects operated within comparable socio-economic contexts and shared similar aims and objectives, the model of provision developed across the six FIP sites was shaped by a number of local factors, including the project managers' professional orientation; leadership and management style; and local governance arrangements.

2. The technologies and rationalities of government developed in one site can be distributed horizontally from one locality to another

Uitermark's model suggests that policy narratives can be distributed horizontally from one locality to another via, for example, local networking and exchanges between policy specialists or institutional actors. While this transfer of knowledge can happen independently from the centre, given that the process of horizontal distribution is marked by the promotion of key concepts and discourses, it can appear to be the case that the strategy has been conceived and implemented at the centre (Uitermark, 2005). In the case of FIPs, as part of their development, there was very clearly a horizontal transfer of knowledge from the Dundee Families Project (Dillane et al, 2001) to each of the six case study sites. This process of distribution was facilitated, in part, by the fact that the children's charity NCH managed five of the six projects as well as the Dundee Family Project, which had been recognised nationally as representing 'good practice' in tackling ASB:

> "What's actually happened is that the manager of our Children's Fund had heard about the Dundee project which NCH managed and we have a fairly strong link with NCH locally so we asked them to, she invited them to come to Salford and do a presentation about the project and have, stimulate, some discussion and we decided that we would like to create something here and they were also actually doing it in some of the neighbouring local authorities as well and I think it was decided that there should be an assistant director who sort of championed this and raised it with councils and things like that, so I got that job." (Project manager)

A direct dialogue also occurred between the six project managers and the Dundee Families Project by phone or email and through visits:

> "We all went up to Dundee, four of us went to Dundee … What we didn't have in the city was a service that was going to do some long, intense work with a few families that probably we all knew as organisations, you know, known to all of us … and it was felt that the Dundee Families' Model was quite a good model to try and look at filling that gap

really. So that, that was, you know that was the reason for everybody's interest in it." (Project manager)

Horizontal networking was further facilitated by the national evaluation (Nixon et al, 2006), which included the provision of a Managed Learning Network (MLN) to provide the six project managers with an institutional and organisational platform to reflect on lessons learned and an opportunity to network between themselves. In practice, the MLN was used to distribute knowledge in a variety of ways, including:

• to provide a forum to legitimate the exchange of views;
• to enable project managers to have a voice and share anxieties;
• to distil concepts of professional practice;
• to provide an opportunity to reflect on what works and what doesn't work and to make sense of both.

Horizontal policy processes provided local actors with access to what were considered useful and functional rationalities and technologies of government, initially developed by the Dundee Families Project. Horizontal networking therefore engendered a process of learning and of assimilating policy from one locality to another.

3. At any one time there will be a number of competing discourses relating to specific problems, based on particular rationalities which inform the technologies – local and national actors try to mobilise support for their discourses through developing interdependencies, which in turn fosters closer central–local interactions and cooperation

Uitermark notes how, at any one time, there are likely to be a number of competing discourses regarding a specific policy problem, and that actors must mobilise support from other local and central actors, creating interdependencies – defined by Uitermark as an arena of struggles and confrontation between actors and strategies. The conceptualisation of ASB that emerged in the six case study areas, and which offered a more nuanced understanding of the policy issue, was not embraced by all actors at a local level in the six sites. Consequently, the process of establishing an appropriate institutional and organisational platform from which projects could operate was not always easy. The six projects therefore needed to develop survival strategies that were specific to local circumstances, and a critical early task was building and maintaining relationships with key actors on whom the projects depended (for resources, information sharing, expertise and support). In some cases, this meant overcoming overt resistance from local agencies who were wedded to the dominant discourse and did not consider the approach 'tough' enough. Developing creative and novel forms of intervention while operating in highly pressured political contexts was seen, however, as a high-risk but necessary activity, as the following comments illustrate:

> "There was so much resistance in agencies and with the public you know, 'why are you rewarding families who are antisocial, why not get rid of them?'.You know, 'they deserve to get evicted, off with their heads', you know, all that sort of stuff. But it's like it [eviction] does nothing more than move the ASB around. It does nothing, it just costs money, you know the families don't change, the children learn that behaviour. When they become parents they behave in exactly the same way. It just is never ending." (Project manager)

> "This project was seen as being too soft, all about the rights of families and not enough about responsibilities." (Project manager)

In order for the projects to become politically acceptable at a local level, project managers reflected on the need to establish a credible narrative that was sufficiently robust to support interdependencies and promote relationships of trust. Indeed, it was necessary to align the projects' interests with those of other actors in order to gain credibility and institutional support. This meant identifying common interests and ensuring that the aims of the projects were discursively formulated in a way that 'fitted' with the strategic interests of other agencies whose 'core business' was not ASB, such as adult and children's services, as well as those tasked with the management of ASB who were more enforcement focused. This required the development of a convincing narrative that would signal the projects' independence and distance from a straightforward, enforcement-led model of intervention, and yet one that would not alienate those agencies more traditionally committed to the use of enforcement. To do this, managers framed the projects' practice model as characterised by a mixture of what was referred to by one project manager as a combination of "support" and "housing" and by another as "support" and "challenge". This reflects a common understanding of housing-led approaches to dealing with ASB as being more focused on enforcement action, in contrast to social services approaches, which are perceived to be more focused on prevention and support. The development of 'challenging' practice models was seen as a defining concept for the identity of the projects and was also perceived as vital to ensuring that the interventions reflected the projects' responsibilities to the wider community. This helped managers to situate the projects somewhere between support and enforcement, and to resist the description of their being a 'soft' option. There was a clear perception, therefore, that projects could not be easily 'pigeon-holed', which helped them to garner institutional support:

> "I do very much promote a culture of we're not messing about, we are going to challenge behaviour." (Project manager)

The projects were also able to gain institutional support and to produce interdependencies, due to their access to resources provided for other organisations:

> "So from our point of view we felt great, another resource, because you know we're always short of resources. So from our point of view a project that would be funded, that would enhance the kind of bag of resources we can offer these families sounded really good, not just the in-house provision but the outreach provision, into the home." (Social worker)

It was only once the projects had established a clear identity and profile, constructed through professional practice, geographical, political and community affiliations and clearly demonstrable outcomes that the 'fledgling' discourses generated by them began to be more widely circulated and started to achieve recognition in other local areas.

4. Discourses can be viewed as a form of resource since they provide conceptualisations and rationales for particular types of intervention that can be distributed through the institutional infrastructure of the state

According to Uitermark's framework, national policies do not determine local outcomes, but nor do they flow from processes of knowledge production and transfer at a local level. Rather, there exist complex interdependencies between local and national actors. One example is the way in which actors at a local level can use institutional infrastructures to influence the decisions of the central state, such that local discourses can be institutionalised and supported as national policy and distributed by the central state. Local discourses on the efficacy of different forms of intervention act as a form of resource, since they provide national actors with useful conceptualisations that help them to perform their tasks. This kind of vertical policy transfer does not occur automatically; rather, the extent to which central actors select a certain discourse and policy is influenced by a number of competing (political, economic, ideological) factors.

Over the period of our research the rationalities and technologies associated with intensive family support were adopted and effectively redistributed by the central state as national policy as part of the Respect Action Plan published in 2006. The six FIPs therefore found themselves to be the focus of intense interest from government ministers and members of the ASB Taskforce, such that project managers were asked to undertake promotional events and 'sell' the FIP idea at Together road shows and were given access to government ministers to promote their work:

> "I believe this is an absolutely excellent service, so I can sell it to anybody. Do you know what I [say], when I've done presentations and I've given presentations to SITRA [a housing organisation providing training and consultancy to others] and to Beacon events on homelessness and conferences and stuff like that, and people say like: 'You know you sound so enthusiastic', I say, 'Its easy. When you go in ... and you can see it working, you know, you can sell it to anybody, it's so easy.'" (Project manager)

Perhaps the most persuasive explanation as to why the FIP model was selected by national actors was the fact that research (Nixon et al, 2006; Jones et al, 2006) suggested that outcomes associated with this form of intervention appeared to be very positive. Moreover, accounts of the efficacy of the FIP approach began to circulate at the same time that national policy makers were seeking to extend measures to control behaviour, in recognition that the government needed to embrace 'support' as a core part of the ASB agenda. National policy makers seized on FIPs as a way of both acknowledging the need to provide perpetrators with support and at the same time retaining a focus on tough disciplining action.

However, as the model of intervention developed at a local level came to be considered worthy of attention and was appropriated at a national level, a process of bargaining occurred. Although the government imported the locally produced rationalities and technologies of governance associated with intensive family support projects, their adoption of these was selective. While on the one hand the new projects were presented as a welfare-oriented form of intervention to tackle the causes of poor behaviour, including domestic violence, poor health, drug dependency and alcohol abuse, on the other hand it was made clear that FIPs were not a 'soft option'. As part of the repositioning of projects, the provision of 'support' was aligned to the threat of sanction and the projects were framed as a 'twin track' approach. Thus it was possible for FIPs to be presented as part of a 'tough' approach involving the enforced rehabilitation and disciplining of 'problem families':

> It is clear from the work of our expert panels on neighbour nuisance that we must now clamp down further on the problem families who, although small in number, cause disproportionate damage to their communities. That is why we are investing £1.25 million to ensure that those parents who persist in letting their kids run wild, or behave like yobs themselves, will face intensive rehabilitation in 50 more areas across the country, backed by the threat of enforcement. (Blears, 2005a)

As the national policy evolved, with a greater emphasis placed on disciplining, the discursive constructs used to describe the projects shifted. While initially they were referred to as 'intensive family *support* projects', reflecting the novel supportive dimension of the intervention, they were subsequently relabelled 'family *intervention* projects' by the Respect Task Force, with an associated repositioning of their role, in which support is reinforced more explicitly by coercive sanctions. The term 'support' in this context has been redefined from its traditional meaning of providing direct help in terms of material benefits, for example income support, to a moral imperative of inclusion, with the onus on those provided with 'support' to change. A similar process can be identified in relation to the regulation of parenting interventions, where, as Gillies (2005) points out, the offer of 'support' barely disguises a form of popular authoritarianism:

> Parents who are regarded as lacking in the necessary reflexivity and knowledge are to be supported back on to

the path of inclusion through advice and parenting classes while those who refuse to conform and acknowledge their moral obligations are to be named, shamed, fined and ultimately even imprisoned. (Gillies, 2005: 83)

Furthermore, while families are defined, by reference to a social exclusion discourse, as having 'multiple problems' requiring 'multiple solutions' and FIPs are rationalised as a response to the inability of agencies to support these families, the national discourse places the emphasis not on the failing of state and non-state agencies but as a failure of families' ability or willingness to engage with welfare agencies. The projects became reconfigured therefore as interventions which 'grip' families:

these projects, a flagship part of the Respect programme, grip families and use enforcement action and intensive help and are proven to turn families around. (Casey, 2007)

The rise to prominence of FIPs as a flagship policy has resulted in the model of intervention being distributed across a wide range of policy fields. Cross-government commitment to the FIP model of working is evidenced in a number of policy initiatives, including the Social Exclusion Taskforce review on 'families at risk' and the Department for Children, Schools and Families' Youth Taskforce Action Plan (DCSF, 2008).

Conclusion

As early as 2000, the government's Social Exclusion Unit promoted as good practice the provision of intensive and, where appropriate, residential support for people who had been evicted from or who had abandoned housing due to ASB (SEU, 2000). It took a further six years, however, for this model of intervention to be adopted as national policy. Using Uitermark's (2005) analytical framework to explore how and why this change in policy direction occurred, this chapter has drawn attention to the role of local actors and the multi-scalar origins of FIP policy. It has demonstrated how the perceived lack of efficacy of enforcement models of intervention, combined with recognition among local practitioners of the value of taking action to address the underlying causes of disruptive behaviour, gave rise to a distinctly local policy for dealing with 'the problem' of ASB, namely intensive family support projects. As 'discourse machines' these local policies embraced complexity and defended a more nuanced conceptualisation of the policy problem, focusing on recognition that ASB is often only one symptom of multiple deprivations and disadvantage.

As has been evidenced in this chapter, the impact of such local discourses on national policy development is illustrative of the fact that government policy formulations are not impermeable to the impact of local contestation or even 'resistance'. At the same time, however, the evidence presented in this chapter also illustrates how local processes of knowledge production and subversion may be manipulated through central strategic interventions. Indeed, the perceived success of the family support projects and the accompanying narrative they generated were subsequently appropriated by and became a 'flagship' policy for the New Labour government in its third term. However, within this process the policy discourse underwent significant changes, with an increased focus on pathology, which served to justify the need for tough sanctions to stimulate behaviour change. This reformulation of the policy's political rationale and associated technologies of government is reflected in the change of name, with projects being relabelled from family *support* projects to family *intervention* projects. Of course, there are possibilities for resistance to and subversion of such a discourse at the level of policy implementation, but such a discussion is unfortunately beyond the scope of this chapter.

EIGHT

Family decision making: new spaces for participation and resistance

Kate Morris and Gale Burford

Introduction

This chapter uses the implementation of an innovative participatory approach to child welfare decision making in England and the US to consider the processes by which professionals and families can seemingly subvert or resist the intended outcomes of a new practice development. This is not to say that interplay between front-line professionals and families is the only place to look in order to explain the discrepancy between the intent of a policy and its outcomes. There is a body of literature that considers the challenges of implementing and managing innovation in public services, but not necessarily the impact of establishing new participative processes at the point of service delivery (Brown, 2007), which is the focus of this discussion. This focus is important because, despite being central to policy formulation in both countries since the mid 1990s, the practice of family engagement remains at best on the margins, with relatively few families having access to these family-led decision-making forums. We suggest the experience of introducing family decision making to be a complex process: professionals are argued to have sought to colonise the model so as to limit family power, and families to have reacted in turn against this process with their own resistance to the professional desire to control family decision making. It should be noted that this is not an exhaustive account of the evolution of family decision making in the UK and the US, rather this chapter is concerned only with particular dimensions of this development. We begin by setting out the history and context of the approach, necessary for understanding the subsequent tensions and difficulties. UK evaluations of local Family Group Conference services are used as illustrative material for the analysis, and the conclusion explores broader messages for innovative and radical social work practice development.

Overview of family group decision making models and history

Historically, in the UK and the US, individuals have been dislocated from their kinship networks in part by the fragmented state welfare services they access or receive (Morris et al, 2008). (While there are complex economic reasons for this separation, which are concerned with productivity and mobility, this is not the focus of this chapter and therefore not explored.) Family group decision making (FGDM) seeks to counterbalance the separation of children from their kinship networks (a term used broadly to include blood relatives and significant others) by enabling the family to lead the planning and decision-making processes. The dislocation of children from their kinship networks during the process of receiving child welfare services impacts their later emotional and psychological health; families are an important connection into a child's heritage, individual histories and identity. However, the involvement of the state in this private domain (the rights of individual family members to both privacy and protection) remains highly contested, and in the UK runs alongside a political discourse that engages in a process of 'othering' those who fail to conform to expectations about family life and who require state interventions in order to fulfil their roles and tasks adequately (Olsen and Clarke, 2003; Gillies, 2005). Thus, families using child welfare services are marginalised both by a historical reluctance on the part of legislators to be seen to interfere in private matters, and by virtue of their needs for help and assistance. Krumer-Nevo (2003) describes such families as defeated families; families who are defeated both by their needs and deprivations and by the services that are meant to assist.

Elsewhere the involvement of the kinship network in child welfare provision sits within a different conceptual and cultural framework. For example, in New Zealand there is a recent history of actively seeking out models for and approaches to the inclusion of extended family in service development, in part as a response to past oppressive state interventions in Maori family life (Doolan, 2007). Thus, FGDM was part of a radical change agenda. In this cultural context Connolly (2007) argues that the inclusion of a child's family in child welfare policies and practices is an extension of a rights-based perspective, and therefore the failure to engage children's networks meaningfully is a contravention of their basic human rights. Drawing on New Zealand's policies and practices, she has developed a conceptual framework for practitioners, bringing together the requirements to remain child centred with the rights of families to participate in assessing and resolving needs. Doolan, drawing on this New Zealand perspective, argues that:

> Families have a right to participate in decision making about matters that concern them and it is at the point where individual and family liberties and freedom of choice are in jeopardy that the state must make its greatest effort to ensure real participation and involvement. (Doolan, 2007: 10)

In the UK, the New Labour agenda has seen a policy discourse concerned with families take an increasingly central role, specifically in the drive to address the consequences of social exclusion. Families have become partners in New Labour preventative initiatives – at times through encouragement, at times through coercion. Policies and the legal frameworks for practice have sought to ensure that some family members, specifically parents, are enlisted in the drive to produce socially and economically viable future citizens (Fawcett et al, 2004; Featherstone, 2006). However, the empirical evidence indicates that for front-line practitioners it is mothers who are the focus of the services (Williams, 2004; Gillies, 2005), thus *family* policies in child welfare are experienced as interventions in mothering and in the parenting that mothers provide. Thus the involvement of the extended family remains a marginal UK practice development, beset with concerns about professional skills, the risks that such developments pose and the challenges that whole family approaches present to fragmented services (Brown, 2007; Morris et al, 2008).

Policy, practice and research efforts surrounding whole family approaches are also confounded in the US, where tensions between family members' rights to privacy and their rights to protection from the behaviour of other family members have often been treated as separate and conflicting discourses. This is especially true for mothers, who have historically been unable to invoke protection from abuse for themselves without simultaneously being blamed for failing to protect their children. In the US, the right to raise one's children as one sees fit is so strongly embedded in policy and practice as to exclude the involvement of extended family unless a child has been placed under the authority of the court. While given an importance in federal legislation that is tied to dollars, family engagement has proved to be highly challenging to mainstream services and to those seeking to evaluate its impact. The various aims of reducing over-representation of specific groups of children, increasing the use of kin care and reducing costs have brought together players from diverse points along the political spectrum at the planning table. Creative workers must still work around legislation and practice cultures that view families with mistrust, while at the same time triaging their efforts to defend themselves and their organisations from errors in the application of procedures. Thus, genuine engagement with families is experienced as challenging and risky.

Family group conferences

This chapter draws on a particular form of family group decision making – Family Group Conferences (FGCs). It is a model of family decision making that originated in New Zealand and was subsequently adopted by policy makers and practitioners in the US and the UK. It is important to note that, despite reflections elsewhere (see for example Holland et al, 2004, 2005), FGCs are not an 'intervention' but are, put simply, a mechanism for families arriving at a plan for vulnerable family members. The model has a series of stages:

Referral: FGCs are used where a child has a set of needs that cannot be responded to without the marshalling of resources. Referrals are made to an FGC coordinator, who will begin by mapping out the child's network.

Preparation: The coordinator will prepare all those concerned for their involvement in the planning process; professionals who are contributing are asked to ensure that they can provide clear information to the family about their assessments, responsibilities and resources.

Meeting: The first stage of the FGC includes professionals and is chaired initially by the coordinator. The family is then left to plan in private, and is charged with three tasks: to arrive at an agreed plan, to arrive at arrangements for monitoring the plan and to set out contingency plans should the original arrangements be unsuccessful. The professionals will rejoin the meeting, and unless the plan compromises their legal responsibilities they should agree the principles and negotiate resources.

The plan: Following the meeting, the family plan is circulated. Established follow-on practices diverge; some areas ask their coordinators to fulfil a follow-up function, and others cease any further involvement.

Therefore the model holds a number of practice principles:

- that families are the appropriate 'context for resolution' (Doolan, 2005) for children's needs and difficulties;
- that professional roles are concerned with facilitation, support and, only if necessary, intervention to ensure safety;
- that families have rights to adequate information about the professional assessments, an understanding of the professional statutory duties and responsibilities, and descriptions of the resources available.

The model is not concerned, in its original form, with the rationing of resources or the implementation of managerial policies. The model is best understood within a rights-based analysis, and therefore is the subject of discussions of power and responsibility. As Holland et al (2004, 2005) describe, the model can present a means of democratising the decision-making processes and empowering families but if misused can result in difficulties facing families in 'holding professionals to account' for the delivery of their commitments within a family plan (Jackson and Morris, 1999).

Implementing family-led decision making

The use of FGCs in New Zealand was embedded within a movement that sought to achieve social change and justice for Maori families who had lost their children to a white 'stranger carer' system (Marsh and Crow, 1998). The model was developed as a means by which Maori families could access social work services without losing their children, or secure the return of their children into their kinship network. Indeed it is argued to have originated in front-line professionals collaborating with local communities to arrive at a responsive model of practice (Wilcox, 1991). Likewise in some states in the US, the model is argued to have been introduced in order to enhance the rights of minority and marginalised families and to deliver on issues of social justice, rather than just to plan for the immediate needs of a child and its family (Crumbley, 2007).

The UK development of FGCs pays little heed to this history of civil rights and oppression. The importing of the model to the UK in the early 1990s was arguably divorced from an understanding of its radical social and political associations (Morris and Tunnard, 1996). Instead, historically, the UK approach by senior policy makers has largely been a pragmatic one – a permissive policy approach to using the model, when judged to be feasible, to arrive at alternative outcomes to those regarded as inadequate. More recently, a series of UK government policy developments and central government guidance has picked up on the potential political value of FGCs. The 'Think Family' policy documents (SEU Task Force, 2007, 2008) produced by the UK government in response to concerns about marginalised families have identified Family Group Conferences as a means of providing a whole-family approach to families with multiple and chronic needs, and thus locating responsibilities for change with the family. In the 2006 Review of Care Proceedings (DCA, 2006), FGCs were promoted as an appropriate means of addressing matters that might otherwise result in care proceedings – the hope here being that they would facilitate informal resolutions and reduce the need for formal interventions. There are ramifications for the model in positioning its use in these ways, and these are explored later in the chapter, but in essence the UK government has slowly warmed to FGCs and now sees them as a useful tool: to facilitate early intervention service delivery, to bring forward alternative resolutions, to exploit kinship care opportunities and as a means of managing professional processes in order to reduce delay in formal decision making for children's future arrangements.

Child welfare in the US is an individual state matter, although the federal government does influence local activity through the allocation of federal monies. State-administered and some county-administered systems adopted FGCs during the 1990s, each with its own personalised mission and, as has become clear in the ensuing years, considerable adaptation and change to the approach. An international survey of FGC and related practices (Nixon et al, 2005) found that in the US local branding resulted in many different names for family engagement strategies, and considerable resultant competition, as has been the historical precedent in the US (e.g. Adams and Nelson, 1995). While this confounds the quality-assurance and evaluation tasks, it does, as Braithwaite (2002) has pointed out, give rise to creative embellishments that would be impossible under conditions that typically force mediocrity in practice, as are often found when over-regulation exists.

In the US, Family Group Decision Making has been used as an umbrella term for a variety of different family-involvement strategies and models. Conceptually, all the models purport to build on family and community strengths (Center for the Study of Social Policy, 2002); however, these models mask a wide variety of practices, for example, varying considerably in the extent of participant preparation for the meeting, the amount of leadership and influence offered to family members, and professional facilitation. Central to each approach is, typically, a face-to-face meeting at which key decisions are rendered by variously defined configurations of stakeholders including family, friends, community members and front-line professionals. Again, in practice significant diversity can mean meetings that include large numbers of professionals with a single family member present, through to meetings that have large numbers of family members present with few professionals.

As with the UK, some efforts in the US to mainstream the practice have resulted in denuding those details of practice most closely associated, in theory, with empowering the family's leadership, including: eliminating categories of 'problem' families from being referred; reducing or eliminating the independence of the meeting coordinator; structuring the meeting with numerous guidelines and high levels of professional facilitation; narrowing the purpose of the meeting to one of manoeuvring the family to 'rubber stamp' the professionals' plan; reduced diligence in efforts to contact family members outside the conflicted household or immediate parents; and elimination of protected time for the family to meet on their own. Critics in the US have anecdotally raised concerns about the amount of preparation time necessary for the New Zealand approach and that it goes too far in handing over important decisions about child safety to the people who have abused them. Neither concern is borne out in evaluation. These arguments have in turn been seen by advocates as colonising the practice to keep power in the hands of the legal, forensic and professional practice industry that has been erected since the late 1970s in US child welfare. One study carried out in Sweden (Sundel et al, 2001) showed that, despite expressing high levels of interest in FGC and agreement with its philosophy, few social workers who were followed up over an 18-month period actually referred a family for an FGC, a pattern that has also been observed in the US and the UK (Brown, 2003; Nixon et al, 2005).

However, the use of family group conferences in some form appears to be on the rise in the US. According to Weigensberg et al (2009), family meetings seem to be used significantly more than non-family interventions in situations where there has been significantly greater severity of harm to the child, substance abuse problems of primary caretakers, and domestic violence. Importantly, studies in the US show that family meetings do not appear to compromise child safety (Edwards et al, 2007).

This review of the evidence nationally and internationally indicates a broad range of practices sitting under the label of an FGC. The evidence indicates that not all meetings called FGCs are family-led decision-making processes and that it is not safe to make cross-country or cross-cultural assumptions about the specific details of the models being adopted (Burford et al, forthcoming). Some themes do emerge from the international review of the evidence and it is important to note here that these themes are significantly positive about the impact of the model on children's well-being:

- Most families have people in their kin and friendship network who are willing and able to become involved in helping to resolve the difficulties.
- Families are able to meet and plan in safety without repercussions for safety or well-being.
- Families are willing to work cooperatively, in partnership with the statutory authorities.
- There is evidence of increased kinship care, formal and informal.
- There are consistently high rates of child and family satisfaction.

It is within this broad context of policy and research that we now consider some specific practice developments in the use of FGCs. In doing so we are able to consider the processes by which professionals and family members respond to opportunities for meaningful participation, but also the complex ways in which intended outcomes are subverted and diverted. As the preceding discussion has highlighted, FGC projects are able to demonstrate positive outcomes for children and families, and are a means of connecting children with their kinship networks – crucial in securing long-term benefits for children. Thus, the relatively low level and uneven nature of their use cannot be explained by adverse or concerning outcome indicators. Drawing on a local FGC service evaluation as illustrative material, we describe the implementation of an FGC service within a UK authority and the tensions produced for staff by the introduction of a participatory model of service delivery. The focus here is the informal processes by which front-line professionals undermined the intentions of the model, and the means by which families sought to step around this professional modification and diminution of the model.

FGCs as democratising processes – subverting the state?

The experience from the US and the UK suggests that where FGC services are developed and supported this development regularly rests on what Edwards et al (2008) refer to as the 'hero practitioner'. Local services are driven initially by individuals or small groups that seek to move their practices into a rights-based framework and identify FGCs as an appropriate means to share decision-making powers and responsibilities.

> It is my personal goal to provide true empowerment (not just a buzz-word for increased funding) to families that I work with. My push is to get this into the community at the grassroots level and inform the public as much as possible, so that they are in a position to demand a conference, when it is not offered. Historically, governments do not relent or share power, without being forced to do so. To me one of the most important things that FGC represents is a vehicle for justice and liberation. (FGC project manager, UK) (Burford et al, 2007)

This role as a hero practitioner places considerable emphasis on individuals for the survival of the services: if the practitioner leaves their post, the capacity of the FGC to continue undisturbed is constrained. In part this is because at local and senior management levels the UK FGC services have usually been funded as pilot projects, set aside from the mainstream and with little active management support (Brown, 2003). It can be argued that management has demonstrated limited understanding of the radical implications of the model, instead either using the projects as evidence for targets concerned with consultation and participation or seeking to fit FGC plans into the performance indicators adopted for professional processes. The attractiveness of FGC in the US can certainly be traced to the federal requirements to demonstrate family engagement as part of the federal review process that is tied to funding. The UK evidence from the 2000s indicates that take-up of the model has been limited and that many FGC services until recently sat outside of mainstream child welfare provision (Brown, 2003). However, the UK guidance issued in 2007 and 2008 (DCSF, 2007; MoJ, 2008) has potentially moved the use of FGCs into the mainstream; this development is considered later in the chapter. The marginal positioning of FGC services reflects an ongoing concern held by local and national policy makers about entrusting families who require child welfare services with decision-making responsibilities (DH, 1999). As Brown identifies, such practice development is experienced by professionals as high risk in a context that seeks to intensively manage any possible adverse outcome for a child or for a professional reputation (Brown, 2007). Local UK FGC practitioner experiences of the barriers and inhibitors to embedding FGCs in core child welfare practices can be clustered around common themes, one of which links directly with the concerns of this text – the reduction of formal powers through informal family/professional collaborations. The model seeks to form effective partnerships and, by doing so, to remove the need for extensive formal intervention. Thus the model requires professionals to respect families as sensible decision makers, and to change their conceptual framework for their work with the family (Morris and Burford, 2007). Repeatedly, local FGC evaluations in the UK have described the anxieties and reluctance of professionals to embrace this change (see, for example, Brown, 2003, 2007; Morris and Burford, 2007).

The empirical evidence from local UK FGC evaluations documents the frustrations of those hero practitioners seeking to use FGCs. The local regulatory arrangements for child protection and for children who are the subject of formal state interventions are experienced as significant blocks, and as mechanisms for strengthening professional power and status.

> There will be a slow shift with the Every Child Matters agenda but it's happening too slowly for me. I think the danger for those of us who have been working in this field for a long time is how we continue to maintain our motivation in the face of agency resistance/undermining of the process. I long for the day that it becomes mandatory either in being resourced fully to meet policy requirements, throughout the country or becomes law – I think the latter is necessary to make it happen – in my view agencies have to be made to give up/share power especially in this culture of hanging out the professional to dry if anything goes wrong. (UK service manager) (Burford et al, 2007)

Complex tensions arise for front-line staff in the US and the UK where the democratisation of decision making hinders or impedes the implementation of established state processes. This sets the limits for the hero practitioner in bending or changing the regulatory arrangements for child welfare provision, and in seeking to relocate responsibilities and rights within the family network (Nixon et al, 2005; Doolan, 2007). Particularly in the US, tensions between social workers and their colleagues in the legal, mental health and domestic violence communities can surface. Fears that the perpetrators can influence and intimidate other family members in ways that professionals cannot discern often get spread to family members spanning branches and generations. Social workers and FGC coordinators find themselves in the role of constantly having to educate their colleagues, and many worry they will be blamed if something goes wrong. This in turn often sets up perfectionist expectations of the worker, their supervisor and the family, with the underlying belief that an investigative or forensic approach is 'more safe' than family engagement.

In the UK, service evaluations indicate that localised attempts by FGC project managers to enhance the efficacy of the model and the planning resources of the families were used by professionals as an opportunity to restrict the work of the family and undermine the participative and democratising principles of the model (Morris, 2007). The service sought to help professionals to lay out clearly their concerns by developing a set of questions for the family. In practice this became a mechanism for professionals to pre-set the agenda for the family and/or to gather further information from the family for professional decision-making processes. Indeed, one family plan begins with the following sentence:

> About the family plan: The questions for the family to address are in bold type followed by the family's response in regular type.

The transformation of the opportunity to present the family with helpful, clarifying questions into a mechanism for guiding and driving the content of the plan suggests that front-line staff remained unconvinced of the value of changing the existing arrangements for working with families. Such subversions of intended 'good practice' guidance by the front-line professionals demonstrate the limited impact of an innovative change model on staff perceptions of their roles and responsibilities when staff are not connected to the original intentions and drivers for the change.

These narratives from practice signify that when FGCs are 'fitted onto' the existing system of services without enabling legislation and clear senior policy endorsement of the shift in decision-making power, the changes are such that legal, managerial and professional colonisation of the approach will be necessary for professionals to resolve the conflicting demands they face. That is, the model itself requires such radical shifts in front-line practice that, unless workers feel they are operating within a permissive framework for these changes, they will seek to adapt the model to retain their pre-agreed roles and powers. Simply trying to deliver training and educating through the piloting of an FGC service cannot be expected to overturn existing cultures of professional practice. Implementation failure will almost certainly follow, suggesting that the shelf life of many programmes (Nixon et al, 2005) that do not settle into place and follow a comprehensive, multi-layered implementation plan will be short.

Families within FGCs: working around the barriers

Local UK evaluations also suggest that there are family actions that seek to challenge the resistance of professionals who are engaged in modifying the FGC model to negate the sharing of power. An analysis of the data contained within the family plans generated by service evaluations (Morris, 2007) points towards families using the meeting of their network as an opportunity to articulate their 'ethic of care'. Williams (2004) described a desire within family networks to 'do the right thing' in supporting and helping other family members. She suggested that empirical evidence from the CAVA research (a major UK project exploring changes in parenting and partnering) revealed families motivated by a concern for each other, rather than individualised preoccupations. She argued that families work within an ethic of care that is concerned with their shared moral and ethical understandings about family life and family commitments. This ethic of care was evident in the analysis of the family plans made during the FGC process – irrespective of the extent to which the decision-making powers of the meeting were subverted by professionals pre-setting the agenda. Families still sought to articulate their commitment to and care for their children (Morris, 2007: 16, 17):

> "Obviously we would like Mum and Dad to get better and live happily ever after but we live in the real world and *our first priority is the children* (family emphasis) ...A and B have a strong family and are very much loved ... We are fully aware of the commitment needed for A and B's future and are prepared to raise them into adulthood if necessary ... we do identify future possible difficulties and would deal with these as any family would do ...
>
> *Just to say which is imperative A and B needs will always be put first. They are much loved children.*" (Family emphasis)

> "I want to care for C full time, give her love and support that she needs ... she is my flesh and blood and I will do

everything to help her. I will take her to nursery or play groups I will go with her to see places ... I will teach her all the things she needs to know ...

We all as a family want what is best for C, we want her to learn how to read, write and interact with other kids. I want her to be herself as C."

Families provided such statements even when they had to deal with an almost exhaustive list of pre-set professional questions. Families would 'add on' a personal statement which allowed them to describe their commitment and their concerns. Professionals were left uneasy and unclear about this twist within the process:

"They may not be answering what they should be answering. When you go back in they give their answers but it wasn't what we were asking." (UK referring social worker) (Morris, 2007)

Excerpts from interviews as part of a US local evaluation echo this theme of family members seeking to manage the FGC process to achieve outcomes that reflect their needs rather than those of the professionals:

Question to young person after FGC: "So you pushed for this to happen?"

Answer: "I was like, 'I want to do that' [FGC] and my social worker was reluctant at first. And then she had to talk to her supervisor because I really pushed for it 'cause I wanted to do it because ... I need this to happen because I cannot stay in foster care until I turn 18." [The young person believed that the FGC would be a means for her to leave the public care system.]

In the US, involving service users in decision making, including in the construction of their own service plans, is not a new idea in education, health, justice or social care services. Where service users have been included, it is in a wide range of ways, from being present so they can be informed about what is happening, to assuming important roles as their own case manager – the former being the prevailing approach. In the statutory services, and particularly for anyone viewed as an abuser or a perpetrator, inclusion in decisions has been more about getting their compliance than their cooperation. In those services, the identity available to the service user tends to be focused on their guilt or innocence during investigation and on their level of compliance.

FGC involves the service users in ways that few other approaches have sought to include them. It makes them architects of their own plans. In doing so, it requires that front-line professionals reconsider how they adjust to greater levels of service-user empowerment. They adjust to innovation that is experienced as reframing their own perceptions of their roles and power, and how those using the services – historically, families with multiple and enduring difficulties – can exercise their own power and responsibilities within a highly regulated and manipulated context. It is these two strands that form the focus of our concluding discussion.

Rights-based practices: FGCs in context

Constructing a space for family participation in public services at the point of service delivery requires professional acknowledgement of the limits of professionals' expertise and knowledge. It also requires a conceptual framework for understanding families that is strength-based, that is, that the problems of one individual are not seen as weaknesses held by all family members. Finally, FGCs demand that front-line professionals make a connection with an analysis of rights-based practice, and use such an analysis to bolster and develop their participatory skills. Despite their apparent initial relevance, current social work debates about the frameworks for understanding the activities of front-line staff may only partially help with the analysis of FGCs in practice. Evans and Harris (2004) dwell on the relevance of Lipsky's analysis of discretion in seeking to understand contemporary social work activity. Their account of the changing regulatory framework for practice and of the implications of this for practitioners provides a useful insight into the context for those social workers expected to work with FGC services. They consider the contested understandings of the frameworks for social work practice, and the extent to which Lipsky's analysis of discretion offers a useful means of reflecting on the contemporary experiences of front-line social workers. However, UK and US FGDM accounts of local experiences reveal a preoccupation with the tensions between hero practitioners driving forward local projects and front-line social workers who resist such radical developments, rather than the impact of senior management activity. The role and effect of management policies and practices become evident at a later stage in the FGC service development, once the work of the hero practitioner is established. Initially the development of FGCs is not primarily concerned with front-line discretion in service and resource allocation (aside of those needed to set up the project); the focal point is the locus of power in decision-making processes, in particular the determining of the issues for deliberation. As such, the analysis of contemporary practice presented by Evans and Harris can only be partially relevant.

In the UK, social work has seen the emergence of new models for service delivery and practice that could usefully frame understandings of family decision making, specifically the emergence of 'personalisation' as a conceptual framework for developing individually tailored services (Leadbetter, 2004). Proponents of this approach suggest that it encourages service users to engage actively in the design and delivery of the services they receive by seeking to develop policies and practices that can be responsive to individual needs and experiences. This, it could be argued, is the focus of family decision making. While personalisation is a highly contested concept with multiple understandings (see, for example, Beresford, 2006; Foster et al, 2006), it can be argued that it is a useful framework for understanding FGCs, given their apparent concern with user-driven services and flexibility. But, while seemingly of relevance to an analysis of the use of FGCs, personalisation fails to engage with the core of the FGC model – the principles of family rights and expertise. FGCs are primarily characterised by a shift in power, and the narratives coming from those developing FGC services suggest that front-line professionals are resistant to changes in their authority and perceived rights to intervene. The danger here is that the complexities of front-line professional resistance to changes in the location of power may be masked in the use of a conceptual framework that does not engage with these debates and tensions.

Thus, attempts to position an analysis of the development of FGCs in existing considerations about the context and arrangements for social work practice are difficult. These difficulties are further compounded when the experiences of families are included in the analysis. Families overwhelmingly report positive reflections on the opportunities presented by FGCs (Marsh and Crow, 1998; Holland et al, 2004). At the same time, local evaluations also demonstrate families' efforts to resist manoeuvres by professionals that would limit or reduce their powers. Importantly, these manoeuvres are seen by professionals as intentional interventions to counteract defences and resistance on the part of families. On the other hand, families are exercising their own discretion in the way in which they respond to the regulatory intentions contained within the professionals' practices. This is a complex sequence of events, and without longitudinal studies it is difficult to ascertain the concluding outcomes for those involved. The family plans presented in the discussion as alternatives to the questions set by professionals may or may not have been pursued, but for the purposes of this discussion it is interesting to note the emergence of a service user-led process of renegotiation and discretion.

Braithwaite (2004: 213-14) argues that:

> Social workers should proceed on their routine work of empowerment not by making judgments that some people are fit to accept responsibility and others not. By assuming that all people have a willingness to take responsibility for securing the rights of vulnerable others with whom they are in close relationships until that presumption is proved wrong, by seeing all people as having multiple selves that include socially responsible and irresponsible selves, social work practice is about empowerment to coax and caress the socially responsible self to the fore. It is about building democratic problem solving, but equally it is about enforcing the democracy's human rights and freedoms when democratic deliberation fails to honour them.

FGC opens up a space, or site, in which rights and justice can be reconciled by the people most affected by the problem, including those charged by society to oversee the protection of the rights of the individuals involved. This chapter has suggested that creation of this space brings with it complex responses at the point of service delivery, which require careful deliberation if skilled practice is to develop.

There can be no 'simple' account here of subversion and resistance, the processes being described are too complex. Social workers can fulfil the roles of hero practitioner and of resistant professional. At times, FGC projects have depended on front-line social workers to drive the work forward, while it is their social work colleagues who are resisting such developments. Likewise, families respond differentially to the opportunities presented by the FGC – some forming alliances with practitioners to plan for change for their children and others, as we have shown, seeking to resist professional attempts to manipulate their decision-making processes.

When Ryburn described FGCs as 'a practice awaiting a theory' (Ryburn and Atherton, 1996), he was referring to the opportunity to connect the practice with social work theories of change and resilience within families. As this chapter has sought to demonstrate, there are also important debates to be had about the theoretical understandings of the implementation processes of FGCs, and within this the responses of the front-line professionals. Family decision making provides a complex picture of radical practice and professional resistance, set alongside evidence of families using the opportunities for participation in anticipated and unanticipated ways. Given these complexities in processes and experiences, it is as yet unclear as to whether this approach to child welfare planning will result in sustained change.

NINE

Subversive attachments: gendered, raced and professional realignments in the 'new' NHS

Shona Hunter

Introduction

Resistance and subversion are not necessarily strategic or conscious, but occur in the everyday negotiations between complex, ambiguous and often hidden desires and conflicts produced through the interplay of the professional and the social (gender, generation, ethnicity, etc). To capture this, this chapter develops a means of thinking about health and social care professionals as emotional actors. It views the emotions as connecting identity and agency, constituted through and constitutive of the social relations of power and inequality. On this view, welfare professionals, their agency and identifications are what I think of as relational. By this I mean that the symbolic and material, structural and discursive dimensions to experience become connected, but also reconfigured through biographical experience. Thus, complex biographical positionings put welfare professionals into conflict with a range of official discourses.

My feminist psychosocial approach in this chapter theorises against the notion of welfare professionals as rational actors. It claims instead that they are 'defended subjects' (Hollway and Jefferson, 2000), maintaining that what they say, do and feel are often quite different. The relational is the point at which this mix of saying, doing and feeling, the cognitive and the emotional, gets negotiated. Relational identifications constitute the felt level of experience, where this range of often-conflicting identifications and commitments is negotiated. The concept of relational agency refers to action which springs from these multiple negotiations which cannot be read from either professional or social location alone. It places as much importance on what these defended subjects do not say as on what they do say, in the belief that not speaking about things often means that they matter more.

This sort of approach provides a novel take on questions of the relationship between service users and health and social care practitioners. As I have argued elsewhere (Hunter, 2003), an important but neglected issue in this debate is that workers and users can be one and the same, in that all health and social care professionals will at some point interact with welfare services *as users*; that these positionings will impact on their experiences as welfare professionals; and that these dual and multiple positionings can constitute sources of subversion and resistance. The value in such an approach is that it can help us to understand why, when it appears that workers have been successfully and *apparently willingly* recruited into the homogenising project of modernisation, they continue to behave in ways which challenge its exclusions. It forces us to think again about the complex interrelations between intent, action and outcome and to rethink health and social care professionals' motivations in a way that can consider them both as friend and as foe to welfare users, other workers and indeed to themselves. It needs to delve into the hidden complex and contradictory nature of experience.

In this chapter I use narrative biographical data to consider how the professional and the social are mutually constitutive in the life of one welfare professional, Navneen, a 42-year-old Indian GP whom I interviewed for research into Primary Health Care Trusts in the Midlands area (Hunter, 2005a, 2005b). Specifically, I am interested not only in the way in which his relational identifications challenge key aspects of modernisation discourse in healthcare, but also in how they challenge the particular *racialisation of modernisation* in the context of primary healthcare. I begin my discussion by considering the ways in which the professional and the social intertwine in public sector modernisation, and in particular how this plays out in the construction of the 'old' and the 'new' professionalisms in primary care. The bulk of the chapter is devoted to a feminist psychosocial analysis of Navneen's narrative, through which I demonstrate the difference between what he *says* (or doesn't say) about gender, race and generation and what he *feels* about them. I rethink his apparent denials of raced and gendered identifications as forms of resistance to the deterministic positionings made available to him as an Asian male GP through contemporary healthcare modernisation. These are either as quality-conscious, modern but de-gendered/racialised GP-manager, or as ineffective, backward-looking, anachronistic Asian male GP.

Modernisation equality and the new public service workers

In their introduction, Barnes and Prior alert us to the variety of practices constituting the technical project of modernisation. But, for New Labour, modernisation was always simultaneously a social project claiming to reconcile economic performance, efficiency and effectiveness with social equality, and the inclusion of a variety of groups that were otherwise excluded on the basis of income, gender, age, ethnicity etc. A key element of this modernisation discourse is its ruptured relationship with the past (Newman, 2001) and a clear rejection of the 'old' *in favour of* the 'new'. It is in some senses true, as John Clarke claims (2004: 65), that there is an 'antisocial' strategy in this rupturing, which relies on historicising concerns for equality as anachronistic, presenting the social struggles of the 1970s and 1980s around inequality as over: settled in the present; confined to the past. As a range of commentators recognise (Franklin, 2000; Newman, 2001; Back et al, 2002), this has often meant a selective appropriation of New Left ideas on equality, to the exclusion of more 'radical' feminist, anti-racist and class-based politics. On the other hand, however, in the context of the recent 'turn to diversity', equality mainstreaming has become a core part of modern governance (Squires, 2006) and a core competence of the new professionalism. Notwithstanding various dilutions, the arrival of mainstreaming has its own set of complex and contradictory effects which are not always straightforwardly reductive (Hunter and Swan, 2007).

New Labour's Primary Care Trusts (PCTs) replaced local health authorities as flagships for devolved collective and professionally led primary healthcare. As core planks in NHS modernisation they were to constitute organisational contexts strongly characterised by the new public management (NPM), in which it was proposed that challenges to traditional hierarchical organisational cultures could thrive. For health and social care professionals they signalled the potential for formal integration into NHS decision-making structures (Peckham, 2000), for increased joint working (DH, 1998b), for user involvement through lay participation, for a move towards a social model of health (DH, 1998a), and for doing 'pioneering work' 'in embedding equality within their structures and activities from the outset' (National Health Service Executive, 2000: 43). As Lutfur Ali, former head of Equality and Diversity in NHS Employment, comments, 'to talk about equality and diversity is basically to talk about effective management and patient centred services' (*NHS Magazine*, 2003). PCTs were to represent the broader 'changing British mood' (DH, 2003: 8) in the health services through the *fusion between quality and equality*. The sort of professionals taking forward this work, the new professionals, would be influenced by more dynamic, transformative and less overtly masculinist working styles (Davies, 1995; Newman, 1995), more flexible, communicative and facilitative of holistic, patient-led care, and used to working in multidisciplinary, horizontally rather than hierarchically structured teams. This is in contrast to the more hierarchically inflexible role- and rule-governed professionalism of yesteryear. My qualitative research with PCTs (Hunter, 2005a) explores how these changes panned out in practice. In this chapter I am less interested in drawing out the specificities of modernisation in primary care and more interested in exploring this context as an example of how attempts to mainstream equalities as part of NPM are negotiated, resisted and more subtly subverted by health and social care professionals.

From early on, commentators had predicted that the value placed on consensus in NPM could be 'bad' for equality where 'internal conflicts are viewed as divisionary at best and at worst destructive' (Newman, 1995: 20; see also Davies, 1995). The feared upshot was an increased homogenisation of difference to fit in with consensus-driven managerial cultures, and a related reluctance to recognise and confront racism and sexism. My discussions with health and social care practitioners suggest that, on the ground, the social relations of gender and race equality and discrimination, their place in primary care and the relationship to their work in PCTs pan out more ambiguously. On one hand, the ongoing presence of structural inequalities in the delivery and practice of healthcare was recognised by participants, as was the need for equalities policies to redress these. On the other hand, however, participants remained largely reluctant to position themselves within the social relations of gender and ethnicity at work, either as 'victim' or as 'perpetrator'. Participants developed a range of strategies in interview to avoid positioning the self in terms of these social relations, a process that I call abdicating voice (Hunter, 2005a, 2009). One approach was to explore gendered and raced experience as something that was relevant to others in the same social category, but not to the participants themselves because of some form of exceptionality; another was to explore its relevance in the past, overcome in the present; yet another was to claim relevance in their personal, but not their professional lives. Participants' ability to recognise the *existence of structural inequalities* coupled with the ability to *overcome the recognition of raced and gendered difference* considered an important characteristic of the 'new' professionalism. Those professionals who were not deemed to achieve this coupling effectively were positioned as stuck in the hierarchical role- and rule-governed ways of the old professionalism, perpetuating structural inequalities through the recognition of social identities. The ongoing presence of these old professionals in the organisation was constituted by participants as an explanation for an ongoing failure to achieve quality/equality within PCTs.

The important point here is the specific way in which the social and the professional coalesce to produce the typical old professional. In the PCTs in this study this failed new professional became *embodied* for participants in the 'older Asian male GPs'. This set of practitioners is constructed by other members of the primary healthcare team as a homogeneous group, still governed by the unequal sexist medical dominance of traditional NHS organisational cultures. They were seen as inflexible, aggressive, didactic, resistant to change, and in particular to working in multidisciplinary teams on equal terms with nurses (viewed only as women) and other women members of the healthcare team. These constructions feed into and off broader discursive trends towards the racialisation of 'poor performance' in medicine (West, 2001) and broader constructions of hyper-masculine, anachronistic South Asian cultures (Alexander, 2002, 2004). Socially constructed differences are combined with the understandings of practice in such a way as to become discursively inseparable. Thus, the assumed 'underperformance' of older Asian male GPs in terms of their assumed resistance to quality/(gender) equality is explained with reference to the particular gendered and generational economies of South Asian communities. It is their 'underperformance' which is used to explain ongoing gender inequalities and poor-quality practice even in contexts where NPM thrives. Thus, in this scenario it is not *all* public service workers in general who appear to be the enemies of modernisation, but one set of workers in particular: older Asian male GPs. This scenario raises questions for those older Asian male GPs who do ally themselves to reform. How can you be for modernisation while apparently embodying all that is against reform?

Navneen's story: family ties, community ruptures and reparation in medicine

Because from a feminist psychosocial perspective emotions are not objects, the methodological aim is not to identify and describe the emotions, but to be alert to their connective power, bringing together or repelling ideas, people, discourses. This means that reading for the emotions is as much about what we don't say, and how we avoid saying it, as about what we do say and how. This goes particularly for issues of social difference, such as gender and 'race', which are often euphemised in everyday talk. Given that feelings about difference are caught up with discursively constructed Manichean positionings as either victim or oppressor, they are often contradictory and ambiguous, requiring a lot of contextual understanding for a robust interpretation. Because of these challenges, narrative methods tend to be favoured in this sort of work, as they favour figurative language and non-literal interpretation in the context of broader stories (Boudens, 2005). In practical terms, my feminist psychosocial approach (Hunter, 2005b, 2005a) brings together principles from Carol Gilligan and colleagues' Feminist Voice Centred Relational methodology (Gilligan et al, 1990a, 1990b), the Free Association Narrative Interview method (Hollway and Jefferson, 2000) and Biographic Narrative Interpretive Method (Wengraf, 2001). I carry out serial interviews with participants in which interview transcripts and my interpretations from our initial interviews form the basis for subsequent conversations, ranging from one to three other interviews, depending on the participant. Rooted in an understanding of participants *and* researcher as multiply positioned in the social relations of power and inequality, where the positioning of neither affords total control or abandonment of agency, the process is designed to produce intra- and inter-subjective dialogue between researcher and participant where both contest one another's perspectives and interpretation explicitly or implicitly throughout the research process. The aim is to analyse power dynamics *within* the research situation as constitutive of and through relations external to the research context. This sort of interpretive approach is, of course, contested and may not be suitable for all research contexts. The ethical challenges are considerable, particularly in terms of the power of the researcher to interpret unspoken feelings into participants and their own stories in any final analysis. I very briefly highlight one challenge in the following discussion in relation to the way I racialise research interviews and analysis. Nevertheless, I have argued elsewhere (Hunter, 2005a, 2005b) that where the research focus is on relatively powerful participants this sort of approach can be useful to 'getting past' strong defences against recognising powerful positioning.

In order to protect against some of the pitfalls of such analysis a feminist psychosocial approach integrates three different levels of analysis – the literal, interpretive and inter-subjective – in order to gain a more holistic understanding of the relationship between the story told about difference and its underlying psychosocial bases. It involves a literal mapping of the story, key characters, plot, events, and so on, and of the way in which the story is told; tone, narrative structure, metaphor, hesitation, repetition, and so on. This is followed by a number of interpretive readings for the participant in the context of social relationships with: 1) other characters in the narrative including the researcher, 2) social structures/groups; and 3) organisations/ institutions. Key images, metaphors, repeated phrases, sudden changes in tone or rhythm, contradiction, omission and silence found in the initial mapping all give clues as to unconscious emotional processes surrounding apparently disparate and unconnected elements of people's lives (see Brown and Gilligan, 1992; Walkerdine et al, 2001). Analysing and interpreting these involves identifying links which illuminate participants' contested meanings, bringing the parts together in order to better understand the whole. These various analyses are recorded in different worksheets and pro forma which can be used for tracking and validating interpretation, and in group analysis form the basis of discussions around data.

The following analysis draws on these principles to interpret two biographical narrative interviews I undertook with Navneen in his surgery (see Hunter, 2005b). Despite our multiple social differences – he an Indian male GP approaching middle age and I a white woman researcher in my mid twenties – our interviews felt relaxed and comfortable. We laughed a lot. Navneen was interested in the research and we found that we had other interests in common, both having a strong commitment to education, which had been the key priority in both our homes growing up, and also being committed to institutional change within our respective professions. In summarising and representing the key points in Navneen's story for the reader I attempt to remain as true to his original wording as possible. Phrases in quotation marks are direct from transcripts, and where my interviewee emphasised words/phrases I have retained this emphasis.

What stands out from these interviews is Navneen's feeling of difference. "It's *very obvious*" that he is visibly different [from the white population] as an Indian man (part of this visible difference may be compounded by his observance of some of Sikhism's five Ks: he wears his long hair (Kesh) in a turban and also wears a steel bracelet (Kara)). He's also different from his [older] "Asian GP colleagues": being a salaried GP in a Primary Medical Services (PMS) practice, he's "not the norm really".[1] These differences are connected to a number of ambiguities and tensions in his story. There are two points in particular. The first, an apparent ambivalence around being "Indian which doesn't bother [him]" – instead he prefers his "family link" with his wife and children, and living near to his brothers, sisters and parents. The second contradiction is that, despite describing himself as laid back and not stressed, he explains that since entering work he has encountered a considerable amount of stress. Things were so difficult in his first GP practice that at one point he felt unable to function.

There is a sense that Navneen was not strongly invested in all his life choices. Although he "plucked up the nerve" to get away from home and go to medical school in another city, "it just happened" that he returned home; "you all *like* moving [back] to where you grew up", he says. There is also a suggestion that medicine was a route more encouraged by his family than chosen by him (Allen, 1998; Min and Kim, 2000). This trend towards South Asian employment within the professional sphere, and especially in medicine (Skills for Health, 2003) has been viewed as reflecting 'the desire and necessity to complete the fragile project of becoming the Western bourgeois subject within the constraints of racism and racist practices' (Walkerdine et al, 2001: 171). Elements of Navneen's story seem to reflect this interpretation. He alludes to the culturally normative character of his decision to enter medicine, framing this field as racialised; as far back as he can remember "my parents always used to tell me 'you're gonna be a doctor'", "it was just ingrained, certainly in the Asian doctors who seemed to be organised". But, after medical school, Navneen found that getting a job where he wanted, in paediatrics, was impossible. When his GP trainer asked him whether he had considered "changing his image" to help in his job search, rather than actively challenging and naming the racism that he experiences, he took a characteristically "pragmatic approach" and opted for the less-prestigious (but racialised; see Ward, 1993) general practice option where, in his view, he was more likely to succeed. Similarly, Navneen's move to focus on his "family link" rather than his "Indian link" could be seen as another move aimed at minimising racialised difference.

In Navneen's opinion his more serious frustrations relate to his lack of 'fit' with the "*old* general practice", imagined as literally older, rigid, inflexible and patriarchal. Navneen, in contrast, is "*very keen*" to make changes, working with a range of people inside and outside the practice. The division between Navneen and these "older" GPs is not clear cut (indeed, Navneen is 42 years old). However, his frustration with the expectation that he should "keep your group happy" – and his refusal do so – suggest that he distances himself from this older Asian patriarchal masculinity. Navneen is proud to emphasise his directorship of the GP out-of-hours service, the first to gain an Investors in People award, presented to him by the British Prime Minister. Hopton (1999) suggests that Investors in People is an exemplar of the move from more traditional, patriarchal cultural forms within public services to more subtle, corporatist masculinity associated with the new managerialism. Navneen's commitment to this award could be read as reflective of his allegiance to the ethos of the latter at the expense of the former, as displayed by the "old" general practice.

Navneen's ambivalence around ethnicity and his distancing from older Asian doctors could be interpreted as symbolic of the current cultural crisis within South Asian communities. Framed within a "caught between two cultures" analysis, in rejecting his Asian "cultural" background (symbolised through medicine in his narrative) in favour of the freedoms of more enlightened English culture (symbolised by modern managerialism), he separates the good, young, vibrant, enlightened, supportive of change Indian (himself), from the bad, patriarchal Indian or Asian (the "other" doctors). Thus, he constitutes one of the South Asian 'model minority'. '[E]conomically successful ... with virtually impermeable family ties', but whose values and behaviour do not significantly disrupt British 'ethos and morality' (Malek, 1998: 127–33).

Speaking in a hesitant voice: racialised ambiguities and ethnicised continuities

In this section I reconsider this analysis of Navneen as an incorporated member of the 'model minority' by exploring his relational negotiations of racialised and gendered difference in more detail.

Extract 1

> (S.H.): "Can you tell me what being an Indian man means to you then?"

> (Navneen): "Well, I think always, *I do* look very different, it's *very obvious*, you know, and I think when I qualified I was very aware that my image is different."

> (S.H.): "Right, OK."

> (Navneen): "My GP trainer sort of highlighted that, cos there was sort of difficulty getting the JOBS, so he said you know, 'have you considered changing your image really?'"

> (S.H.): (laughs) "*What on earth* did ..."

(Navneen): (laughs) "Umm, I was *very*, very surprised at that really. I suppose he was saying you're more likely to get a job, cos, it was difficult, getting through doctors, cos there was an excess of doctors."

(S.H.): "I mean when did you qualify?"

(Navneen): "Um, '83, highlighting my age, I finished in '83, so at that time it was very difficult getting jobs really. Er, and I was *aware*, that it would be difficult really, *I knew* it was difficult getting jobs, but I think, I think you get to a stage where you *have to be you, don't you, I didn't want* to change just for the sake of it. Er, and I think, as it progressed, I didn't find it a *problem*, and I was aware of it, but then I think as I started progressing and *leading* the things, and I felt *comfortable in myself*, and I'm happy the way I am, and I didn't find it a hindrance, I, I don't think it's a problem, I don't think it's an issue, em, being an Indian, or an Asian, *er, I think*, cos I'm happy *with it*, I have no problems relating with other people, and I think, I think if I wasn't, wasn't happy with my body image other people would be able to pick it up really, so I haven't got a problem with it."

(S.H.): "Did they qualify that, or did they just say you need to change your image?

(Navneen): "Well, I think, I think he's, you know, saying maybe I should cut my hair, I mean I think it was really, I think, uhuh and you know he *did* say to me, that I should take them, you know in a sense he was trying to say, to me, that I'd be more likely to get a job, if I didn't look different or anything ..."

Although Navneen has "always been aware" of his difference, the starting point for his response here suggests that it is his physical difference that positions him in terms of 'race'; that it is others (his GP trainer) who position him in this way; and that his entrance into the medical labour market was important in marking this positioning. The construction of his difference as "image" related, while having a literal meaning in terms of his observance of the five Ks, also operates as a more benign euphemism for racialised difference.

Overall, this narrative resolves a number of Navneen's ambivalences around racialised difference. It recognises the problematic 'reality' of his visible positioning as different *in the past*, but also establishes that *in the present* this is no longer problematic. The extract is split into two parts: the first half focuses on his awareness of the inevitable difficulty that he would have on entering the medical labour market. His use of "it" here serves to create ambivalence in the meaning of this part of the narrative. Where he discusses "it", he refers to the difficulty in "getting jobs", related to an excess of doctors and to his visible difference, which must be interpreted in terms of past and current evidence of racism on entry to the medical labour market (see Esmail and Dewart, 1998). The tone changes where Navneen takes up the first person, "I *didn't want* to change just for the sake of it." He begins to emphasise his own agency with the repetition of "I didn't find it a problem/hindrance", rejecting an analysis of difficulties related to his visible difference. At this point he makes the first move to explicitly reference this difference as racialised, "an Indian or an Asian". While Navneen does not deny the fact that others identify his difference, he constructs himself as able to overcome any potential disadvantages because he is confident, able to be happy with himself, and is successful at work "*leading* things". Navneen goes on to make a link between his ability to overcome people's "preconceived ideas that they always have" through his "*reputation*", demonstrating that he "can deliver" at work; "where I am now", he says, "it's *better*". He continues:

Extract 2

> (Navneen): "... and I suppose it's something that you have to do, and yea. But I think that it hasn't been a problem. Yea, yea, I think initially probably would have, when people didn't know me, and I mean I had to try, and I think I probably did have to *try* a little bit *harder really*."

This use of the second person plural "you" in the first phrase is significant here, in that it is racialised. It signals a reality, but one reality from which Navneen struggles to detach himself, moving to end with a seemingly unavoidable first person admission that he did have to "*try* a little bit *harder really*".

Navneen's relationship to racism remains the unspoken focus of this narrative in extracts 1 and 2. One way of reading this is as a reverse version of "I can't be racist, my best friends are Black". Here, "I don't experience racism because people accept me when they know me as being very good at my job." This serves to reduce racism to the level of the individual and demonstrates one of the classic ways in which participants abdicate voice. Becoming an effective professional served to erase difference, positioning participants outside of racialised and gendered social relations. However, another important element to the narrative is Navneen's active refusal to conform to the normative expectations of his white trainer in extract 1: "You get to a stage where you *have to be you,* don't you, I *didn't want* to change just for the sake of it." This suggests that while Navneen knew that he would experience racism, that it might "*be harder*" as part of a broader Indian/Asian "you", he did not want to deny his visible difference, which is an important part of his identity.

Navneen's response (extract 3) to my move to reintroduce discussion around "race" in our second interview is important to re-evaluating the ambiguities in our first discussion.

Extract 3

> (S.H.): "... one of the things that you'd thought about that might have been relevant was all that stuff around work, when somebody had asked about, changing your image at work ... but what we skirted over was what does being an Indian man mean to *you?*"

> (Navneen): (laughs) "I didn't, I mean I (sighs) I mean, I didn't, in my *work?*"

After I clarify "Yes, if that's important, but also more generally *to* you as a person", Navneen, despite his clear discomfort, eventually responds at a very general level: "My *cultural* upbringing, and my social circle, is Indian really", "I don't follow the religion even though I've got the *image*", "I think that's probably I feel *more comfortable,* that's the way I've been brought up really", "I've got a close link with my *family,* more than anything". The reference to being comfortable links the two discussions. Taken together, these discussions complicate the relations between the personal, cultural, familial, community and raced identifications so often conflated in analysis of South Asian subjectivities. They suggest a sense of continuity derived from *ethnicised* (or "cultural" in Navneen's terms) identification, but the rejection of any particular relevance to the totalising effects of a more clearly *raced* (Indian) identification (see Werbner, 1997a; Matthews, 2001). Thus, rather than the abdication of voice on Navneen's part, these discussions suggest a failure to understand on my part. Through my moves to create a centrality to being Indian in Navneen's narrative, I fail to understand the importance of more complex ethnicised identifications, racialising Navneen in precisely the way his comments are resisting.

Following Navneen's focus on his "family link", a number of important connections can be made within his account. The repetition of the key phrase "I have an interest in" and its variant "because I had a personal interest" can also be traced back to his "family link". This occurs frequently in relation to both medicine and education. This key phrase provides the terms of Navneen's 'personal myth' (Chanfrault-Duchet, 2004), in which the personal and the professional cohere around education. In my analysis of Navneen's account I pick up on this continuity and I ask him about it in our final interview.

Extract 4

> (Navneen): "I think, um I think, um I've always liked education, and I think its *changed the way I think, and the way I work* really, I've become much more *reflective*, and *I've* done that while I've been educating myself and I've found, it's made me develop as an *individual*, and I *enjoy* education and I think I've met a lot of interesting people through education, er, and so it's certainly made my *view of medicine* very different, meeting *different people*, um and I, that's what I, have probably been *very keen to do things other than*, just doing general practice, and I, I've always, find it interesting, and I find it *quite challenging*, mmm, maybe I think of, think of myself as an academic, I don't know (laughs)."

Navneen's response suggests that education represents both continuity and change. Rather than being foisted upon him, this is something he has actively pursued and found potentially enabling throughout his career. Education has also prompted the reassessment of his relationship to medicine more generally.

Developing medicine through ethnicised continuities

On the basis of Navneen's understanding of education as linked to his family and ethnicity, a more complex interpretation of his relationship to the "old" general practice can be made. In extract 4 Navneen makes a direct link between the role of education and his difference from medicine. In our first interview, when I ask Navneen about a time when he felt let down at work, he constructs a narrative around the point at which he began to experience difficulties with the "old" medicine when working in his previous medical practice. Embedded in his narrative is a reference to the importance of an assertiveness course he attended. This incident is important because it links both rupture and reconciliation with his "older" GP colleagues.

His attendance on this assertiveness course marks the point at which things at work in his previous practice "got much worse" and eventually were "broken down". Navneen suggests that things were difficult because he and his GP partner had different ways of "moving forward". However the "break down" occurred because "I learned some techniques", "I was able to say *what I wanted to do*", "said what I had to say", but "[I] *found that* those techniques helped me to reduce my *stress*" because "I was 'well I'm not gonna compromise'". Through this course Navneen was able to relieve the stress he felt from the "old" general practice. His explanation as to why he went on this course makes a number of further important links.

Extract 5

> (Navneen): (laughs) "I mean, I have to, I dunno *why* I went, I can't you know, I'm thinking back, why did I go on that? I mean I've always been interested in training, and I've always wanted to go on a different training, you know I like going on different training courses, and this *particular one, I went to*, and I was the *only doctor*. In the middle of the nurses, and the managers, I don't know why I went onto this er ... but obviously this was very non-clinical, very *management* oriented and obviously whoever sent the information to me, obviously I found it attractive, er, and I don't know why I went on."
>
> (S.H.): "Maybe it was divine intervention?"
>
> (Navneen): "Maybe, *absolutely*, and I must admit, I *needed* the change, and I suppose it taught you techniques, how to deal with, difficult situations, and I must say I found them, *very, very* useful from then on."

The extract serves to link three of the key points of differentiation between himself and other GPs. He is positioned among other professionals and in a non-clinical setting. This event represents

Navneen's first foray into management. The extract also highlights another pattern in his account, his ability to deal with "difficult situations" (the euphemism used throughout the text for Navneen's difficult relations with older male GPs). Navneen's concern to pinpoint why he attended this course, coupled with his inability to remember, signals a strong emotional response complicating his remembering – one interpretation being that he finds it difficult to claim any active engagement in challenging "older" medicine, creating an explicit rupture between himself and "his group".

Paradoxically, this assertiveness course can also be viewed as enabling Navneen to connect with and construct less-divided relations with "older" GPs. The narrative around assertiveness links Navneen's discussions of his previous practice to those concerned with his role as medical director of the GP out-of-hours service. This was a "big change for GPs", and it has been a real challenge for Navneen, as he deals with complaints against colleagues' "very difficult situations". Sometimes "*It's a mess*" and really stressful, especially when his "older" GP colleagues have "done something outrageous" and "won't apologise". An important element of Navneen's attendance on the assertiveness course was the ability it gave him to reinterpret his own situation. Navneen's experiences *after* undertaking the assertiveness course are mirrored in his approach to working with his GP colleagues. While dealing with complaints, Navneen helps his colleagues to "*find the right words*". In the same way that he was able to stand up and speak out within his old practice, he supports his GP colleagues to do the same. What is important is that Navneen can "understand from their point of view it's quite frightening, er, I think if I can *support them*, get them to, to you know, *think more about it*" by adopting a more holistic approach to the situation. In making this analysis I am not claiming any evaluation on the general effectiveness of assertiveness training in achieving restorative relations (for a critique see Clegg, 1999). What I am claiming is that in Navneen's account assertiveness training becomes symbolic for education, which he then associates with the ability to create more space to engage in reparative relations with his older GP colleagues.

Overall, this analysis is not to suggest that Navneen's account is unambiguous, that he does not defend against a recognition of racialised identification or, even more so, gendered identification (which we do not discuss at all); nor that his account does not contribute to the collective racialisation of older Asian GPs. In all of these senses he can be read as having succumbed to the call of the new professionalism, suppressing (anachronistic) racialised difference in favour of the new, modern, forward-looking, deracialised, more cohesive professionalism. However, on closer inspection Navneen does not necessarily choose "British freedoms" *over* his own cultural belongings. His ethnicised subjectivity provides a coherent emotional logic which stands in contrast to fractured 'identity crisis' narratives often attributed to second- or third-generation British South Asians. He derives strength from this culture through its connections to education, family and medicine, enabling a more nuanced understanding of his GP colleagues. Navneen is best viewed in a position of 'organic hybridity', involving unconscious cultural borrowings (see Werbner, 1997b, 2004) through which he potentially subverts racist images, even as he may be seen to perpetuate them.

Conclusions

Through Navneen's account I have sought to demonstrate that there is a complex emotional politics to resistance which welfare professionals grapple with throughout their working lives. These workers are rarely straightforwardly for or against modernisation. This is because, just as the process of modernisation is multifarious, so are the points of connection to this process as a man, GP, Asian, Indian, Sikh. Workers may identify with and support some elements of change and reject others, and these multiple identifications may produce conflict. In this example, where the reproduction of inequality and "bad" practice becomes associated with Asian masculinity, this presents dilemmas for Navneen, positioned as a new, modern GP, but also as an Asian/Indian man. As we see in his case, categorical positionings have deeply rooted biographical significance, which means that behaviour that is seen from the 'outside' appears as conforming – for example, the refusal to identify as Indian/Asian man – can also from the 'inside' be a means of resisting the strait-jacketing created by inflexible social categories, which in this case construct older Asian male GPs as sexist, patriarchal and unequal. Although the recognition of social difference is still problematic within the context of NPM, regardless of or perhaps because of mainstreaming equalities, this does not mean that participants do not live profession through such differences.

Nevertheless, it is important not to conflate the sort of personal contestations and negotiations discussed in this chapter with more pronounced individual or collective challenges and systemic rupturing of social patterns. But ignoring these complex relational contestations means misunderstanding the significance of multiple meanings and contested contradictory personal engagements with broader social meanings. In this chapter I have argued for the importance of the intricate emotional logics underpinning professional identifications and related agency. This is an argument for paying attention to the more amorphous elements of feeling and experience, often less well articulated by social subjects but which are crucial to how discursive patterns are articulated and contested, how these patterns feel to subjects, what they mean to them and why they connect with some patterns and not with others. Because a feminist psychosocial approach insists on exploring multiple levels of experience, the collective, individual *and* relational, it enables more fluid analysis of people's movement between different positionings. This multiple, layered, analytical approach stays closer to participants' meanings negotiated at the relational level; it also goes some way to guarding against analysts' blind spots and failures to hear complex emotional connections.

More broadly, the claim that professional relations get lived through gendered and raced biographies has important implications for approaches to organisational change which have not been fully understood in policy terms. For example, recent advice for managing organisational transitions in relation to equality and diversity recommends that 'before you can start something new, you must end the old system and so you need to understand who is losing what. What is over? It is helpful to acknowledge the losses and be clear about what has finished and what has not' (DH, 2008: 45). However, biographically rooted emotions, values and feelings cannot be switched on and off at a whim, jettisoned in favour of the new way of doing things. The challenge is to better understand the ways in which they influence the dynamics of change and connection to new ideas. Emotions will always be important connectors to the past and to intermingling this with new ways of working in the future. While the connections they foster may not always seem to produce the most radical challenges to homogenised managerialist futures, in a context where past welfare resistances and struggles organised around social identities are constantly being written out of histories of welfare service provision, maintaining emotional connections to those past struggles, however small, is an important victory.

Note
[1] The slippage between skin colour, religion, country and continent of family origin are deliberate here, representing slippage in Navneen's story and our conversations. The significance of these is considered in more detail in the following section.

TEN

Managerialism subverted? Exploring the activity of youth justice practitioners

Nathan Hughes

Since the election of the New Labour government in 1997, the landscape of youth justice policy and practice has altered dramatically. A variety of significant changes illustrates a continued trend towards a 'corporatist' or 'managerialist' approach to youth justice provision within the UK, characterised by a new mode of governance for youth crime (see, for example, Pickford, 2000; McLaughlin et al, 2001; Muncie and Hughes, 2002; Smith, 2003; Grimshaw, 2004).

Significant reform of the infrastructure of the system has seen the 'simultaneous centralisation and devolution of state responsibility' for youth justice (Muncie and Hughes, 2002: 5). The establishment of the Youth Justice Board (YJB) as a non-departmental public body sponsored by the Home Office to oversee the performance and functioning of the system is paralleled by changes to the local organisation of youth justice services, requiring each local authority to set up multi-agency Youth Offending Teams (YOTs) to coordinate the provision of services (Gordon et al, 1999: 26–7).

Since its inception, the YJB has overseen a proliferation of initiatives, ranging from early interventions aimed at preventing the onset of offending, through to significant changes to disposals for persistent and serious offenders. Each initiative is implemented by local YOTs or associated agencies through grants awarded by the YJB, typically accompanied by substantial guidance and explicit performance management targets (Muncie and Hughes, 2002: 5).

The implementation of a managerialist approach to youth justice provision is clearly problematic. The translation of standardised programmes and prescribed practices within complex local contexts brings unavoidable challenges, contradictions and tensions. Such an agenda has clear potential to conflict with existing practice within an institution, as professional identities, priorities and assumptions about desirable outcomes intersect with managerialism, rather than being replaced by it. This conflict is evidenced in Michael Lipsky's (1980) theorisation of 'street-level bureaucracies', in which he emphasises the role of the individual professional in implementing law and policy through the provision of services. Such conflict is further complicated where different professional or stakeholder groups are involved in the implementation of a policy or initiative – as is so commonly the case. Here the possibilities for contradiction and tension are multiplied, with each group potentially prioritising different objectives or purposes.

It is this tension between the development and implementation of policy, both in the macro-management of government and in the interaction of a diverse range of professionals, that guided the study of the implementation of a Bail Support and Supervision (BSS) Scheme within one Youth Offending Team. In this chapter I explore how the intended aims of this policy are interpreted by two key local stakeholder groups. The official aims and guidance associated with this policy represent just one of three competing perspectives and influences on the development of BSS policy within the locality, as the intended outcomes of the initiative are challenged and the processes and procedures designed to control its functioning are either ignored or resisted. It thus provides an illustrative example of the complex processes through which centralised, managerialist policy can be resisted and subverted by those charged with its implementation.

Bail support and supervision

One aspect of youth justice that has been subjected to substantial recent managerialist reform is the bail and remand system. Within the youth justice system, the remand process serves a dual purpose. It seeks to ensure minimisation of the risk to the victim and to the public caused by the alleged offender, and at the same time to protect the young person and respecting their rights as an unconvicted minor assumed to be innocent before trial. Emphasising the latter of these purposes, the 1998 Crime and Disorder Act outlined a statutory duty to provide Bail Support and Supervision so as to reduce the 'inappropriate' use of custodial remand for young people.

BSS is defined within the Youth Justice Board's *Guide to the national standards for bail supervision and support schemes* (Thomas and Goldman, 2001) as:

> Community based activities in programmes designed to help
> ensure that defendants awaiting trial or sentence successfully
> complete their period of bail by returning to court on the

due date, without committing offences or interfering with the course of justice, and to assist the bailee to observe any conditions of their bail.

As such, the schemes seek to provide courts with the option of granting bail, with sufficient conditions for those charged with serious offences or with persistent offending habits to satisfy any concerns as to the possible behaviour of the young person during the bail period.

The official aims of such schemes, as stated within the *National standards for bail supervision and support schemes* (YJB, 2001) are to:

a) Prevent offending on bail
b) Ensure the appearance of the young person at court to reduce delays in the court process
c) Ensure remands to custody and secure remands are kept to the essential minimum.

It is these aims that form the basis of performance management for the scheme, setting clear targets against which monitoring should occur. Despite the focus within the Crime and Disorder Act on reducing the use of custody, in line with the general shift in youth justice policy, it is the first of these objectives that has taken on more prominence 'as the result of growing concern about high levels of offending on bail by the juvenile age range' (Nacro, 1998).

The following discussion draws on three years' study of the implementation and development of a BSS scheme within a city with a traditionally high custodial remand rate, which is therefore a key target area for the initiative. This chapter describes the development of the scheme within the locality, focusing on the interaction of YOT workers and magistrates in making decisions about the nature of bail and remand interventions. I will illustrate how the bail scheme workers are engaged in a process of adapting or subverting policy goals and processes in order to achieve legitimation as accepted participants in the court process. In parallel, I will show how magistrates circumvent bureaucratic rules and assessment processes by emphasising 'gut reaction'. In order to do so, I draw on a strand of activity theory and the concept of collective, object-oriented activity.

Activity theory

Activity theory provides a framework through which to consider human actions as 'object-oriented' and collective (Engeström, 1987;

Engeström et al, 1999). Figure 10.1 illustrates the unit of analysis: an activity system composed of a number of interrelated elements that the research must explore.

Figure 10.1: The structure of a human activity system

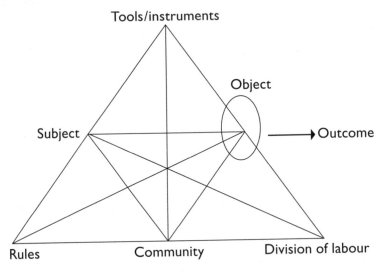

In this framework the 'object' refers to the 'problem space at which the activity is directed' (Popova and Daniels, 2004: 196). All activity is connected to an object: 'there is no such thing as objectless activity' (CATDWR, 2008). This becomes the focus of the analysis.

The 'subject' refers to the individual or group from whose perspective or agency the activity is to be viewed. 'Tools' or 'instruments' refer to those physical or symbolic artefacts that have been developed to allow the subject to work towards the object. This might include physical objects such as the 'QWERTY'-style keyboard, the postage stamp and money, as well as less tangible concepts, such as beliefs, procedures, language and mathematics – all of which serve a number of purposes in allowing us to carry out activities.

The subsequent 'outcome' represents the change to the object through this activity. It is the conceptualisation of the intended outcome that functions as the motivation for and gives meaning to the activity.

The theory holds that all activity is collective; that the action of an individual is only made meaningful if it is understood in the context of the collective activity; and that it is through the collective activity that individuals' actions are mediated. A commonly used exemplar of collective activity explores the role of the bush-beater in the primeval hunt (Leont'ev, 1981: 210–13; Tolman, 1999: 73; Virkkunen and Kuutti, 2000: 301). As an individual action, the disturbance of the animals appears to be irrational, and counter to the overall objective. The logic only emerges if someone else shares the bush-beater's goal and anticipates the animal's attempted escape. 'The sense of his action lies not in the action itself but in his relation to other members of the group' (Tolman, 1999: 73).

The base of the triangle incorporates 'the social/collective elements of the activity system' (Warmington et al, 2004: 10). 'Community' is included to place the subject(s) within a larger group comprising different subjects with the same or similar general object, or with an interest in the activity. Relations between subject and community are seen to be regulated and constrained by 'rules' 'that specify acceptable interactions between members of the community' (Virkkunen and Kuutti, 2000: 300). These rules include the formal and the informal norms, conventions, laws and expectations of a community. The model is completed with the inclusion of the 'division of labour' between the members of the community, through the implicit and explicit organisation and distribution of actions in relation to the activity. This applies 'to both the division of tasks and the status relations between actors' (Daniels, 2004: 123). This also raises the idea of multiple perspectives on an activity among those participating.

This framework for exploring collective, object-oriented activity was used to examine the implementation of BSS in a context incorporating multiple communities of interest with varied professional perspectives. It is employed to illustrate how a policy objective is enacted within a complex system influenced by other competing aims, pressures and influences.

The youth court involves the interaction of a range of subjects with various professional and specialist roles, ensuring a breadth of perspectives and influences on decision making. Such roles include the magistrate, clerk, defence and prosecution solicitors, and YOT workers, as well as witnesses and defendants. Moore and Smith (2001: 44) follow other commentators in comparing court processes 'to theatrical performances, with a fixed range of formal roles, prescribed scripts, and very explicit stage directions', with each participant therefore 'performing one's assigned role'. However, this analogy downplays the power differential that exists within the interactions between stakeholder groups, such that, even when seen to be performing a defined role, each actor may seek to influence not only the decision of the magistrate but also the position of each of the other contributors to that decision.

Within the setting we must therefore consider the division of labour between the relevant professional groups, each with specific objects and intended outcomes, as well as formal roles, and with a distinctive and at times confrontational perspective. We must also consider the range of tools employed by various subjects in attempting to ensure that these objects are addressed. In both the formation of objects and the contravention of the tools and rules through which the activity system is intended to operate, we see the subversion of the statutory aims of the policy.

Object formation: the reinterpretation of statutory aims

Tracing the process of object formation within the case study site demonstrates how the official aims of a policy can be challenged during its implementation. In the discussion below, I highlight two key means by which such aims can potentially become subverted. First, I demonstrate a tension between government aims and the professional perspectives of those charged with their implementation. Here the rules and tools governing professional practice in working with young people at risk of remand can be seen to be at odds with the targets and performance indicators determined by central government. Second, I show how the interaction of different stakeholder groups and communities of interest involved in implementing policies can lead to priorities and assumptions being contested. In this example, the particular power relations within the activity system are such that the desired outcomes as defined by magistrates dominate those of the BSS team, and even those of the government.

The three principal aims of BSS, as defined by the YJB, were recognised locally as being contradictory. If priority was given to reducing the numbers being remanded into custody, then there was likely to be an associated increase in numbers offending while on bail and of young people being breached for failure to comply. In addition, as those more at risk of these negative outcomes would be placed on bail, there was a greater risk of non-attendance in court. The primary emphasis on preventing offending on bail therefore suggests that attempts to reduce the use of custody should adopt a low-risk strategy in providing support.

Recognising this contradiction, in an early interview the team's coordinator suggested a reversal in the prioritisation stated in the scheme's official documentation, with her focus primarily on "providing a service for children and young people who are unlikely to be granted bail by the court and are therefore at risk of remand to prison custody or secure accommodation or local authority accommodation ..." (Interview with coordinator, September 2000)

The coordinator described these young people as facing "a wide range of difficulties and problems". "By addressing these problems in the community the damaging, and costly, effects of custodial remands can be avoided while the risk of further offending is also tackled" (Interview with coordinator, September 2000).

Here we can see the initial ideal object of the BSS team. In this professional perspective it is the needs of the young person that are prioritised as the focus of activity, with each case to be addressed individually through the intended production of a tailored package of support and supervision (seen as the 'tool' for this activity). The intended outcome of the local team's activity is therefore not expressed in aggregated performance indicators regarding reducing offending on bail or even in the numbers remanded in custody. Instead, these are replaced by an aspiration 'to achieve the least intensive restrictions of their liberty before sentence consistent with public safety' (from a promotional leaflet for court users, 2000). In this representation, it is not only those at risk of custody who are seen as needing protection from unnecessary (perhaps damaging) restrictions to their liberty, but all young people facing a remand hearing.

However, the unfolding narrative of the scheme's development suggests that this ideal representation of the object of activity does not accurately reflect actual practice, due to the influence of other stakeholders within the system. As well as attempting to harmonise professional perspectives with statutory 'rules' and requirements, those charged with implementing the BSS scheme are also influenced by the perspectives of those involved in the youth court decision-making processes which determine whether a young person is placed on BSS.

The division of labour within the system ensures dependency on the bench for the successful realisation of the intended outcomes of the scheme. This was explicitly recognised by the team. Due to this relative power, the intended outcomes of the YOT are realised to depend on appeasing the bench. Achieving the desired outcome for any particular young person is dependent on convincing the magistrates that this is an appropriate course of action. This requires the magistrate to agree with the prioritisation of the team in relation to the three potentially contradictory functions, and to have confidence in the decisions of the BSS team. Before seeking to influence other professionals within the youth court so as to work towards the aims of the scheme, the team was therefore forced to be reactive to the context and setting, rather than proactive in changing it to meet the requirements of the scheme.

Magistrate representations of the effectiveness and value of the bail worker within the courtroom focused on the bail worker's effectiveness in supporting the bench in reaching an appropriate decision and, in doing so, facilitating the court. "Professionalism" among the YOT staff therefore equated to "timeliness", a lack of unnecessary delays, and being able to "answer all questions [from magistrates] appropriately"; all of which are seen as key to creating the "right environment" for the young people within the court and as the basis for any subsequent programmes of intervention (quotes from various interviews with magistrates, December 2003–March 2004). We therefore see a change in the object of the team, and with it the continued adaptation and subversion of the policy goals and processes. Rather than addressing the stated object, we instead see a new transitory object, that is, to portray professionalism and effectiveness in contributing to the functioning of the youth court. The intended outcome becomes the legitimation of the BSS scheme and its workers as accepted participants in the court process. This involves not only a further change of object from the initial intent of the initiative, but also the adoption of a professional identity that is other than that implied by policy statements, and significant changes to the tools and rules to be used. This is particularly evident in perceptions of the assessment procedures carried out by the BSS team and in the increased emphasis on supervision within the packages of support put together for those young people made subject to BSS.

Resisting the rules and tools

As the object of activity in local implementation of policy may commonly involve subversion of the aims of an initiative, so the tools and rules contained in guidance regarding the implementation of new policies are in turn adapted or resisted. As discussed above, the object is the basis for exploring and understanding the operation of an activity system. If an object is changed, the other components of the system will necessarily change also, responding to inevitable tensions and contradictions between what a system intends to achieve and the means by which it can achieve it. A shift in focus from meeting the needs of a young person to appeasing the concerns of magistrates therefore inevitably leads to a reconsideration of the tools and rules on which the system functions. The processes and procedures (tools and rules) intended by the YJB to determine practice within the youth court are therefore ignored or resisted in practice. The role they are intended to play is not valued in relation to the intended outcome of activity as determined by those implementing the policy. The continued relative power of the magistrates means that through this activity they are able to resist the imposition of particular ways of working, and therefore once again subvert the intended functioning of the initiative.

When first instigated, the statutory requirements of the BSS scheme brought with them a set of processes or rules to be followed in making a decision to bail or remand a young person. However, the extent to which such procedures were adhered to during day-to-day activity was repeatedly refuted by magistrates.

> "I think decision making is a bit of a gut reaction and anyone who says you go through this magnificent scheme that the Judicial Studies Board has produced for decision making, well ... I don't think you do. You've heard what's been said. OK, the prosecution have said that because of these points the young person should be in custody, and I guess it then depends on how inclined you are to grant bail." (Interview with senior magistrate, January 2004)

This is a lucid articulation of a much more extensive set of issues. While not admitting to "breaking any rules", to varying degrees each magistrate discusses "informal" methods of reaching decisions, drawing upon what is variably termed by magistrates as "common sense" or "intuition". In particular, for the more senior or experienced magistrates, this scheme was viewed as a repetition of past working arrangements or aims, and therefore as "ultimately nothing new", "one of the sort of schemes that come and go" without affecting the overall functioning or mentality of the court (interview with senior magistrate, February 2004). Such new schemes, when first instigated, are seen to create new procedures and paperwork that are "religiously" followed. However, it was argued, once the purposes of the scheme become established and understood, the formality and rigidity of working processes are relaxed, people relying instead on old ways of working, with new initiatives and procedures "not ignored but not taken as seriously as they should be" (quotes taken from various interviews with magistrates). Thus, magistrates commonly admitted to circumventing "bureaucratic rules".

In this representation of activity the following of rigid procedures and processes is seen as counter to the effective functioning of the youth court – the primary intended outcome of activity. The procedures and practices imposed on the court for such cases are therefore resisted, as, once again, are the intended outcomes for the initiative. In reaction we observe the reaffirmation of the autonomy of the bench, and its easy assimilation of new procedures into long-established ways of working. In this blasé depiction of magistrates' decision-making procedures we not only observe the relative power of the two groups of professionals, and therefore the considerable influence of local magistrates over the activity system, but also the relative ease with which this powerful stakeholder group is able to resist the implementation of nationally determined policies.

However, the original aims of the initiative and the means by which the scheme was intended to operate were not defended by the BSS staff or YOT management. Indeed, far from being defended, such a positioning of the team was used to work towards the object of assimilation and integration of the BSS scheme into the long-established working practices and decision-making processes. As such, when confronted with the above quotes, rather than perceiving a challenge to the scheme, the coordinator was "heartened" by the idea that BSS procedures had been "developed" such that they could be "absorbed into the court's workings", allowing BSS to operate and influence decisions "from within" rather than "battling from the sidelines". This was (rather philosophically) presented by the coordinator as an attempt to ensure BSS "enters the subconsciousness [of youth court users] rather than being in a constant battle to stay in the conscious", and thus as a deliberate long-term strategy in working towards the advancement of their own aims for the scheme (quote from the coordinator recorded in field note from visit to YOT, March 2004).

Such a strategy was seen to require flexibility and negotiation within the youth court, so as to develop working practices appropriate to daily interactions. An obvious example of the willingness of the BSS team to bend if not ignore its own YJB-prescribed rules and tools comes in the reaction to criticism of the formalised nature of the decision-making process and the unnecessary time taken up by assessments where decisions were seen to be uncontested, "obvious" or "common sense". This is reflected in the monitoring of the work of the bail team in the courtroom.

The Bail ASSET form is a structured assessment framework for assisting practitioners in identifying whether a programme of intervention is necessary to manage risks, address needs and meet objections to bail. The tool is intended to form the basis of any recommendations to the youth court as to appropriate bail status and conditions. The introduction of such assessment tools is a useful example of the YJB's attempts to regulate professional practice in youth justice and encourage 'transparency and accountability' (Baker, 2005: 106). Although its use is strongly advised in the *Guide to national standards for bail support and supervision* (Thomas and Goldman, 2001), its completion is not mandatory. Indeed, such tools are presented as a means to support professional judgement rather than an attempt to limit or replace professional discretion (Baker, 2005).

In the early stages of the scheme a Bail ASSET assessment form was completed for every case – with 100% completion for all referrals in the first nine months of the scheme's operation. In the final three quarters for which the monitoring data was collected, the percentage of completion dropped to 81.25%. Almost one in every five referrals was no longer assessed. While there is no statutory obligation to use Bail ASSET in assessments, the figures suggest that comparable cases were no longer being assessed with such rigour. When questioned, bail workers admitted that this practice resulted from what they labelled "additional pressures" on them during the working day, based on demands placed on the YOT workers by other court users as to the timely availability of their assessments. In terms of the order of the day's cases, there was an expectation that the youth workers would keep to the timetable decided by the court clerk and solicitors. As such, information for a particular young person had to be made available when a particular case was called, guiding the order in which assessments were carried out.

By rejecting the formal basis upon which the policy intends the BSS staff to communicate their professional judgement, the risk management agenda imposed by the YJB is itself rejected. The means by which the BSS team is intended to influence decision making and, in doing so, to work towards the aims of the initiative, are therefore challenged and impeded. Instead, the specific conditions attached to the package must satisfy the bench that its concerns regarding the likelihood of bail being breached should be met.

"... at the end, I suppose we have to satisfy ourselves: are we taking a risk by giving this young person freedom? Do we honestly believe that he's not going to commit a further offence while he's on bail before his next hearing? Because the wording is that there are 'substantial reasons' for us to believe that given bail he would either fail bail or commit further offences." (Interview with senior magistrate, January 2004)

Accordingly, the range of factors contained in the Bail ASSET form is replaced by a list of "headline issues of concern" (interview with senior magistrate, January 2004) based on the reasons for possible refusal of bail, as opposed to the potential causes of offending identified in the Bail ASSET.

This was further reflected in the nature of the packages put to the bench in order to support recommendations for bail – a further tool by which the team worked towards the intended outcomes of the scheme. Seeking to address the obvious preoccupations of many magistrates by placing the packages of support within the common supervisory discourse of the bench, the team developed a "menu" of packages through which the court representative of the team offered incremental levels of bail conditions. Three packages were developed by the team. 'Level One' was restricted to residency conditions, with 'Level Two' also incorporating a doorstep curfew. Within 'Level Three' the young person would also be monitored, either by having to report regularly to the police or by wearing an electronic tag. The packages aimed to address directly the call for conditions that met the 'headline' concerns of the bench by explicitly highlighting those issues considered most salient in deciding whether a case was fit for bail or required a custodial remand. The complex assessment form that was supposed to be the basis for professional judgement was thus reduced to three choices of supervisory package, the language encapsulated in the Bail ASSET being entirely absent, to the point where the Bail ASSET assessment seemed insignificant to the decision of the bench.

This change in the rules governing the decision as to whether a young person should receive bail thus runs counter to the ideal object presented by the coordinator at the outset of the initiative for addressing the needs of each young person. Instead, the emphasis is on suitable methods of control and surveillance so as to deter offending while on bail.

This approach is a further attempt to develop perceptions, first, of trust in the perspective of the team in relation to a case, and second, of legitimacy of the professional assessment carried out – again emphasising the aims of the magistrate over those of the policy or the BSS team.

A further means by which the BSS team attempted to appease magistrates, while apparently working counter to its own stated aims and objectives to minimise restrictions while on bail, was the increased use of surveillance and supervision. A basic requirement of attendance at three sessions per week was included as part of any BSS programme, from the outset of the scheme. However, during later periods, and with growing regularity, magistrates were found to be increasing this commitment to as many as five sessions, meaning one contact a day for some young people. This was presented by magistrates as a means to "ensure a suitably arduous package of supervision" (interview with senior magistrate, December 2003), allowing for a frequency of contact that enabled the team to monitor any particular concerns that the bench might have and that otherwise might have resulted in the need for custody. As such, the increased contact was very much presented as a means for additional supervision rather than as additional support.

The potential effect of these new requirements on the nature of the support provided to the young person was apparent to the BSS team. Concern was expressed among the team that this extra contact was not transferring directly into extra work being undertaken with the young person, or even into extra time being spent with the young person per week. Indeed, it was even feared that there might be a decline in positive support, this being replaced by a relationship based primarily on surveillance. This model of provision was therefore seen as being detrimental to the establishment of a supportive and communicative relationship with the young person, which was in turn seen as being important to the scheme's success with the individual. This represents another clear example of how the BSS team was content to appease magistrate concerns, despite a clear contradiction of its own intended aims via the intervention.

Conclusion

The implementation of policy commonly takes place within activity systems involving a number of different subjects and a complex community of interest. In the example presented here, the official aims and guidance associated with this policy represent just one of three competing perspectives and influences on the implementation of the initiative in the locality. From its inception, the professional perspective of the BSS staff led to the aims of the scheme being challenged, reprioritised and therefore subverted. However, even this perspective is countered by the relative power and influence of magistrates within the local area. In order to work towards the outcomes intended by the BSS staff, the magistrate perspective must be appeased. This powerful stakeholder group is able to override the aim of this and other specific schemes to fit its own overarching object of a well-functioning youth court. The operation of the BSS schemes is therefore adapted to fit this overall object, leaving the YOT staff to replace their own intended activity outcome with a transitory object of appeasement, even where this is counter to their own original and formally stated aims.

This change in object for the initiative brings parallel changes in its operation. The tool provided by the YJB in order to manage assessments and guide subsequent support for the individual young person is sidelined by the need to respond to magistrates' concerns. As such, assessments and presentations become premised on the imagined or predicted concerns of the bench, as opposed to the professionally assessed needs of the individual: the focus is on the creation of packages to suit all cases, rather than on the development of a particular package to suit a particular individual. This is in tension with the idealised representation of the aim of the scheme at the outset (and consistently presented throughout the evaluation period) of minimising the restrictions placed on the liberty of any young person to those that are necessary. In place of the multiple aims described at the outset we therefore see a primary focus on the seemingly discrete goal of reducing custodial remands.

Such a strategy is of course in keeping with the formal aim outlined by the YJB. However, the emphasis and means to achieve this policy are changed in line with the pressures on the scheme within the local context. The central aim of the scheme is therefore maintained, but the means by which it is achieved are significantly altered because the rules in operation at the local level are controlled not by the YJB but by the immediacy of the magistrates' control over the courtroom. Thus, rather than being focused on the needs of the young person it is focused instead on the concerns of the magistrates.

This narrative surrounding the development of BSS provides an illustrative example of the complex processes through which centralised, managerialist policy can be resisted and subverted by those charged with its implementation. In particular, it demonstrates two processes through which policy and practice can be subverted. First, where such policy contains different assumptions about desired outcomes these assumptions can be contradictory or in tension. As a result, interpretation can be subjective, dependent on the perspective and discourse applied by those charged with their implementation. Further to this, in circumstances where different professional groups or workers from different agencies are involved in the policy implementation (as appears common, if not the norm), these groups will prioritise different outcomes, purposes or objectives. Which of these comes to dominate in practice is, at least in part, a function of power relations existing between those groups.

The framework for analysis provided by activity theory allows for exploration of how such a range of pressures and competing perspectives can impact on the object formation arising out of the policy aims. Further, consideration as to how the activity system is formed around this object provides the basis for understanding how the procedures and processes that typically accompany such policy initiatives are adapted or rejected so as to work towards the achievement of intended outcomes. This theoretical approach has therefore provided useful insight into an exploration of managerialist policy implementation and the potential role of subversive professionals and other stakeholders in the process.

The value of activity theory lies in its focus on the actual endeavours of the people charged with implementing policy, as opposed to the policy itself. Through a focus on 'object' as opposed to 'objective' this framework looks beyond the officially stated account of the scheme, towards an understanding of how this translates into day-to-day functioning. The conceptualisation of the system at the level of object-oriented, collective activity provides explicit consideration of the interaction between the different subjects involved in the implementation of a policy. From this perspective, activity theory provides a means to understand power relations between professional groups interacting in the implementation of social policy, and perhaps competing to prioritise desired outcomes and objectives. Through this approach, a seemingly simple managerialist aim of addressing a particular objective, presented as though discrete and isolated, can be seen as being enacted within a complex system where such an aim cannot be disentangled from a web of other competing pressures and influences. Such a focus shows how the formal aims of an initiative, as defined by government, are necessarily altered or circumvented in order to address the more immediate concerns of influential local stakeholders. As such, in response to the pressures of the local context, the policy goals of a managerialist intervention are subverted by those charged with their implementation.

ELEVEN

Awkward customers? Policing in a consumer age

Louise Westmarland and John Clarke

In this chapter we explore the problematic relationship between the consumerist orientation of New Labour's approach to public service reform and the organisation of the police as guardians of law and order. Police reform has always been a contentious issue, often provoking resistance and recalcitrance within the police service itself. In this case, the reform process creates potential tensions between the remit of serving the public and the responsibility of exercising legal authority. We draw on empirical work in two English urban settings to consider how both police and public view ideas of a consumer/customer orientation in policing to examine the unsettled relationships between publics and police. We give particular attention to how local communities may be engaged in the process of policing through more or less institutionalised notions of 'voice'. In the context of this book, we draw attention to how both members of the public and police officers may be seen as 'subversive' citizens but may be subverting very different aspects of policy. As we indicate in the following section, practices of subversion – resistance, recalcitrance, negotiation and translation – take place within a complex field of forces. The chapter concludes by reflecting on the problematic relationship between publics, politics and power in policing.

Resisting reform

Policing has not been immune to the significant policy discourses of consumerism and choice that have shaped public service reform in the UK in the early 21st century. The longer history of police reform demonstrates a range of barriers to new policies and their implementation. The response of police officers to reform has involved an expansive repertoire of resistances: forms of occupational recalcitrance, the skilled mobilisation of public and political opinion, the judicious translation of policy into practice and, as we shall see, a thoroughgoing organisational scepticism about 'reform' in all its guises.

Equally, this history of police shows that it is not only the street-level or 'blue coated' bureaucrats who can effectively block new policies and ways of working. Senior officers acting in defence of their jobs or their rank, status and titles have also been significant forces in shaping the course of reform. For example, a review of police organisational structures in 1993 (the Sheehy Inquiry) proposed a flattening out of the senior rank structure, but resistance to this was 'swift, well-orchestrated and effective' (Leishman et al, 1996). Similarly, the aftermath of the London terrorist activities in 2005 and the threat of organised crime produced proposals for the merging of smaller forces, but again this was resisted and finally abandoned. In a different way, the Metropolitan Police have eroded constraints on stop-and-search practices, intended to limit the racist use of discretionary powers. Lower down the rank structure, the methods of resistance and recalcitrance may be less public but are no less effective. Front-line staff often view attempts to change their organisation as trends and fashions that come around again in a slightly changed form. They are sceptical about bursts of political enthusiasm for police reform, or about the innovations put forward by 'new high-flying senior officers' who are 'merely ships that pass in the night on their journeys to even more glorious ports of call' (Young, 1993: 84).

There are complex relations between these different levels and forms of resistance within the police service and processes of policy and organisational reform (see Skogan, 2007 for a fuller discussion). In this chapter we explore ways in which customer/consumer-orientated policies have been inflected through different organisational and occupational discourses. We trace how these policy initiatives and organisational responses construct engagements with publics who bring diverse expectations and identifications to their encounters with the police. We borrow from our book on public service reform a framing device (Figure 11.1) that distinguishes some of the different relations and dynamics that might be at stake (Clarke et al, 2007b; see also Clarke and Newman, 2008).

Rather than the conventional hierarchical/linear model of policy formation and implementation, the model here points to different potential alignments of alliance and antagonism. The diamond allows us to see that governmental reform initiatives may be separate from the demands and desires of different publics. Indeed, we can see how publics may be engaged, solicited and represented by all three of the other points. Governments claim to embody the (democratically expressed) public will; organisations claim to know what the public wants (especially through surveys, consultations etc); while the

Figure 11.1:Alignments of reform and resistance

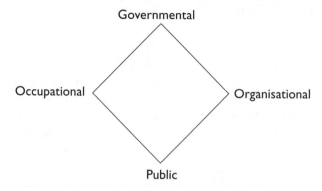

occupation (front-line officers, especially) claims to know the public by virtue of face-to-face encounters. Each of these claims may be deployed to legitimate particular orientations, strategies and practices. The diamond allows us to think about how governmental reform programmes may bear differently on the organisation, the occupation and the supposed beneficiaries (the public). But it also makes it possible to see the dynamics *within* policing where organisational pressures may be different from, or even in tension with, occupational ones. For example, there have been recurrent ambitions to enhance managerial control over the processes and practices of policing or to reform the 'canteen culture' of front-line officers.

Serving the public?

As part of New Labour's public service reform programme, the police needed to be brought into line with the 'modern' world. The conception of modernity was an important theme in New Labour discourse and in terms of public services. Britain was seen as having become a 'consumer society' in which a proliferation of goods and services enabled a wide variety of wants and needs to be satisfied:

> Thirty years ago the one size fits all of the 1940s was still in the ascendant. Public services were monolithic. The public were supposed to be truly grateful for what they were about to receive. People had little say and precious little choice. Today we live in a quite different world. We live in a consumer age. People demand services tailor made to their individual needs. Ours is the informed and

enquiring society. People expect choice and demand quality. (Milburn, 2002)

Elsewhere we have explored the importance of the different institutional formations and trajectories of specific public services (Clarke et al, 2007b). Nowhere is this more significant than for policing. Whereas services such as the NHS have received largely positive public support, since the late 1970s policing has undergone a crisis of confidence. From the mid 1970s, policing has been marked by an increasingly fraught relationship with at least some of its publics. In the 1970s high-profile cases of miscarriage of justice shook public belief in the 'British bobby' as the public discovered that officers had routinely lied, beaten and tortured in order to obtain false confessions in cases such as the Birmingham Six (Blom Cooper, 1997). Confidence declined further in the 1980s, when officers were denounced as (individually and institutionally) racist and, perhaps worse in the eyes of some sections of the public and press, seemed unable to contain public disorder such as the Brixton riots. By the 1990s, the police had been viewed by some as political puppets for their role in the miners' strike and other disputes, and were experiencing a series of high-profile sex discrimination cases, including allegations of sexual assault and psychological brutality towards women serving in the police. They were also seen as failing to support women who reported being raped or suffering domestic assault. In these different ways, policing encountered an increasingly differentiated and difficult public whose deference to police authority could not be taken for granted. In this public, lines of political and social fracture became both a focus of policing (from Irish republicanism to industrial relations) and a focus for complaint, challenge and conflict (particularly around divisions of race, ethnicity, gender and sexuality). The police came to embody a particular version of the crisis of social order in the UK and were in the front line of conflicting attempts to challenge, rearrange and restore that order (Hall et al, 1978).

Demands for police 'modernisation' began under Conservative governments during the 1980s and 1990s but were dominated by 'managerial' rather than 'consumerist' imperatives. This focus changed with the arrival of New Labour, who shifted focus to more participatory, more consumerist and more community-centred principles of modernisation. This coincided with changing orientations among senior police officers. According to observers who were analysing their media presentational style (for example, Heward, 1994), by the mid 1990s senior officers were adopting new strategies and public rhetorics. Heward reported a move from demanding ever more public disorder and riot control weapons towards senior officers talking about wanting to improve customer care. The symbolic move from 'force' to 'service' had begun and its tactics included rebranding the police as developing a more consultative, less authoritative (or authoritarian) style of public policing. The impetus to change, then, came both from senior levels within the police and from government reform programmes. Both pointed to a change in the image *and* style of policing. The rhetoric of change which talked about 'giving the public what they want' has been developing since then and has culminated most recently in the rolling out of a national programme of 'neighbourhood policing'. As the Prime Minister announced in his foreword to *The Home Office Strategic Plan 2004–08*:

> Firstly, we want to revive the idea of community policing, but for a modern world. That means a big increase in uniformed patrols on our streets but linked to 21st century technology to make sure they have the biggest possible impact on crime and the public's fear of crime ... And we'll give local communities a real say in deciding the priorities for the new neighbourhood policing teams. (Home Office, 2004: foreword)

Appealing to the idea of 'community' and the public's apparently insatiable desire for more uniforms on the street, the Strategic Plan had a number of characteristics that might be seen as promoting 'choice'. In terms of confidence building and giving the public what it wants, community policing promises a locally controlled, accountable service. This was powerfully articulated in the 1998 Crime and Disorder Act and has continued as a central theme in policing policy since then (see, for example, Flanagan, 2008). Home Office guidance to local forces and front-line staff stated that community policing would provide a dedicated team for each neighbourhood to work with the community, 'intelligence led' targeting of community concerns, and 'joint action and problem solving' with local partners to improve community quality of life (ACPO Centrex, 2006: 4). As we have argued elsewhere, policing develops a multiple conception of the public in the development of a customer/consumer orientation. There is a strong emphasis on a 'customer care' culture in interactions with members of the public, while the community is evoked as a sort of 'collective consumer' endowed with some forms of both choice and voice. As we shall see, this creates a complicated terrain for processes of negotiation, translation and resistance.

Our research explored New Labour's attempts to modernise public services, building upon the previous Conservative governments' reforms, including managerialism, fiscal retrenchment, privatisation, decentralisation and marketisation (Clarke and Newman, 1997). For the police this had included the use of targets to assess and quantify performance, which threatened traditional habits of working and 'easing': core elements of occupational culture. The police, then, shared in many of the tendencies of public service reform over the last three decades but they experienced them in distinctive ways because of the particular structure, culture and functions of the service. In our study (Clarke et al, 2007b) we focused on four aspects of the citizen/consumer relationship through our questionnaires, interviews and focus groups: challenge, choice, responsibility and inequality. Because of the centrality of 'authority' to the policing role, we give particular attention here to the issues of choice and challenge. How can an authoritative public institution – charged with maintaining order – adapt to demands for choice and the possibility of challenge from the public it serves?

Keeping a distance?

We begin with questions of choice and challenge because the idea of choice seems far from what the police can provide, and challenge is what policing has traditionally suppressed, even in democratic societies. The police are typically viewed in a Hobbesian way, expected to uphold the law in the 'war' when one set of men fights another (Hearn, 1992). Such institutionalised and embodied authority finds challenge difficult to contemplate – and it is often seen as potentially subversive. It has been taken for granted that 'law-abiding' or 'upstanding' members of the public would not contemplate challenging police authority and the Rule of Law. It can be seen as a personal affront to authority, as the following front-line officer observes:

> "... the younger generations, the youths will confront me. They will say to me that – they can be quite rude and aggressive and say 'you can't do that to me, I know my rights'." (Newtown police front-line staff 05)

When another front-line officer from Newtown was asked whether he was willing to be challenged, he replied:

> "Yeah. One of the biggest things they tell us is, um, if you make a decision, that's fine as long as you can justify the

reason for why you made that decision. So if someone on the street wants to challenge my decision that's fine, they can do that, it's not gonna change it." (Newtown police front-line staff 01)

Being challenged can be tolerated as long as it is framed – and contained – within the parameters of these officers' authoritative view of the police role. Their authority is based both on their knowledge of 'law' and on their decisive embodiment of it: they are the law in practice. Equally, we found that police view the idea of choice with scepticism about how it might work in practice. There were claims of inappropriate comparisons, and inapplicability when they are confronted with notions of consumerism or of a service catering to the desires of a 'customer'.

"We are all things to all people and it is a job unlike no other job. Er, so to try and, er, make it too business orientated you're gonna lose the whole principle of what policing's about. But to give you an example where we do – and I start – started to think about offering choice, er, is – and I've got to say before I go on and lose the thought, because of those things that takes our opportunity to give choice away because tomorrow, if another organisation decides to go on strike, with the best will in the world we need to respond like no other organisation responds. We don't have the choice, we have to respond urgently and rapidly and be very professional at it. So we can't offer any choices when we're doing that because we have to respond to things such as the riots that happened at the prison, such as – do you understand what I mean?" (Oldtown police front-line staff 02)

Resistance to such consumerist ideas was widespread among both front-line and senior officers. Their responses combined scepticism about policies (condemned as either the latest fashion or simply unrealistic), doubts about politics (hyperactive governments) and a desire to defend key features of public service in policing from erosion (see Clarke et al, 2007b). One of the justifications for this combination of scepticism and resistance can be found in the notion of the "awkward", "difficult" or "slippery customer". Indeed, the managers we interviewed suggested that many officers would use the terms of consumerism sarcastically – mocking the language of consumer, choice and customer-centredness.

However, another senior officer observed that changes were becoming visible:

> "So whereas a few years ago we might have said we don't have customers, we are the police force, and that is what we do – we police the streets and keep order, we did not necessarily look upon people as providing a service to them and that they consumed our service." (Newtown police senior officer 01)

Senior officers wondered how to get this "public service" message across to their staff, given the tensions it creates with occupational cultural notions of a "thin blue line" upholding the law, preventing chaos and stopping the "dangerous classes" taking control. From such a starting point, the notion that they should "hand over" control in relation to priorities and resources contravened many deeply held cultural expectations of serving police officers:

> "I think it depends when you join. I mean, for me, I have never got my head round this customer idea and I never will do. They're not customers out there. For me they're just members of the public, you know. And if I was using the police service or whatever or any other service – or any like official body I wouldn't think of myself as a customer, I'd hate that. Um, no, it's just members of the public, you know…" (Oldtown police front-line staff 01)

Here established occupational conceptions of the process and relationships of policing combine with a "citizen" view of the world of public services more generally in refusing the consumer/customer model of service relationships. Elsewhere scepticism about the consumer/business model of reform abounded:

> "Er, but I still think the organisation of policing is very difficult. If you want to treat policing like business, er, which previous Home Secretaries have done, er, then it's fraught with danger because it is such an unusual job and there – it's not a job you can negotiate, we need to police the streets otherwise we've got anarchy. So it's a constant thing 7 days a week, 365 days a year, 24 hours a day. It never ever – you can never ever not be there. You know, it's unlike no other job. We don't make money, it's a total loss. From a business

perspective you throw money at policing, you don't get it back ...You can adopt business principles at the time and put them into policing but I don't think you can – as some of them, try and run the police service like a typical business because it will fail." (Oldtown police front-line staff 02)

However, one officer articulated a rather different view of the relationship between policing, the public and forms of choice:

"Um, I don't think the majority of the public are interested. I really don't think they're bothered. You know, I think if they, you know, I think most people's lives aren't touched too much by crime and disorder and I think so long as they can just phone somebody up they don't really care who it is. So long as somebody can solve their problem ... The switched-on ones will go to their MPs, you know ... or they'll go to the police complaints authority or they might phone up a department of the local authority, you know. Actually, I suppose they have got a lot of choices of the people they can speak to to try and get things done actually when you think about it. But unless you sat down and thought about it no, you probably would think your options are limited. But there are – for those that want it they do have choices." (Oldtown police front-line staff 01)

This turns to a much broader conception of choice – in terms of who has the social or cultural capital to make connections and thus expand their possibilities of choice (discussed more extensively in Clarke et al, 2007b). But if choice is a limited concept in relation to the individual user of police services, then how has it been articulated in relation to the 'collective consumers': local communities? A beat inspector from Oldtown explained how important community feedback and opinion had now become, not least because it now formed part of his career appraisal (and hence promotion) system. He explained that the police now survey public views and hold public meetings to invite feedback:

"And we ask those kind of questions now, it's not all centred around, er, you know, we're doing great for crime and feeding back to them in crime, which is quite clearly important to them. What we've now gotta say is 'you tell us what are the problems, you tell us how you think we're doing, you tell us how you think we can do it better'. So we're trying to listen more and respond more to local concerns." (Oldtown police front-line staff 02)

User-led policing?

Our decision to investigate choice and challenge in terms of the delivery of police services was partly a result of New Labour's claims about being the 'People's Champion' in providing public services that were consumer led:

> All four principles [national standards, devolution, flexibility, choice] have one goal – to put the consumer first. We are making the public services user-led, not producer or bureaucracy led, allowing for greater freedom and incentives for services to develop as users want. (Blair, 2001)

As we have indicated, this puts a particular strain on the integral formation of knowledge and power in policing, given the officer as the authoritative embodiment of the law (and order). Meanwhile Sir Ian Blair, then Metropolitan Police Commissioner, had argued that a 'culture war' was taking place about what the police should do and how: "I think we are in a culture war: what is this service for, how does it deliver its service. Is it customer shaped?" (quoted in Dodd, 2005). What were the outcomes of this 'culture war'? In what ways was policing being reshaped in 'user-led' ways? The beat inspector from Oldtown quoted above explained how his local community are offered 'choices' and are encouraged to challenge police officers at meetings if they are unhappy with what is decided. He identified the central role of a local action plan, drawn up in consultation with the public and officers from the local authority to establish policing priorities:

> "So it could be robbery, it could be burglary, it could be antisocial behaviour which is the big issue for most people in most cities. So that's very high on our agenda, linked to juvenile nuisance cos it's in their face day in, day out. That's what affects people's quality of life and that's what wears people down. So that's what's important to the community. And what we do is we draft that up and we present that to the local community for them to rubber-stamp that action plan. We go to a forum called Community Committee Group which is chaired by a member of the

local community. Er, it has a constitution, it can draw officers and call upon officers from a number of agencies to come and they're answerable to that forum as to what is happening in their area, why things aren't as they are or why things are as they are. And what we said is the emphasis of that plan is 'over to you'. You say – if you're happy with the police to be doing this in the next three years you say. If you're not happy then there's dialogue and there's negotiation. And that plan is set to police that area how they want it to be policed. So we're already doing that, we've been doing that for five years." (Oldtown front-line police staff 02)

This points to some of the characteristic ambiguities of new sites and forms of public governance (Newman and Clarke, 2009). Consultation, negotiation and dialogue jostle uncomfortably alongside the 'rubber-stamp' by the community forum. Exactly how power is being redrawn in such settings is difficult to see. But such priority setting and planning clearly requires the participation of communities and publics, however elusive or attenuated their power might be. This more active view of engagement was reflected in the members of the public whom we surveyed and interviewed about using police services. In contrast to the ambivalence of some front-line police, the public we encountered were largely in favour of choice and challenging the police. They viewed it as something potentially positive in their current relationships, even where they claimed to be satisfied with local policing. Hardly anyone claimed to believe that the 'police know best' and should be left to make the decisions. Where trust and satisfaction were expressed, they seemed to have been hard won or were 'co-produced'. One of the residents' groups where we held a focus group told us that they had for some time been operating a system such as the one to be introduced countrywide called 'Neighbourhood Policing', which meant they had the local sergeant's mobile phone number.

(Resident):"All I've got to do is ring the sergeant up and I get him, unless he is in a meeting, he'll see me immediately and … we'll discuss what went on and he'll 'go on the swim', that's what they call it, and he will find out what went on."

(Int):"That sounds like you have got a good relationship with the police."

(Resident): "We've got a fantastic relationship with them."
(Resident A, Oldtown police focus group 1)

The group were clear that they had invested time and effort in building a sustained engagement with the local police that resulted in them being taken very seriously when they raised issues or complaints:

> "The reason we know the chief inspector and stuff is because we go to the actual police meetings and it's very rare we call the police because we have no need to call them. One time I came home and my windows were covered in mud, not just mine, the whole street and my next-door neighbour had rung the police and no one came and we were at a meeting that night praising the police, but the next day I went in the police station and the sergeant said 'I know what you're here about' and the chief inspector actually rollicked every police officer that was on duty that night because he went past the police station and they were all in and we've had a fantastic response ever since."
> (Resident A, Oldtown police focus group 1)

As the power of this group illustrates, having local officers "rollicked" for not looking after the estate is part of the process of bending of police resources to their demands, perhaps to the exclusion of other parts of the town, and to the needs of the 'problem' families that have been displaced from the estate. Their combination of multiple roles – as consumers of police services, able to make demands, and as public-spirited 'citizens' (being the "people who go to police meetings") – confers upon them a certain power and status to demand (and apparently receive) police time and resources. In contrast, a residents' group in Newtown was less positive and had a number of individual examples of a lack of response or following-up of problems they had raised. For this resident, police consultation processes were a source of frustration:

> "I wanted to say that, the police surgeries they are a joke because for those few hours, they are all standing there and they talk to you like they've got this service that they are providing you with and a couple of times I've challenged them on a political front ... They keep pushing it back on us ... They talk as if they are there but they are not. Even if you get through to them on the phone they

don't provide the service people in this country need."
(Resident A, Newtown police focus group 1)

This respondent contradicts what the officers quoted above have said about consultation and engagement. But perhaps her comments reveal the subtext of the officers' words: that they can listen and take views into account, but are not always willing to implement the public's choices. We encountered another group of residents who were also less than satisfied customers. One elderly woman recounted a story of years of low-level abuse, culminating in her being threatened with a gun. As a result she wrote a letter to Tony Blair (then Prime Minister), leading to a visit from the local Chief Superintendent. Afterwards she was reasonably satisfied in that the people were prosecuted, but the residents' group as a whole were still not happy because before she complained "to the top", nothing had happened.

> "That was the only reason he came out. He wasn't even aware that Margaret was getting abuse, because his officers hadn't passed on a *minor* thing like that. Nothing was got done until she went to the top." (Resident A, Oldtown police focus group 2)

Resident B, a former shop owner, had a similar experience of inaction, and unsatisfactory responses from senior officers:

> "I'm going back a few years but what happened to me made me realise that you cannot depend on the police. I still have that reservation ... I had a store and one Sunday, I wasn't in and they said the people were taking the beer, and there is nothing you can do. So a police lady came, 'I'll go and see them on Tuesday'. They were in a flat round the corner, they could have got the evidence. So I closed that shop that day, because I felt I could not rely on the police. They took away all my support. I wrote to the Chief Constable, and he said – I'm sorry. SORRY! So, me, I do not depend on the police, that might sound awful, but it is only because of the experiences I've had that made me like that."

Another resident in the group was more positive:

> (Resident C): "See my experience of the police is different to these two because of what I am and what I do. When I

phone the police they come out and do pretty much what I ask them to do."

(Int): "Because?"

(Resident C): "Because I am the chairman of the residents' committee and I talk to their bosses as well, but would I get the same treatment if I was just a member of the public?"

This more powerful sense of engagement was also visible in a Newtown focus group involving a local parish councillor and two women who had set up a residents' group. During the focus group the parish councillor explained how the action had changed relations between police and the local community:

(Parish councillor): "What they [the two women] did was set up a residents' action group because they perceived nothing was being done for the estate. They started to get people to tell them what was being done, but more important than that they started to get people to listen to them and do what it was they wanted …"

(Int): "So how do you tell people what you are doing?

(PC): "A newsletter, public meetings, this building is a one-stop shop that people can come in. It is not that the council doesn't do anything, it is that there are some pretty awful residents who just don't want to learn."

(Resident A): "When we first opened the complaints on the first day and there were loads, it was bin bags and cars. But there has been loads of money gone into it, but you've got one or two recalcitrant families and the kids, that won't learn and just don't want to learn …"

(PC): "The parish council, in response to the residents, put aside a budget of £4,000 a year, which goes straight to the police inspector and that pays for overtime when we've got a problem that we think needs addressing."

(Resident A): "We get more than that back."

(PC): "Yes, we get more than that back, because we put something in."

(Resident A): "Yes, it is because we put something in. We work with them you know."

(PC): "Yes we work with them and if we say there is a brothel starting in X,Y and Z then they will target it .... We don't always see them, but they are there."

(Int): "So I suppose what you are saying is that you have quite a lot of power and control over the police. I mean in the nicest possible way."

(PC): (talking over others) "We have input, not control."

(Resident A): "It is not control, it is cooperation."

(Resident A): "We bought them mountain bikes because at one point area beat officers had to patrol from the [main road] to the motorway on foot, that is a hell of a long way." (Newtown police focus group 2)

So the "pretty awful families who just won't learn" are presumably, as in the Oldtown estate, identified and ASBOed or moved on to another estate. The power to claim the right to demand what you want from the police and the system more generally can be viewed as, variously, people power, community action, democracy in action or alternatively the abuse of social and cultural capital, given the inequalities that are apparent in these discussions. The power of money to "buy" police services in the last example may be seen in terms of 'choice', resulting in the residents having a version of control and authority over the police. But is this the version of a customer culture or 'having a real say' that the Blairs had in mind?

The People's Police?

The residents quoted above see themselves as exercising power through combinations of voice, money, cooperation and consultation. But how do the police see such changes towards user-led services?

(Officer): "Um, again it depends what they're asking. I mean just recently we were contacted quite a lot by some members of the ... Parish Council for my beat area, saying there was constant problems outside one of the local shop centres on and off. And in the end they plagued us so much about it, cos we went up there did mobile patrols, you know, um, what do you call it – when you pass by and have a look, didn't see anything notable. In the end we went up there with a mobile CCTV and watched for two evenings and gave them a complete report back on it. Um, as it was we didn't see anything. So I guess we can be pressured into responding to people if they're demanding something that they see as a problem. We try to do what it is they want as best we can, yeah.

(Int): Those initiatives. I mean what's the feeling among – for want of a better word, front-line police officers about the kind of things that come down from above with regard to customer focus, consumerism, what kind of –"

(Officer): "Well, we usually say to each other 'well yeah it's a nice idea but it's never gonna happen'. The people that are at the top are under a lot of pressure to, um, meet the government's targets and they have to fight for their part of the budget to get to finance their own force at the top. So they are – they want to pull the right strings and say the right things to, um, get the money that they need to function well. And, um, as I say, our Chief Constable at the moment is all for area beat officers and yes, he says, the focus is gonna move more towards community policing cos that's the way forward! Well, the people that have been in service for 20-odd years in my department say 'yeah and it won't make any difference to us cos nothing's gonna change at this end of the chain'." (Newtown police front-line staff 05)

Perhaps the police and their publics are involved in the co-production of a form of policing that keeps both sides satisfied: the public feeling they have wrested some control from a powerful or indifferent organisation, and the police feeling they have given some ground, perhaps just enough to be able to tick any relevant boxes on their individual and corporate appraisal forms. However, the place of 'community' in these changes is problematic, in part because it is unclear as to who is represented in these processes (Hughes, 2007; Mooney and Neal, 2009). The groups we talked to were clear that without communal mobilisation, and political involvement in some cases, "nothing would happen" regarding the troublesome families and individuals who were the motivating force behind their mobilisation. Nevertheless, the community-based, neighbourhood-focused model suffers from another difficulty: local communities may contain many different identities, tensions and antagonisms.

Questions of power and agency are central to these processes of reform and resistance – but they do not align in any simple or singular way. We have tried to show how both senior and front-line police officers have tried to resist, translate or bend government initiatives, although not necessarily in the same direction. Senior officers may have organisational concerns and objectives that differ from those of the occupational culture of 'ordinary coppers'. Equally, both the organisational and occupational dynamics may be resisted, subverted or exploited by groups within the public to shape the priorities and practices of local policing. The Flanagan report (2008) indicates how such local involvement is a focus of both desire and anxiety in police reform. The participation of citizens, customers and communities is avidly sought, but such localism is always vulnerable to tipping over into 'politics' or the pursuit of specific 'interests' (see Clarke, 2009). The encounters between governmental, organisational, occupational and public imperatives are thus profoundly unstable. Governments, police forces and front-line officers each make claims to know 'what the public wants' – and to be able to see how best it should be served. These sit uncomfortably alongside claims by parts of the public to know what they want – and their demands to be served differently.

One senior officer addressed the challenge of the police having to engage more fully with communities while holding onto the power and authority that came from their professional knowledge. This officer moved beyond the 'we know best' approach of conventional professional paternalism, to reflect on how debate between police and public might be shaped. He offered a more 'dialogic' view of relations between public and police in which he sought to

> "open up the debate about looking at the public as consumers and having an understanding of what their needs are, and then in return for that being able to move from what I describe as an ill-informed community to an informed community, then you can actually have some logic to your debate with them." (Newtown police senior officer 02)

This is a powerful expression of the ambiguities of power and agency that we have been tracing. Is it a cynical engagement – such that informed communities know what the police want them to know (and can thus approve police priorities)? Is it a view of the political and social dangers of ill-informed communities making regressive demands of the police? Or is it a view of dialogic engagement as a learning process that reshapes both the police and the public?

Part Four
Conclusion

TWELVE

'Subversion' and the analysis of public policy

David Prior and Marian Barnes

This book is concerned with understanding variations in the processes and outcomes of public policies and services. The focus is, however, a very specific one. Although 'large' questions of policy change and development are touched on in a number of the chapters, the primary focus of the book is not on the macro level, that is, on the attempted and actual transformations in the purposes and outcomes of the various services of the welfare state or in the relationships between the state and its citizens. We are not examining, for example, the capacity of public services to achieve social justice or well-being among citizens, nor to ensure safety and social cohesion within diverse communities. Rather, the principal concern addressed here is what happens to produce particular kinds of outcomes at the micro level of interactions between different individuals and groups in a variety of policy development and service delivery contexts. The focus has been on the way in which both officials charged with the delivery of policy and those citizens and service users who are the focus of policy intervention negotiate and shape processes of decision making, and thus what constitutes policy in practice. We have sought to open up the question of 'what happens' when these interactions occur through the idea of 'subversion'.

It is important to emphasise that the analyses and case studies in this book do not identify subversion as a heroic, revolutionary or necessarily even conscious act deliberately intended to undermine a particular purpose or outcome of public policy. Rather, from careful analysis of what actually goes on when front-line workers interact with service users, when citizens and officials come together in spaces designed for policy deliberation, when policy makers attempt to characterise particular groups within the population for policy action – the contributors identify subversion as an almost inevitable aspect of the policy process. However, this does not mean that subversion is always devoid of normative content. In many of the analyses presented here, it is identified as capable of generating consequences that, in normative terms, may be viewed as either progressive or regressive. Thus, there are examples of action by both workers and service users that is intended to promote elements of social justice by countering the perceived stigmatising, victimising, exploitative or undemocratic effects of official policies. But there are also examples of subversion where action is defensive or reactionary, intended to preserve or enhance the vested interests of certain groups of professionals or citizens or to prevent the development and realisation of 'progressive' forms of practice. We draw attention to these normative issues in the discussion that follows.

We want to conclude by considering what it is that is particular about the concept of subversion and to what extent the concept is helpful in developing our understanding of how public policies and services can produce unexpected outcomes. First, however, it will be helpful to summarise what each chapter says about what subversion means, what it is that is being subverted, in what locations and contexts subversion takes place (is this usually in spaces where there is interaction between different actors – both provider/user and worker/worker?) and what processes/mechanisms are implicated. We also consider how our authors have sought to understand/explain these questions using different conceptual, theoretical and analytical frameworks. Our aim here is not to attempt synthesis but to identify the kinds of insights that can be generated using different perspectives.

Dimensions of policy subversion

In this section we address questions of the meanings, objects, locations and processes of subversion through four dimensions that feature in the preceding chapters: citizenship; policy and service objectives; professional and citizen identities; and modes of governance.

Constructing/contesting citizenship

While the title of this book highlights 'citizens' as key actors in processes of subversion, 'citizen' is an ambiguous identity and 'citizenship' is both a contested status and a negotiated form of practice. This is, in part, because the categories 'citizen' and 'citizenship' acquire much of their meaning from the particular sets of rights and responsibilities that they invoke and these rights and responsibilities are subject to revocation, change or expansion. Marshall's (1950) classic discussion distinguished between the legal, political and social rights and responsibilities of citizenship and showed how each of these was the focus of historical struggles. Not only do these dimensions of citizenship remain sites of contestation, as the chapters by Flint and by Newman and Clarke illustrate, but new sites of struggle are being added, for example in relation to the environment and to non-human life (Roche, 1992). Moreover, what are perceived as appropriate practices of citizenship – what it is that a citizen should actually do – are not defined solely by the formal, legal status of citizenship. Thus it is arguable that in contemporary Britain, as in many other countries, the formal responsibilities of the citizen (obeying the laws, paying taxes, etc) result in a very thin practice of citizenship, in contrast to the exhortations of successive recent governments that people should be 'active citizens' engaged in fulfilling a range of moral, social and political obligations to each other, to their community, to their country, to future generations and to the world. The definition of these practices of active responsible citizenship, what their limits are, what rewards and sanctions might accompany them and what rights they bring with them, are the subject of repeated claim and counterclaim and are continually in the process of negotiation and resettlement. It is no coincidence that three of the chapters (by Flint, Prior, and Parr and Nixon) focus on aspects of policy and practice in response to 'antisocial behaviour' (ASB). The rapid rise of ASB as a priority concern for the UK government can be read as a particular attempt to establish a notion of citizenship as embodying certain ways of behaving and, more specifically, to provide a strategy for regulating and disciplining those whose behaviour threatens to subvert that notion.

In the struggle over citizenship, then, government attempts to act as citizenship's gatekeeper – to control which social groups can legitimately claim the title 'citizens' and what kinds of behaviour are to be associated with 'good citizenship'. As John Flint argues in Chapter Six, one way in which government does this is by creating a discourse of an imaginary national community, united by a consensus on the acceptable values and behaviours of community life, and then identifying as potentially subversive (and therefore justifying specific corrective policies and interventions) those groups or individuals who do not or cannot conform to the ideal. Here, use of the label 'subversive' becomes a technology of government, enabling the setting of particular goals or conditions which certain groups must achieve if they are to be rewarded with the benefits of citizenship, or the construction of legal barriers which ensure the continued exclusion from citizenship of other groups. In the story of the campaign for voting rights for non-naturalised residents of Cambridge, Massachusetts, recounted by Janet Newman and John Clarke in Chapter Five, the threat of national legal and cultural traditions being subverted is deployed as a means of preventing the campaign from succeeding; thus, again, certain groups are prevented from obtaining at least one of the rights of citizenship because of their alleged potential for subversion.

Newman and Clarke's other story, of the struggle over public service reductions in Norway, illustrates the ambiguity of the identity of 'citizen' even among those who have full citizenship status. Here, people involved in opposition to the service reductions moved between different identities (resident; service user; consumer; volunteer; activist; citizen) as they engaged in different forms of relationship with politicians and service managers and used different types of technique to exert power. While the consequence of their actions might have been the 'subversion' of a policy decision, such actions originated in a multiplicity of identities and capacities; they could not, as Newman and Clarke argue, be categorised simply as 'subversive citizens'. This raises a more general issue about the way in which analysis of policies and services often uses categories that identify and group people. Citizenship, as a status and a practice, tends to be located in the public sphere, denoting something about the relationship between the individual and institutions of public life such as the state, community or neighbourhood. Yet many public service users, who may be discursively constructed by policies as citizens with public rights and responsibilities, are primarily concerned with 'private' matters – their own health and social care requirements, the well-being of their children and other family members, their relationships with their neighbours. It is in this confused space of slippage between the public and the private that multiple and hyphenated identities arise (for example, see Clarke et al, 2007b on the 'citizen-consumer') and ambiguous identities become apparent. This can have consequences for the way in which public officials interact with service users: are the families engaged in formally recognised decision-making processes about their children's futures, discussed by Kate Morris and Gale Burford in Chapter Eight, to be understood as 'citizens'? If so, does this suggest a qualitatively different way of approaching their rights and capacities to determine the support they need rather than a construction of them *either* as 'problem families' *or* as 'service users'? And, since officials are citizens too (Marian Barnes, Chapter Three), in what circumstances do they draw on their identities as citizens rather than, or in addition to those of public service workers?

Subverting policy discourse and service objectives

A number of the chapters identify and analyse 'subversion' in the process of delivery of public services, in which the key actors are service users and/or front-line service providers: social workers and other project staff and the families with whom they are engaged; police officers and people making use of policing services; antisocial behaviour officers and both perpetrators and victims of ASB; youth justice workers, magistrates and young offenders. Here, the focus is on relationships of power and agency at the point of service delivery, identifying the possibilities for subversion of policies and practices in the moment when service users and providers encounter one another.

David Prior, in Chapter Two, explores these subversive possibilities through the notion of 'counter-agency': action by service delivery staff, or by users, or by a combination of the two that produces outcomes other than those intended by or prescribed in policies. He suggests that counter-agency can take different forms, such as revision – when staff adopt alternative strategies and technologies that modify or 'bend' official policy and practice towards outcomes more suited to their assessment of the situation they are confronted with; resistance – when it is citizens/users (with or without the support of service staff) who develop alternative ways of acting to address a need or resolve a problem rather than the action defined in official policy; and refusal – when citizens/users flatly reject not just formal service strategies, but the official view that they should be engaged in addressing a particular problem or need at all.

While not necessarily sharing the same conceptual language, other contributors to this collection identify and describe similar kinds of 'subversive' responses at the point of service delivery. Sadie Parr and Judy Nixon's analysis of Family Intervention Projects (Chapter Seven) showed how some project workers were consciously engaged in critically revising the official discourse that defined 'antisocial families'. They sought ways of talking about and interacting with the families involved in the projects that avoided both the condemnatory description of certain forms of behaviour as simply 'antisocial' and the ascription of individual blame and personal responsibility. Instead, they gave recognition, in both discourse and practice, to features of the families' lives that were suppressed in official policy statements: poverty, poor housing, mental illness, and so on.

The accounts by Louise Westmarland and John Clarke (Chapter Eleven) and Kate Morris and Gale Burford (Chapter Eight) each reveal complex dynamics of agency and counter-agency in relationships between service providers and users. In Westmarland and Clarke's study of the impact of consumerist strategies in policing, there is evidence of front-line police officers undermining the objectives of the consumer-oriented 'modernisation' of the police service by reasserting the necessity of police–public relationships being based on the authority of the former, as against the empowerment of the latter through mechanisms of 'choice'. However, the police are also faced with having to implement strategies that prioritise public 'voice' through the development of forms of consultation and shared decision making. The study suggests that some more senior officers may be appearing to support such developments in order to meet performance criteria against which they are judged, while adapting or bending the process of engaging with the public in order to preserve their internally defined operational priorities. Particular sections of an increasingly differentiated and demanding public, meanwhile, attempt to redefine the purpose of new channels of communication with the police and use them to establish policing priorities that meet their own particular purposes. Initiatives to promote public service reforms based in increasing consumer 'choice' and 'voice' are revealed as sites of multidimensional relationships of power and agency.

Morris and Burford demonstrate similar struggles to revise and resist both the discursive and practical elements of a new policy development in their account of family group decision making (FGDM) initiatives in social work. The introduction of such initiatives, recognised and supported in government policy, in which decisions over a child's welfare are entrusted to family members, is itself subversive of established professional values and practices, implying a shift of power and authority away from social workers. In a context of heightened 'fear of failure' in relation to the protection and well-being of children, workers are resistant to the efforts of certain of their colleagues, the 'hero practitioners', to promote more democratic forms of decision making in which family members are positioned as key participants; such resistance is manifest both in a reluctance to engage in the new initiatives and, when they do engage, through attempts to introduce mechanisms of professional control to the FGDM process – steering, shaping and setting parameters to the family group discussions. However, Morris and Burford cite evidence which suggests that these attempts at reasserting professional control are themselves resisted by families, who find ways of modifying the procedures in order to give prominence to the values and outcomes that are important to them. The chapter highlights the complexity of such situations, in which 'subversion' cannot be understood in terms of linear dynamics of 'cause and effect' or simple oppositional relationships between workers and citizens.

Nathan Hughes' analysis in Chapter Ten of the local implementation of the national model of Bail Support Schemes tells a similarly complex story, although here the processes of revision and resistance are all between different groups of official stakeholders. Support scheme workers revise national policy aims, viewed as contradictory, in order to more adequately respond to their perception of local needs; their strategy, however, along with the technologies of assessment they adapt from the national model, is in turn resisted by magistrates, who draw on long-established discourses that value intuition and experience-based judgement over 'objective' criteria and systematic procedures. This results in further revision by the workers in order to enhance and secure the scheme's credibility in the eyes of the magistrates. Official policy and practice is thereby doubly subverted: by professional workers exploiting its inherent contradictions and ambiguities in the context of local implementation, and by magistrates taking advantage of their dominance in power relationships among local stakeholders.

All of these studies emphasise the point we made in the introduction to this chapter, that, in normative terms, 'subversion' cannot be viewed simply as either progressive or regressive in its consequences. Each of the examples indicates the significance of conflicts between sets of values and struggles involving relations of power between groups of participants in the service delivery process; and the results of such struggles will be widely variant when judged against any concept of social justice.

Subverting professional and citizen/user identities

We have seen how the notion of 'the citizen' is itself a matter of discursive construction and contestation. Our interest in the particular dynamics of subversion in the context of public policy making and service delivery led us to invite contributions that addressed the role of public officials as subversive actors as well as considering the resistances and refusals of service users and citizens. We argued in the introduction that Lipsky's analysis of the resistances adopted by those he referred to as 'street level bureaucrats' needed to be revisited in a context in which they are exhorted to work 'in partnership' with users and citizens in delivering policy, and to understand service users as 'co-producers' of the services through which policy objectives are to be achieved. While considerable attention has been given to the potential and limitation of new spaces and practices intended to 'empower' users and citizens, there has been rather less attention to the way in which public sector workers negotiate their roles and identities in the context of the 'new' practices of governance and service delivery.

A number of chapters have shown how front-line workers can adopt both defensive and progressive strategies towards public policy, appealing to their perceived role in ensuring needs are met and, perhaps, social justice is delivered, and/or to their roles as guardians or protectors of both individuals and communities. The chapters by Marian Barnes and Shona Hunter suggest that it is important also to adopt a rather more personal perspective on these negotiations and strategies. Their analyses suggest that we need at least to be asking whether it remains appropriate to reserve the term 'citizen' to considerations of those who are the intended recipients or beneficiaries of public policies, and whether we can understand the stances taken by public officials solely by reference to their official identities: as social worker, police officer, doctor or other public role.

Barnes provides an analysis of the contested and creative spaces of public participation to identify ways in which both officials and citizens use these spaces to work out 'who they are' and determine what they want from such engagement. Such negotiations may be influenced but not determined by identities and interests shared between citizens and officials: it is not inevitable that an official from a minority ethnic community will 'take the side' of community representatives, nor is it inevitable that 'community representatives' will prioritise lay over expert knowledge. She argues that participative spaces contain both conservative and subversive potentials, but that it is too simplistic to understand these as spaces of co-option or subversion. They are spaces in which the binary separations between official and citizen and between expert and lay knowledge can themselves be subverted through processes of deliberation and contestation which may, or may not, lead to a new framing of policy issues and problems.

Shona Hunter, in Chapter Nine, adopts a different theoretical and methodological approach to an analysis of health professionals as emotional actors. She takes a detailed look at a male Indian GP and the way in which he negotiates his identity as a (particular type of) doctor, a Sikh, a family member and as a man in relation to official constructions of 'old' and 'new' professionals within primary care. Hunter's purpose here is to demonstrate the emotional dimension to the resistances that health and social care professionals grapple with in their working lives. She argues that within any process of change in public services there will be some aspects that workers identify with and others they resist. Hence they will experience personal conflict in their response to change. In those cases where change ('modernisation', the 'new') is seen as deliberately designed to challenge 'old' or obstructive professional identities, and where such identities are also conflated with raced or gendered identities (in this case 'older Asian male GPs') the professional and personal processes of adaptation or resistance may be particularly problematic.

Subverting modes of governance

The final dimension of subversion that we want to highlight from the contributions to this book is the style and practice of governance itself. In our introduction we identified transformations in governance, in particular the move to governmental arrangements based in the participation of a wide range of institutional actors connected through networks of coordination, as a key factor in generating new kinds of conditions in which officials and citizens, service providers and users, engage with policies and services. Clearly, concepts such as 'participation' and 'network' identify only the most general features of the new governance; in practice, in different policy and service settings, particular forms of governance involve specific sets of participants in specific types of relationships in order to meet distinctive policy objectives. In a number of the chapters in this collection we can see that it is a particular mode of governance that is liable to be subverted through the actions of participants.

This is most explicitly the focus of Helen Sullivan's Chapter Four on the emergence of the neighbourhood as a distinct level of governance. While the policy rationale in favour of neighbourhood-level governance is couched in terms of greater efficiency and effectiveness in delivering public services and closer involvement of local citizens in achieving policy goals, Sullivan argues that such outcomes are frequently unrealised because of tensions between different visions of what neighbourhood governance should mean in practice and competing understandings of the roles of key neighbourhood players: local politicians, professionals involved in public service management and delivery, and the local public. It is in the 'dissonance' created by the interaction between these different conceptions of neighbourhood governance that the conditions exist in which local actors, whether politicians, professionals or public, can revise or subvert the goals of neighbourhood policy; the result may be the assertion of alternative, or the restoration of pre-existing, relations of power at the local level. Similarly, the chapter by Barnes indicates that the creation of new forms of participatory governance does not inevitably lead to specific outcomes that either challenge or support existing policy and ways of doing things. While there is a continual search for models of 'good practice' that can be seen to deliver specific outcomes through public participation, Barnes' analysis suggests that we should rather view these as spaces with uncertain and sometimes contradictory potentials.

Other chapters identify the conditions for and possibilities of resistance to attempts to impose specific modes of governance. In the stories analysed by Newman and Clarke, struggles over the values, forms and practices of governance seem as significant as the conflicts over the meaning of citizenship – in the one case (US), over the fundamental question of 'how to govern' in the context of a highly differentiated and diverse population, and in the other (Norway), over an approach to citizen and user participation in the governance of an individual public service. Westmarland and Clarke also discuss governance issues in a particular service context, examining the ambiguities and conflicts that characterise the introduction of new governance arrangements and practices into policing. Similarly to Sullivan's analysis, these conditions of uncertainty generate new relationships of power and agency as front-line police officers resist a consumerist model of governance and sections of the local public take advantage of opportunities to increase their influence.

Explaining subversion

Subversion exposes the ambiguities, contradictions and tensions that exist within public policies. It highlights the difficulties, perhaps impossibilities, of attempts to define or classify both the objects of policy and those who implement or deliver them by reference to singular characteristics. Thus subversion demonstrates the inadequacy of a rational, linear approach to understanding policy making and implementation, and the poverty of positivist approaches to policy analysis. Rather, the possibility of subversion and the variety of forms it can take, revealed in the contributions to this book, draws attention to the significance of intricate and multiple relations of power, of the competing values and motivations of different actors, and of the complex relationships between institutional context and individual agency in analysing and explaining the outcomes of public services.

While the authors in this collection draw on a number of distinct theoretical and conceptual approaches, they can all be situated in an analytical orientation that seeks 'an understanding of the discursive struggle to create and control systems of shared social meanings' (Fischer, 2003a: 13). In other words, what is going on in the various accounts of policy implementation and service delivery in Chapters Two to Eleven are attempts to analyse public service policies and practices as sites for the construction and reconstruction of agreed purposes, objectives, outcomes and consequences through continuing interaction between officials and citizens, practitioners and users, policy makers and providers.

Within this notion of the policy process as an ongoing struggle to establish settled meanings, the particular dynamic of 'subversion' can be viewed from a number of perspectives. Thus it can, for instance, be identified as a deliberate strategy of government, as in Sullivan's account of the promotion of neighbourhood-level initiatives by central government as a means of destabilising and subverting the power of local politicians and professionals. It can also be seen as part of the 'natural' evolution of policy, when government is able to appropriate and incorporate what appeared to be the 'subversive' outcomes or processes of challenge and resistance into a new iteration of the original policy – there are suggestions of this in the chapters by Prior and Parr and Nixon.

It is possible to see subversion as a consequence of the development of 'network governance', as a potential outcome of the more complex processes of negotiation, joint planning and coordination between different kinds of agencies and stakeholders required in the delivery of policy and service goals though partnership-type relationships. Such negotiation is shaped by differential power relations between 'partners', which vary from setting to setting, and by new alliances that can form between partners. Such alliances may be temporary and partial and may draw on different identifications that undermine an easy separation between service providers and service users (as Barnes elaborates in her chapter). But this can result not only in the development of new kinds of services or policy initiatives and the creation of new governmental spaces, bringing in yet more potential contributors to the process of policy negotiation; but also in different ways of framing the problems and issues that are the focus of policy and practice. Both can lead to the modification or recasting of the original policy intentions of government. In a sense, this is an updated recognition of the significance of the 'politics of implementation' in shaping policy outcomes identified many years ago by Pressman and Wildavsky (1973), but in a quite different institutional context in which the 'creative tension' of complex inter-agency relationships, and assumptions that users and citizens should be partners and co-producers rather than passive objects of policy, are viewed as key drivers of effective and efficient policy outcomes.

Governance based in relationships between separate and formally independent agents linked together in a network is an aspect of the 'governing at a distance' identified by Miller and Rose (1990), following Latour and others, as a core characteristic of how modern governments operate to achieve their goals in the absence of the possibility of direct and coercive control from the centre. Here, 'the local' becomes of great significance in demarcating a particular space of governmental relationships, which is by definition distinct from the space of national or central government, but through which a range of diverse agents are engaged in processes of negotiation, translation and construction in attempting to align national policies and associated resources with the particular needs and potentialities of their local context. The uncertain and unstable qualities of these local processes of negotiation and translation, involving temporary alliances between 'partners' who bring varying degrees of power to the table, and provisional but vulnerable agreements on joint objectives and the means of achieving them, are – in different ways – identified in a number of the chapters in this book as providing the conditions in which the subversion of policy goals occurs. Thus, Prior refers to the necessarily contingent nature of the 'configurations of power' through which, in particular local and service-specific contexts, policies and practices are constructed that can generate outcomes other than those intended in national policy discourse; Newman and Clarke use the notion of 'assemblages' to capture the multiple, contested and fragile mobilisations and alignments of relationships of power and authority, including acts of subversion, that characterise particular local struggles; Sullivan sees the distinctiveness of the local in the aims and methods of 'small' government initiatives focused on the neighbourhood, contrasting and often conflicting with the aims and methods of 'big' (national) government – a contrast which generates the possibility for different positionings and relationships of power between key sets of local actors, and the undermining of the original intentions of neighbourhood policy. The contextual specificities of 'the local' are also significant in some of the case study chapters in Part Three: in the translation of national policy discourse on problem families into less stigmatising local practices by the Family Intervention Project workers studied by Parr and Nixon; in Hughes' account of how, within a discursive framework supplied by national policy on bail support, local actors arrive at an accommodation of different values and perspectives that enables working relationships to be sustained; and in Westmarland and Clarke's study of the ways in which a national policy imperative to 'modernise' relationships between the police and the public is modified and subverted by different groups of stakeholders responding to particular local contexts.

The particular shift in state–citizen relationships embodied in multiple practices of participatory governance and co-production in service delivery provides a distinctive context and opportunity for subversion. There is a long-established body of research and analysis that explores the strategies that may be adopted by citizens and service users who seek to challenge, influence, frustrate or possibly undermine official policy (see, for example, Taylor, 2003; Wainwright, 2003). Community organisations, social movements, user groups and sometimes NGOs have all sought to subvert the power of the state to define policy and to determine what are appropriate responses to policy problems. The development of 'invited spaces' for such groups to take part as collaborators in policy development and service delivery has been seen by some as deliberately neutralising the oppositional stances adopted by such groups and as part of a broader process of creating responsible citizens who are actively and collaboratively engaged in delivering shared objectives in pursuit of the 'common good'. The issue of whether such invited spaces embody the potential for subversion requires detailed empirical study. As Barnes' contribution demonstrates, the theorisation of the development of alternative framings of issues and an associated oppositional consciousness in the context of social movement organisation shares similarities with ideas of discursive deliberation more familiar to the analysis of participative governance. Deliberative forums can generate contention as well as consensus – and not always along anticipated axes. Sullivan's suggestion that neighbourhood governance, at least in part, is designed to fracture established relationships between professionals and service users offers a similar insight into the potential for new forms of participatory governance to create spaces which not only enable the performance of existing roles and rules, but also generate new ones. Similarly, Morris and Burford demonstrate the way in which families resist the importation of professionally determined rules of procedure into spaces that are intended to enable alternative ways of resolving problems.

A final approach to explaining subversion in public services links back to the point, noted by both Flint and Sullivan in their chapters, that it is government itself that sometimes seeks to subvert established policies, practices and identities. One way in which government can create the conditions for subversion is by encouraging and enabling 'officials' to adopt deliberately challenging and innovatory roles in order to transform how public services are delivered. This approach was endorsed by Tony Blair in his vision of public service practitioners as 'entrepreneurs':

> I want power devolved down in public services, so that the creative energy of our teachers, doctors, nurses, police officers is incentivised and released. They are the social entrepreneurs of the future. (Blair, 2001)

This suggests a move towards the 'empowerment' of public service workers, in parallel to the initiatives in public participation intended to 'empower' citizens and service users. To the extent that public services staff can take on the qualities of 'transformational leaders' (Newman, 2005), there is the potential for them to subvert entrenched models of practice and professional values and identities. This potential was clearly recognised and pursued by the 'hero practitioners' in Morris and Burford's account of attempts to legitimise family members as responsible decision makers in the context of childcare interventions and who, perhaps predictably, encountered resistance from social workers whose professional identities were bound up with a model of practice that denied the capacity of family members to take appropriate decisions about a child's well-being. However, the construction of practitioners as 'transformational leaders', challenging the established professional identities and practices of colleagues, can generate ambivalence and conflict at the personal level, involving the emotional engagement of the practitioner and perhaps subverting their own sense of self. This is demonstrated in Hunter's study of the attempts by a male Asian GP to reconcile his professional role as a modernising manager and agent of change within primary care, involving him in confronting issues of race and gender as obstacles to change, with aspects of his personal biography, cultural values and individual identity. There is also a particular way of understanding what is expected from the entrepreneurial officials encouraged by New Labour. As we discussed in the introduction to this collection, Blair's other characterisation of public service workers is as conservatives seeking to resist the 'new' in terms both of service delivery and of public governance. We have argued that subversion can have both defensive and innovative potential, but we should not assume that professional values and identities are inevitably conservative and frustrating of the pursuit of public service values.

Conclusion: stories of agency, resistance and subversion

We have highlighted the different dimensions of subversion and sought to explain the various processes that operate to create the revisions, resistances and refusals that both citizens and officials generate in policy and service delivery processes. Many of our contributors approach these issues through specific theoretical or analytical frameworks. We have not, however, attempted in this conclusion to construct an overarching theory of subversion, and are doubtful about the feasibility, or indeed the value, of this. Rather, we wish to conclude by reflecting on the different ways in which our contributors have offered accounts, narratives or stories of subversion in practice. For example, in Newman and Clarke's chapter these accounts are explicitly presented as narratives told to the authors by another researcher. Hunter constructs an account from one-to-one interviews about one doctor's attempts to make sense of his personal and professional identity in the context of official discourses of modernisation in primary care. Barnes offers accounts of the way in which both citizens and officials work out 'who they are' and how they can make use of the possibilities created by participatory forums to secure their objectives for change. And Parr and Nixon recount the way in which local practitioners reconceptualised governmental discourses regarding the 'problems' posed by 'antisocial' families in order to construct support services that could respond to what they perceived to be the most pressing problems experienced by such families.

In these and other accounts we can see evidence of competing potentials within processes of governance and service delivery. Policies do not arrive 'fixed', uncontested or uncontestable. Rather, they contain multiple and often contrasting ways of conceptualising or framing policy issues and problems; 'new' practices do not sweep away the 'old' ways of doing things, and both the workers and the citizen-users bring to these practices beliefs, values and identities through which they seek to make sense of the possibilities available to them. In spite of attempts to banish the 'anecdotal' from evidence-based policy making, narratives retain their power to enable people to make sense not only of their own lives and circumstances (such as the families, in Morris and Burford's account, who construct moral stories about their concern for their children and how they can express this), but also of collective goals and how these might be realised (as is evident in Hughes' account of the way in which youth justice workers perform different roles in the process of seeking acceptance for their way of constructing the purpose of a Bail Support Scheme).

Narrative is not only a process through which participants construct a story that makes sense to them of what public policies are for and how they should be delivered, it is also an analytic resource. The narrative focus enables the analyst to understand the context in which policy and service delivery take place, the significance of actors' intentions and motivations, and the ways in which interactions and negotiations develop and construct particular consequences from these particular forms of social encounter (see Fischer, 2003a). Narratives encompass not only meanings but also values. Public officials are not only social workers, or health service managers, or police officers; they are also raced and gendered citizens who hold commitments to specific sets of values, and whose biographies will often encompass their own experiences of interaction with public services. Analysis that simply examines the 'roles' of public officials and citizens is inadequate to an understanding of the way in which policy becomes subverted. The accounts collected together here demonstrate the necessity of analyses that enable an understanding of the conscious and unconscious agency of both officials and citizens in the process of interpreting, deliberating, accepting or rejecting policy objectives (Mayo et al, 2007). They demonstrate that neither purely cognitive schema nor sophisticated analytical frameworks will do in determining an explanation for the policy failure that we have here conceptualised as subversion.

The studies discussed by our contributors show how both officials and citizens are actively engaged in a process of working out what is 'the right thing to do' in particular contexts, drawing on both professional and personal identities and values, personal and professional identifications and experiences, and assessing the possibilities and limitations of the institutional context in which they are operating. They are both subject to the impact of institutional rules and norms and actively engaged in determining how and indeed whether they should be applied in specific contexts. They operate within, but also reflect on and rework, policy discourses and regimes of practice. They are, inevitably, faced with the challenge of resolving the contingencies that characterise situations of public service development and delivery. It is this process of 'working out' that we mean by agency and which is illustrated by the stories told in this book; an agency that is influenced but not determined by both local and broader structures and which often has the consequence of subverting official intentions regarding policy and its implementation.

References

ACPO (Association of Chief Police Officers) – Centrex (2006) *Practice advice on professionalising the business of neighbourhood policing*, Wyboston: National Centre for Policing Excellence (Centrex).

Adams, P. and Nelson, K.E. (eds) (1995) *Reinventing human services: Community- and family-centered practice*, New York: Aldine de Gruyter.

Alexander, C. (2002) 'Beyond black: re-thinking the colour/culture divide', *Ethnic and Racial Studies*, vol 25, pp 552–71.

Alexander, C. (2004) 'Imagining the Asian gang: ethnicity, masculinity and youth after "the riots"', *Critical Social Policy*, vol 24, pp 526–49.

Allen, A. (1998) 'What are ethnic minorities looking for?', in T. Modood and T. Acland (eds) *Race and higher education: Experiences, challenges and policy implications*, London: Policy Studies Institute.

Allen, J. (2003) *Lost geographies of power*, Oxford: Blackwell.

Allen, J. and Cochrane, A. (2007) 'Beyond the territorial fix: regional assemblages, politics and power', *Regional Studies*, vol 41, no 9, pp 1161–75.

Anderson, B. (1983) *Imagined communities: Reflections on the origin and spread of nationalism*, London: Verso.

Andersson, E., Tritter, J. and Wilson, R. (eds) (2008) *Healthy democracy: The future involvement in health and social care*, NHS Centre for Involvement, www.nhscentreforinvolvement.nhs.uk

Atkinson, R. (2003) 'Addressing urban social exclusion through community involvement in urban regeneration', in R. Imrie and M. Raco (eds) *Urban renaissance? New Labour, community and urban policy*, Bristol: The Policy Press, pp 101-20.

Atkinson, R. and Carmichael, L. (2007) 'Neighbourhood as a new focus for action in West European states', in I. Smith, E. Lepine and M. Taylor (eds) *Disadvantaged by where you live?*, Bristol: The Policy Press, pp 43–64.

Back, L., Keith, M., Khan, A., Shukra, K. and Solomos, J. (2002) 'The return of assimilationism: race, multiculturalism and New Labour', *Sociological Research Online*, vol 7, www.socresonline.org.uk/7/2/back. html

Baggott, R., Allsop, J. and Jones, K. (2005) *Speaking for patients and carers: Health consumers and the policy process*, Basingstoke: Palgrave.

Baker, K. (2005) 'Assessment in youth justice: professional discretion and the use of Asset', *Youth Justice*, vol 5, no 2, pp 106–22.

Ball, S. (2008) *The education debate: Policy and practice in the 21st century*, Bristol: The Policy Press.

Bang, H.P. and Sørenson, E. (1999) 'The everyday maker: A new challenge to democratic governance', *Administrative Theory and Praxis*, vol 21, no 3, pp 325–42.

Barnes, M. (2002) 'Bringing difference into deliberation. Disabled people, survivors and local governance', *Policy and Politics*, vol 30, no 3, pp 355–68.

Barnes, M. (2008) 'Passionate participation: emotional experiences and expressions in deliberative forums', *Critical Social Policy*, vol 28, no 4, pp 461–81.

Barnes, M. and Bowl, R. (2001) *Taking over the asylum: Empowerment and mental health*, Basingstoke: Palgrave.

Barnes, M. and Prior, D. (1995) 'Spoilt for choice? How consumerism can disempower service users', *Public Money and Management*, vol 15, no 3, pp 55-8.

Barnes, M. and Prior, D. (2000) *Private lives as public policy*, Birmingham: Venture Press.

Barnes, M., Matka, E. and Sullivan, H. (2003) 'Evidence, understanding and complexity: evaluation in non-linear systems', *Evaluation*, vol 9, no 3, pp 263–82.

Barnes, M., Bauld, L., Benzeval, M., Judge, K., Mackenzie, M. and Sullivan, H. (2005) *Health Action Zones: Partnerships for health equity*, London: Routledge.

Barnes, M., Newman, J. and Sullivan, H. (2006) 'Discursive arenas: deliberation and the constitution of identity in public participation at a local level', *Social Movement Studies*, vol 5, no 3, pp 193–207.

Barnes, M., Newman, J. and Sullivan, H. (2007) *Power, participation and political renewal: Case studies in public participation*, Bristol: The Policy Press.

Barnes, M., Skelcher, C., Beirens, H., Dalziel, R., Jeffares, S. and Wilson, L. (2008) *Designing citizen-centred governance*, York: Joseph Rowntree Foundation.

Barton, A. (2008) 'New Labour's management and audit and "What works" approach to controlling the "untrustworthy" professions', *Public Policy and Administration*, vol 23, no 3, pp 263-77.

Beckett, K. and Herbert, S. (2007) 'Dealing with disorder: social control and the post-industrial city', *Theoretical Criminology*, vol 12, no 1, pp 5–30.

Beresford, P. (2006) 'The White Paper and prospects for social care: a personal view', *Journal of Integrated Care*, vol 14, no 3, pp 1–6.

Bevir, M. (2007) 'The construction of governance', in M. Bevir and F. Trentmann (eds) *Governance, consumers and citizens: Agency and resistance in contemporary politics*, Basingstoke: Palgrave Macmillan, pp 25–48.

Bevir, M. and Trentmann, F. (2007) 'Introduction: consumption and citizenship in the new governance', in M. Bevir and F. Trentmann (eds) *Governance, consumers and citizens: Agency and resistance in contemporary politics*, Basingstoke: Palgrave Macmillan, pp 1–22.

Blackwell, T. and Seabrook, J. (1993) *The revolt against change: Towards a conserving radicalism*, New York: Vintage Books.

Blair, T. (2001) Speech to public sector workers at the British Library, London, 16 October.

Blair, T. (2005) 'Improving parenting', Speech, Meridian Community Centre, Watford, 2 September.

Blears, H. (2005a) 'Rehabilitation for neighbours from hell', Home Office press release, 14 February.

Blears, H. (2005b) 'New measures will tackle the causes of ASB', Home Office press release, 29 June.

Blom Cooper, L. (1997) *The Birmingham Six and other cases*, London: Gerald Duckworth and Co.

Boudens, C. (2005) 'The story of work: a narrative analysis of workplace emotion', *Organization Studies*, vol 26, pp 1285–306.

Bradford, M. and Robson, B. (1995) 'An evaluation of urban policy', in R. Hambleton and H. Thomas (eds) *Urban policy evaluation: Challenge and change*, London: Paul Chapman, pp 37-54.

Braithwaite, J. (2002) *Restorative justice and responsive regulation*, Oxford: Oxford University Press.

Braithwaite, J. (2004) 'Families and the republic', *Journal of Sociology and Social Welfare*, vol 31, no 1, pp 199–215.

Brown, L. (2003) 'Mainstream or margin? The current use of family group conferences in child welfare practice in the UK', *Child & Family Social Work*, vol 8, no 4, pp 331–40.

Brown, L. (2007) 'The adoption and implementation of a service innovation in a social work setting – A case study of family group conferencing in the UK', *Social Policy and Society*, vol 6, no 3, pp 321–32.

Brown, L.M. and Gilligan, C. (1992) *Meeting at the crossroads: Women's psychology and girls' development*, New York: Ballantine Books.

Burford, G., Morris, K. and Nixon, P. (2007) 'Family decision making international survey' (unpublished).

Burford, G., Connolly, M., Morris, K., and Pennell, J. (forthcoming) *Family involvement strategies: An international review of the evidence*, Englewood, CO: American Humane Association.

Burleigh, M. (2005) *Earthly powers: Religion and politics in Europe from the Enlightenment to the Great War*, London: Harper Perennial.

Burnett, R. and Appleton, C. (2004) *Joined-up youth justice:Tackling youth crime in partnership*, Lyme Regis: Russell House Publishing.

Burney, E. (2005) *Making people behave:Anti-social behaviour politics and policies*, Cullompton:Willan Publishers.

Burns, D., Hambleton, R. and Hoggett, P. (1994) *The politics of decentralisation*, London: Macmillan.

Butler, J. (1993) *Bodies that matter: On the discursive constitution of 'sex'*, NewYork: Routledge.

Callon, M. (1986) 'Some elements of a sociology of translation: domestication of the scallops and the fishermen of Saint Brieuc Bay', in J. Law (ed) *Power, action and belief: A new sociology of knowledge?*, London: Routledge.

Cameron,A. (2007) 'Geographies of welfare and exclusion: reconstituting the "public"', *Progress in Human Geography*, vol 3, no 4, pp 519–26.

Campbell, J. and Oliver, M. (1996) *Disability politics*, London: Routledge.

Casey, L. (2007) 'Innovative new help to tackle "neighbours" from hell', Home Office press release, 11 April.

Castello, G., Lavalle,A.G. and Houtzager, P.P. (2007) 'Civil organisations and political representation in Brazil's participatory institutions', in A. Cornwall andV. Schattan Coelho (eds) *Spaces for change*, London: Zed Books, pp 114-30.

CATDWR (Center for Activity Theory and Developmental Work Research) (2008) *About the Center*, www.edu.helsinki.fi/activity, accessed 9 December 2008.

Center for the Study of Social Policy and Center for Community Partnerships in Child Welfare (2002) *Bringing families to the table: A comparative guide to family meetings in child welfare*, Washington, DC: CSSP/CCPCW.

Chanfrault-Duchet, M.-F. (2004) 'In quest of teacher's professional identity: the life story as a methodological tool', in P. Chamberlayne, J. Bornat and U. Apitzsch (eds) *Biographical methods and professional practice:An international perspective*, Bristol:The Policy Press, pp 265-83.

Church, K. (1996) 'Beyond "bad manners": the power relations of "consumer participation" in Ontario's community mental health system', *Canadian Journal of Community Mental Health*, vol 15, no 2, pp 27–44.

Clarke, J. (2004) *Changing welfare changing states: New directions in social policy*, London: Sage.

Clarke, J. (2005) 'New Labour's citizens: activated, empowered, responsibilized, abandoned?', *Critical Social Policy*, vol 25, no 4, pp 447–63.

Clarke, J. (2009) 'The people's police? Citizens, consumers and communities', in R. Simmons, M. Powell and I. Greener (eds) *The consumer in public services*, Bristol: The Policy Press, pp 157-77.

Clarke, J. (forthcoming) 'Talking citizenship? Governmental and vernacular discourses', *Anthropologie et Sociétés*.

Clarke, J. and Newman, J. (1997) *The managerial state: Power, politics and ideology in the remaking of social welfare*, London: Sage.

Clarke, J. and Newman, J. (2008) 'Elusive publics: knowledge, power and public service reform', in S. Gewirtz, P. Mahony, I. Hextall and A. Cribb (eds) *Changing teacher professionalism*, London: Routledge, pp 43-53.

Clarke, J., Newman, J., and Westmarland, L. (2007a) 'Creating citizen-consumers? Public service reform and (un)willing selves', in S. Maasen and B. Sutter (eds) *On willing selves: Neoliberal politics vis-à-vis the neuroscientific challenge*, Basingstoke: Palgrave, pp 124-43.

Clarke, J., Newman, J., Smith, N., Vidler, L.E. and Westmarland, L. (2007b) *Creating citizen-consumers: Changing publics and changing public services*, London: Sage.

Clegg, S. (1999) 'Professional education, reflective practice and feminism', *International Journal of Inclusive Education*, vol 3, pp 167–79.

Clement, M. (2007) 'Bristol: civilising the inner city', *Race and Class*, vol 48, no 4, pp 97–114.

Cockburn, C. (1977) *The local state, management of cities and people*, London: Pluto Press.

Coleman, R. (2004) *Reclaiming the streets: Surveillance, social control and the city*, Cullompton: Willan Publishing.

Coll, K. (2004) 'Necesidades y problemas: immigrant Latina vernaculars of belonging, coalition and citizenship in San Francisco, California', *Latino Studies*, vol 2, no 2, pp 186–209.

Coll, K. (2005) '"Yo no estoy perdida": immigrant women (re)locating citizenship', in B. Epps, K. Valens and B. Gonzalez (eds) *Passing lines: Sexuality and immigration*, Cambridge, MA: Harvard University Press, pp 389–410.

Coll, K. (forthcoming) 'Citizenship acts and immigrant voting rights in the US', in C. Neveu (ed) *Questions de Citoyenneté/Questioning Citizenship*, Paris: Maison des Sciences de l'Homme.

Connolly, M. (2007) 'Practice frameworks: conceptual maps to guide interventions in child welfare', *British Journal of Social Work*, vol 37, no 5, pp 825–37.

Contandriopoulos, D., Denis, J.L. and Langley, A. (2004) 'Defining the "public", in a public healthcare system', *Human Relations*, vol 57, no 12, pp 1573–96.

Cornwall, A. (2004) 'New democratic spaces? The politics and dynamics of institutionalised participation', in A. Cornwall and V. Coelho (eds), *New democratic spaces?* Institute of Development Studies Bulletin, vol 35, no 2, pp 1–10.

Cornwall, A. and Coelho, V.S.P. (2004) *New democratic spaces*, Institute of Development Studies Bulletin, vol 35, no 2.

Cornwall, A. and Coelho, V.S.P. (2007) *Spaces for change? The politics of citizen participation in the new democratic arenas*, London: Zed Books.

Cowan, D. and Hunter, C. (2007) *Governing the ungovernable: Private sector landlords and anti-social behaviour*, Paper presented to ESRC Seminar 'Governing Anti-Social Behaviour Through Housing', Sheffield: Sheffield Hallam Univeristy, November.

Crawford, A. (2003) '"Contractual governance" of deviant behaviour', *Journal of Law and Society*, vol 30, no 4, pp 479–505.

Crewe, B. (2007) 'Power, adaptation and resistance in a late-modern men's prison', *British Journal of Criminology*, vol 47, no 2, pp 256–75.

Crossley, N. (2002) *Making sense of social movements*, Buckingham: Open University Press.

Cruikshank, B. (1999) *The will to empower: Democratic citizens and other subjects*, Ithaca, NY: Cornell University Press.

Crumbley, J. (2007) 'Impacting institutions and policies through family group decision making', Keynote address to the American Humane Association International Conference Washington, DC, June.

Curry, G. (2007) 'Football spectatorship in mid-to-late Victorian Sheffield', *Soccer and Society*, vol 8, no 2–3, pp 185–204.

Dahl, R. and Tufte, E. (1973) *Size and democracy*, Stanford, CA: Stanford University Press.

Dale, J. (1987) 'Decentralization: grounding the debate', *Community Development Journal*, vol 22, no 2, pp 152–8.

Daniels, H. (2004) 'Activity theory, discourse and Bernstein', *Educational Review*, vol 56, no 2, pp 121–32.

D'Arcus, B. (2004) 'Dissent, public space and the politics of citizenship: riots and the "outside agitator"', *Space and Polity*, vol 8, no 3, pp 355–70.

Davies, C. (1995) *Gender and the professional predicament in nursing*, Buckingham: Open University Press.

DCA (Department for Constitutional Affairs) (2006) *Review of care proceedings in England and Wales*, London: DCA.

DCLG (Department of Communities and Local Government) (2007) 'An action plan for community empowerment: building on success', www.communities.gov.uk/publications/communities/communityempowermentactionplan, accessed 1 July 2008.

DCLG (2008a) *Communities in control: Real people, real power*, London: DCLG.

DCLG (2008b) *Communicating important information to new local residents*, London: DCLG.

DCLG and I&DeA (2008) *Integrating new migrants: Communicating important information*, London: DCLG.

DCSF (Department for Children, Schools and Families) (2007) *Care matters: Transforming the lives of children and young people in care*, London: DCSF.

DCSF (2008) *Youth task force action plan*, Nottingham: DCSF.

Deacon, A. (2004) 'Justifying conditionality: the case of anti-social tenants', *Housing Studies*, vol 19, no 6, pp 911–26.

Dean, M. (1999) *Governmentality: Power and rule in modern society*, London: Sage.

Della Porta, D. and Diani, M. (1999) *Social movements: An introduction*, Oxford: Blackwell.

Department for Work and Pensions (2008) *No one written off: Reforming welfare to reward responsibility*, London: Department for Work and Pensions.

DH (Department of Health) (1998a) *Our healthier nation: A contract for health*, London: The Stationery Office.

DH (1998b) *Partnership in action (new opportunities for joint working between health and social services), a discussion document*, London: DH,

DH (1999) *Working together to safeguard children*, London: The Stationery Office.

DH (2003) *Equalities and diversity: Strategy and delivery plan to support the NHS*, London: DH.

DH (2004) *Choosing health: Making healthy choices easier*, London: The Stationery Office.

DH (2008) *Making the difference: The Pacesetters beginners' guide to service improvement for equality and diversity in the NHS*, London: The Stationery Office.

Dillane, J., Hill, M., Bannister, J. and Scott, S. (2001) *Evaluation of the Dundee Families Project – Final report*, Edinburgh: Scottish Executive.

Dodd, V. (2005) 'The top policeman branded too PC rides storm of criticism', *The Guardian*, 2 July (http://guardian.co.uk/UK/2005/jul/02/race.ukcrime, accessed 19 April 2009).

Doolan, M. (2005) *Family group conferences and social work: Some observations about the United Kingdom and New Zealand*, www.frg.org.uk.

Doolan, M. (2007) 'Duty calls: the response of law, policy and practice to participation right in child welfare systems', *Protecting Children*, vol 22, no 1, pp 10–18, American Humane Association.

Dwyer, P. (2004) *Understanding social citizenship*, Bristol: The Policy Press.

Edwards, A., Apostolov, A., Dooher, I. and Popova, A. (2008) 'Working with extended schools to prevent social exclusion', in K. Morris (ed) *Social work and multi agency working: Making a difference*, Bristol: The Policy Press, pp 47-66.

Edwards, M., Tinworth, K., Burford, G., and Pennell, J. (2007) *Family team meeting (FTM) process, outcome, and impact evaluation phase II report*, Englewood, CO: American Humane Association.

Elias, N. (2000) *The civilizing process*, Oxford: Blackwell.

Engeström, Y. (1987) *Learning by expanding*, Helsinki: Orienta-konsultit.

Engeström, Y., Miettinen, R. and Punamaki, R.L. (1999) (eds) *Perspectives on activity theory*, New York: Cambridge University Press.

Esmail, A. and Dewart, P. (1998) 'Failure of Asian students in clinical examinations: The Manchester experience', in T. Modood and T. Acland (eds) *Race and higher education: Experiences, challenges and policy implications*, London: Policy Studies Institute.

Evans, T. and Harris, J. (2004) 'Street-level bureaucracy, social work and the (exaggerated) death of discretion', *British Journal of Social Work*, vol 34, no 6, pp 871–95.

Ewick, P. and Silby, S. (2003) 'Narrating social structure: stories of resistance to legal authority', *American Journal of Sociology*, vol 108, no 6, pp 1328–72.

Fawcett, B., Featherstone, F. and Goddard, J. (2004) *Contemporary child care policy and practice*, Basingstoke: Palgrave Macmillan.

Featherstone, B. (2006) 'Rethinking family support in the current policy context', *British Journal of Social Work*, vol 36, no 1, pp 5–19.

Feely, M. and Simon, J. (1992) 'The new penology', *Criminology*, vol 39, no 4, pp 449-74.

Field, S. (2007) 'Practice cultures and the "new" youth justice in (England and) Wales', *British Journal of Criminology*, vol 47, no 2, pp 311–30.

Fischer, F. (2000) *Citizens, experts and the environment: The politics of local knowledge*, Durham, NC, and London: Duke University Press.

Fischer, F. (2003a) *Reframing public policy: Discursive politics and deliberative practices*, Oxford: Oxford University Press.

Fischer, F. (2003b) 'Beyond empiricism: policy analysis as deliberative practice', in M. Hajer and H. Wagenaar (eds) *Deliberative policy analysis: Understanding governance in the network society*, Cambridge: Cambridge University Press, pp 209–27.

Flanagan, R. (2008) *The final report of the independent review of policing, conducted by Sir Ronnie Flanagan*, London: Home Office.

Flint, C. (2008) Speech to Fabian Society, London, 5 February.

Flint, J. (2002) 'Social housing agencies and the governance of anti-social behaviour', *Housing Studies*, vol 17, pp 619–37.

Flint, J. (2003) 'Housing and etho-politics: constructing identities of active consumption and responsible community', *Economy and Society*, vol 32, no 3, pp 611–29.

Flint, J. (ed) (2006) *Housing, urban governance and anti-social behaviour*, Bristol: The Policy Press.

Flint, J. (2009, forthcoming) 'Cultures, ghettos and camps: sites of exception and antagonism in the city', *Housing Studies*, vol 24.

Flint, J., Jones, A. and Parr, S. (2008) *An evaluation of the sanction of housing benefit: Scoping report*, London: Department for Work and Pensions.

Forbes, J. and Sashidharan, S.P. (1997) 'User involvement in services – incorporation or challenge?', *British Journal of Social Work*, vol 27, pp 481–98.

Fording, R.C., Soss, J. and Schram, S.F. (2007) 'Devolution, discretion and the effect of local political values on TANF sanctioning', *Social Service Review*, vol 81, no 3, pp 285–316.

Foster, M., Harris, J., Jackson, K., Morgan, H. and Glendinning, C. (2006) 'Personalised social care for adults with disabilities: a problematic concept for frontline practice', *Health & Social Care in the Community*, vol 14, no 2, pp 125–35.

Foucault, M. (1978) *History of sexuality, vol 1: The will to knowledge*, New York: Pantheon.

Foucault, M. (1980) *Power/knowledge: Selected interviews and other writings 1972–1977* (edited by C. Gordon), New York, Pantheon.

Foucault, M. (1991) 'Governmentality', in G. Burchell, C. Gordon and P. Miller (eds) *The Foucault effect: Studies in governmentality*, Hemel Hempstead: Harvester Wheatsheaf, pp 87–104.

Franklin, J. (2000) 'What's wrong with New Labour politics?', *Feminist Review*, vol 66, pp 138–42.

Fraser, N. (1997) *Justice interruptus: Critical reflections on the 'postsocialist' condition*, New York, Routledge.

Garrett, P.M. (2007) '"Sinbin" solutions: the "pioneer" projects for "problem families" and the forgetfulness of social policy research', *Critical Social Policy*, vol 27, no 2, pp 203–30.

Gaventa, J. (2004) 'Towards participatory local governance: assessing the transformative possibilities', in S. Hickey and G. Mohan (eds) *Participation: From tyranny to transformation*, London: Zed Books.

Gillies, V. (2005) 'Meeting parents' needs? Discourses of "support" and "inclusion", in family policy', *Critical Social Policy*, vol 25, no 1, pp 70–90.

Gilligan, C., Brown, L.M. and Rogers, A.G. (1990a) 'Psyche embedded: a place for the body, relationships, and culture in personality theory', in A.I. Rabin, R. Zucker, R. Emmons and S. Frank (eds) *Studying persons and lives*, New York: Springer.

Gilligan, C., Lyons, N.P. and Hanmer, T.J. (eds) (1990b) *Making connections: The relational worlds of adolescent girls at Emma Willard School*, Cambridge, MA: Harvard University Press.

Gilmour, D. (2007) *The ruling caste: Imperial lives in the Victorian Raj*, London: Pimlico.

Gil-Robles, A. (2005) 'Report of the Commissioner for Human Rights, on his visit to the United Kingdom 4th–12th November 2004', www.statewatch.org

Goldsmith, P. (2008) *Citizenship: Our common bond – Lord Goldsmith QC citizenship review*, London: Ministry of Justice.

Gordon, W., Cuddy, P. and Black, J. (1999) *Introduction to youth justice*, Winchester: Waterside Press.

Greener, I. (2009) *Healthcare in the UK: Understanding continuity and change*, Bristol: The Policy Press.

Griffin, C. (2007) 'Protest practice and (tree) cultures of conflict: understanding the spaces of "tree maiming", in eighteenth- and early nineteenth-century England', *Transactions of the British Institute of Geographers*, vol 33, no 1, pp 91–108.

Grimshaw, R. (2004) 'Whose justice? Principal drivers of criminal justice policy, their implications for stakeholders, and some foundations for critical policy departures', Paper presented at British Criminology Conference, Portsmouth, July, www.britsoccrim.org/volume7/005.pdf

Gutmann, A. and Thompson, D. (1996) *Democracy and disagreement*, Cambridge, MA: Belknap Press.

Hajer, M. (2003) 'A frame in the fields: policymaking and the reinvention of politics', in M.A. Hajer and H. Wagenaar (eds) *Deliberative policy analysis: Understanding governance in the network society*, Cambridge: Cambridge University Press, pp 88–110.

Hall, S., Critcher, C., Jefferson, T., Clarke, J. and Roberts, B. (1978) *Policing the crisis: Mugging, the state and law 'n' order*, London: Macmillan.

Hearn, J. (1992) *Men in the public eye: The construction and deconstruction of public men and public patriarchies*, London: Routledge.

Helms, G., Atkinson, R. and Macleod, G. (2007) 'Securing the city: urban renaissance, policing and social regulation', *European Urban and Regional Studies*, vol 14, no 4, pp 267–76.

Heward, T. (1994) 'Retailing the police: corporate identity and the Met', in R. Keat, N. Whiteley and N. Abercrombie (eds) *The authority of the consumer*, London: Routledge, pp 240-52.

Hewitt, M. (2000) *Welfare and human nature: The human subject in twentieth century social politics*, Basingstoke: Macmillan.

Hillyard, P. (1993) *Suspect community: People's experience of the prevention of terrorism acts in Britain*, London: Pluto Press.

Hirschman, A. (1970) *Exit, voice and loyalty*, Cambridge, MA: Harvard University Press.

Hirst, P. (1994) *Associative democracy: New forms of economic and social governance*, Cambridge: Polity Press.

HM Government (2008) *Youth crime action plan*, London: Home Office.

Hodge, M. (2007) 'A message to my fellow immigrants', *Observer*, 20 May.

Hodge, S. (2005) 'Participation, discourse and power: a case study in service user involvement', *Critical Social Policy*, vol 25, no 2, pp 164–79.

Holland, S., O'Neill, S., Scourfield, J., and Pithouse, A. (2004) *Outcomes in family group conferences for children on the brink of care: A study of child and family participation: Final report*, Cardiff: Cardiff University, School of Social Sciences.

Holland, S., Scourfield, J., O'Neill, S. and Pithouse, A. (2005) 'Democratising the family and the state? The case of family group conferences in child welfare', *Journal of Social Policy*, vol 34, pp 59–77.

Hollway, W. and Jefferson, T. (2000) *Doing qualitative research differently: Free association, narrative and the interview method*, London: Sage.

Holt, A. (2008) 'Room for resistance? Parenting Orders, disciplinary powers and the production of the "bad parent"', in P. Squires (ed) *ASBO nation: The criminalisation of nuisance*, Bristol: The Policy Press, pp 203–22.

Home Affairs Select Committee (2005) *Select Committee on Home Affairs Fifth Report: Anti-social behaviour*, London: House of Commons.

Home Office (2003) *Respect and responsibility – taking a stand against anti-social behaviour*, London: The Stationery Office.

Home Office (2004) *Confident communities in a secure Britain: The Home Office Strategic Plan 2004–08*, Cm 6287, London: Home Office.

Home Office Border and Immigration Agency (2008a) *The path to citizenship: Next steps in reforming the immigration system*, London: Home Office.

Home Office Border and Immigration Agency (2008b) *Introducing compulsory identity cards for foreign nationals*, London: Home Office.

Hopton, J. (1999) 'Militarism, masculinism and managerialisation in the British public sector', *Journal of Gender Studies*, vol 8, pp 71–82.

Hughes, G. (2007) *The politics of crime and community*, London: Palgrave Macmillan.

Hunter, C. and Nixon, J. (2001) 'Taking the blame and losing the home: women and anti-social behaviour', *Journal of Social Welfare and Family Law*, vol 23, no 4, pp 395–410.

Hunter, S. (2003) 'A critical analysis of approaches to the concept of social identity in social policy', *Journal of Social Work Practice*, vol 23, pp 322–44.

Hunter, S. (2005a) *Negotiating professional and social identities: 'Race', gender and profession in two primary care organisations*, Birmingham: University of Birmingham.

Hunter, S. (2005b) 'Negotiating professional and social voices in research principles and practice', *Journal of Social Work Practice*, vol 19, pp 145–58.

Hunter, S. (2009) 'Feminist psychosocial approaches to relationality, recognition and denial', in M.P. Ozbilgin (ed) *Theory and scholarship in equality, diversity, inclusion and work: A research companion*, Cheltenham: Edward Elgar, pp 179–92.

Hunter, S. and Swan, E. (2007) 'The politics of equality: professionals, states and activists', *Equal Opportunities International*, vol 26, pp 377–86.

Hupe, P. and Hill, M. (2007) 'Street-level bureaucracy and public accountability', *Public Administration*, vol 85, no 2, pp 279–99.

Innes, J.E. and Booher, D.E. (2003) 'Collaborative policy making: governance through dialogue', in M.A. Hajer and H. Wagenaar (eds) *Deliberative policy analysis: Understanding governance in the network society*, Cambridge: Cambridge University Press, pp 33–59.

Issitt, M. (2000) 'Critical professionals and reflective practice: the experience of women practitioners in health, welfare and education', in J. Batsleer and B. Humphries (eds) *Welfare, exclusion and political agency*, London: Routledge, pp 116–33.

Jackson, S. and Morris, K. (1999) 'Family group conferences: user empowerment or family self-reliance? – a development from Lupton', *British Journal of Social Work*, vol 29, no 4, pp 621–30.

Jacobs, K., Kemeny, J., and Manzi, T. (2003) 'Power, discursive space and institutional practices in the construction of housing problems', *Housing Studies*, vol 18, no 4, pp 429–46.

Jenks, C. (2003) *Transgression*, London: Routledge.

Jessop, B. (2002) *The future of the capitalist state*, Cambridge: Polity Press.

Jones, A., Pleace, N. and Quilgars, D. (2006) *Addressing antisocial behaviour: An independent evaluation of Shelter Inclusion Project*, London: Shelter.

Kennedy, P. and Kennedy, C.A. (2007) 'Control and resistance at the ward face: contesting the nursing labour process', in G. Mooney and A. Law (eds) *New Labour/hard labour? Restructuring and resistance in the welfare industry*, Bristol: The Policy Press, pp 93–116.

Kneale, J. (2001) 'The place of drink: temperance and the public, 1856–1914', *Social and Cultural Geography*, vol 2, no 1, pp 43–59.

Kooiman, J. (2003) *Governing as governance*, London: Sage.

Krumer-Nevo, M. (2003) 'From "a coalition of despair" to "a covenant of help" in social work with families in distress', *European Journal of Social Work*, vol 6, no 3, pp 273–82.

Kundani, A. (2007) 'Integrationism – the politics of anti-Muslim racism', *Race and Class*, vol 48, no 4, pp 24–44.

Latour, B. (2005) *Reassembling the social*, Oxford: Oxford University Press.

Lavalette, M. (2007) 'Social work today: a profession worth fighting for?', in G. Mooney and A. Law (eds) *New Labour/hard labour? Restructuring and resistance in the welfare industry*, Bristol: The Policy Press, pp 189-208.

Leadbetter, C. (2004) *Personalisation through participation: A new script for public services*, London: Demos.

Leadbetter, C., Bartlett, J. and Gallagher, N. (2008) *Making it personal*, London: Demos.

Leishman, F., Cope, S. and Starie, P. (1996) 'Reinventing and restructuring: towards a "new policing order"', in F. Leishman, B. Loveday and S.P. Savage (eds) *Core issues in policing*, London: Longman.

Leont'ev, A.N. (1981) 'The problem of activity in psychology', in J.V. Wertsch (ed), *The concept of activity in Soviet psychology*, Armonk, NY: M.E. Sharpe, pp 15–37.

Lepine, E. and Sullivan, H. (2007) 'More local than local government: the relationship between local government and the neighbourhood agenda', in I. Smith, E. Lepine and M. Taylor (eds) *Disadvantaged by where you live? Neighbourhood governance in contemporary urban policy*, Bristol: The Policy Press, pp 83–104.

Lepine, E., Smith, I., Sullivan, H. and Taylor, M. (2007) 'Introduction: of neighbourhoods and governance', in I. Smith, E. Lepine and M. Taylor (eds) *Disadvantaged by where you live? Neighbourhood governance in contemporary urban policy*, Bristol: The Policy Press, pp 1–20.

Levitas, R. (2005) *The inclusive society: Social exclusion and New Labour*, Basingstoke: Palgrave.

Li, T. (2007) 'Practices of assemblage and community forest management', *Economy and Society*, vol 36, no 2, pp 263–93.

Lipsky, M. (1980) *Street-level bureaucracy: Dilemmas of the individual in public services*, New York: Russell Sage Foundation.

Lowndes, V. and Sullivan, H. (2004) 'Local partnerships and public participation', *Local Government Studies*, vol 30, no 2, 51–73.

Lowndes, V. and Sullivan, H. (2008) 'How low can you go? Rationales and challenges for neighbourhood governance', *Public Administration*, vol 86, no 1, pp 53–74.

Malek, B. (1998) 'Not such tolerant times', in J. Rutherford (ed) *Young Britain: Politics, pleasures and predicaments*, London: Lawrence and Wishart.

Mansbridge, J. and Morris, A. (eds) (2001) *Oppositional consciousness: The subjective roots of social protest*, Chicago, IL: University of Chicago Press.

Marne, P. (2001) 'Whose public space was it anyway? Class, gender and ethnicity in the creation of the Sefton and Stanley Parks, Liverpool: 1858–1872', *Social and Cultural Geography*, vol 2, no 4, pp 421–43.

Marsh, P. and Crow, G. (1998) *Family group conferences in child welfare*, Oxford: Blackwell Science.

Marshall, T. (1950) *Citizenship and social class and other essays*, Cambridge: Cambridge University Press.

Marshall, T. (1977) *Class, citizenship and social development*, London: University of Chicago Press.

Martin, G.P. (2007) '"Ordinary people only": knowledge, representativeness and the publics of public participation in healthcare', *Sociology of Health and Illness*, vol 29, no 2, doi:10.1111/j.1467-9566.2007.01027.x.

Mason, P. and Prior, D. (2008) 'The Children's Fund and the prevention of crime and anti-social behaviour', *Criminology and Criminal Justice*, vol 8, no 3, pp 279–98.

Massey, D. (2004) 'Geographies of responsibility', *Geografiska Annaler*, vol 86 B, no 1, pp 5–18.

Matthews, R.N. (2001) *Mixed ethnicity, health and healthcare experiences*, Birmingham: University of Birmingham.

Matthews, R., Easton, H., Briggs, D. and Pease, K. (2007) *Assessing the use and impact of Anti-social Behaviour Orders*, Bristol: The Policy Press.

Maynard-Moody, S. and Musheno, M. (2003) *Cops, teachers, counsellors: Stories from the front line of public service*, Ann Arbor: University of Michigan Press.

Mayo, M., Hoggett, P. and Miller, C. (2007) 'Navigating the contradictions of public service modernization: the case of community engagement professionals', *Policy and Politics*, vol 35, no 4, pp 667–81.

McCafferty, T. and Mooney, G. (2007) 'Working "for" welfare in the grip of the "iron" Chancellor: modernisation and resistance in the Department of Work and Pensions', in G. Mooney and A. Law (eds) *New Labour/hard labour? Restructuring and resistance in the welfare industry*, Bristol: The Policy Press, pp 209–32.

McLaughlin, E., Muncie, J. and Hughes, G. (2001) 'The permanent revolution: New Labour, new public management and the modernization of criminal justice', *Criminal Justice*, vol 1, no 3, pp 301–18.

Melucci, A. (1996) *Challenging codes: Collective action in the information age*, Cambridge: Cambridge University Press.

Milburn, A. (2002) Speech by the Secretary of State for Health to the Annual Social Services Conference, 16 October 2002, Cardiff, www.dh.gov.uk/en/News/Speeches/Speecheslist/DH_4031620, accessed 10 August 2008.

Miller, P. and Rose, N. (1990) 'Governing economic life', *Economy and Society*, vol 19, no 1, pp 1–31.

Miller, P. and Rose, N. (2008) *Governing the present: Administering economic, social and personal life*, Cambridge: Polity Press.

Millie, A. (2007) 'Looking for anti-social behaviour', *Policy and Politics*, vol 35, no 4, pp 611–27.

Millie, A., Jacobson, J., McDonald, E. and Hough, M. (2005) *Anti-social behaviour strategies – finding a balance*, York: Joseph Rowntree Foundation and The Policy Press.

Min, P.G. and Kim, R. (2000) 'Formation of ethnic and racial identities: narratives by young Asian-American professionals,' *Ethnic and Racial Studies*, vol 23, pp 735–60.

MoJ (Ministry of Justice) (2008) *The public law outline*, London: MoJ.

Mooney, G. and Law, A. (eds) (2007) *New Labour/hard labour? Restructuring and resistance in the welfare industry*, Bristol: The Policy Press.

Mooney, G. and Neal, S. (eds) (2009) *Community: Crime, welfare and society*, Maidenhead and Milton Keynes: The Open University Press/ The Open University.

Moore, S. and Smith, R. (2001) *The pre-trial guide: Working with young people from arrest to trial*, London: The Children's Society.

Morgan, A. (2005) 'Governmentality versus choice in contemporary special education', *Critical Social Policy*, vol 25, no 3, pp 325–48.

Morgen, S. (2001) 'The agency of welfare workers: negotiating devolution, privatization, and the meaning of self-sufficiency', *American Anthropologist*, vol 103, pp 747–61.

Morris, K. (2007) *Camden FGC service: An evaluation of service use and outcomes*, London: London Borough of Camden.

Morris, K. and Burford, G. (2007) 'Working with children's existing networks – building better opportunities?', *Social Policy and Society*, vol 6, pp 209–17.

Morris, K. and Tunnard, J. (1996) *Family group conferences: Messages from UK practice and research*, Aldershot: Ashgate/FRG.

Morris, K., Hughes, N., Clarke, H., Mason, P., Burford, G., Galvani, S., Tew, J., Lewis, A. and Becker, S. (2008) *Whole family approaches: A literature review*, London: Social Exclusion Unit/Cabinet Office.

Muncie, J. (2008) 'The punitive turn in juvenile justice: cultures of control and rights compliance in Western Europe and the USA', *Youth Justice*, vol 8 no 2, pp 107–21.

Muncie, J. and Hughes, G. (2002) 'Modes of youth governance: political rationalities, criminalization and resistance', in J. Muncie, G. Hughes and E. McLaughlin (eds) *Youth justice: Critical readings*, London: Sage, pp 1–18.

Nacro (1998) *Bail support*, London: Nacro.

National Health Service Executive (2000) *The vital connection: An equalities framework for the NHS: working together for equality*, London: Department of Health.

NCSN (National Community Safety Network) (2005) *Anti-social behaviour, key issues and recommendations: A practitioner perspective*, Chester: NCSN.

Newman, J. (1995) 'Gender and cultural change', in C. Itzin and J. Newman (eds) *Gender, culture and organizational change: Putting theory into practice*, London: Routledge, pp 11–29.

Newman, J. (2001) *Modernising governance*, London: Sage.

Newman, J. (2005) 'Introduction', in J. Newman (ed), *Remaking governance, peoples, politics and the public sphere*, Bristol: The Policy Press, pp 1–16.

Newman, J. (2007) 'Governance as cultural practice: texts, talk and the struggle for meaning', in M. Bevir and F. Trentmann (eds) *Governance, consumers and citizens: Agency and resistance in contemporary politics*, Basingstoke: Palgrave Macmillan: pp 49–68.

Newman, J. and Clarke, J. (2009) *Publics, politics and power: Remaking the public in public services*, London: Sage.

Newton, K. (1982) 'Is small really so beautiful? Is big really so ugly? Size, effectiveness, and democracy in local government', *Political Studies*, vol 30, no 2, p 203.

NHS Magazine (2003) 'Positive outlook', www.nhsmagazine/ primarycare/archives/sept2003/feature3.asp

Nixon, J. and Hunter, C. (2009) 'Disciplining women and the governance of conduct', in A. Millie (ed) *Securing respect: Behavioural expectations and anti-social behaviour in the UK*, Bristol: The Policy Press, pp 119-38.

Nixon, J. and Parr, S. (2006) 'Anti-social behaviour: Voices from the front line', in J. Flint (ed) *Housing, urban governance and anti-social behaviour: Perspectives, policy and practice*, Bristol: The Policy Press, pp 79-98.

Nixon, J., Parr, S., and Sanderson, D. (2008) *The longer-term outcomes for families who have worked with intensive family support projects*, London: Department of Communities and Local Government.

Nixon, P., Burford, G., Quinn, A. with Edelbaum, J. (2005) *A survey of international practices, policy and research on family group conferencing and related practices*, www.americanhumane.org/site

Nixon, J., Hunter, C., Parr, S., Myers, S., Whittle, S. and Sanderson, D. (2006) *Anti-social behaviour intensive family support projects: An evaluation of six pioneering projects*, London: Office of the Deputy Prime Minister.

North Lanarkshire Council (2008) *Anti Social Task Force Support Service client book*, Coatbridge: North Lanarkshire Council.

ODPM (Office of the Deputy Prime Minister)/DfT (Department for Transport) (2006) *National evaluation of LSPs: Formative evaluation and action research programme, 2002–2005*, Warwick Business School/Liverpool John Moores/OPM/UWE, London: ODPM.

ODPM/HO (Home Office) (2005) *Citizen engagement and public services: Why neighbourhoods matter*, London: ODPM.

Olsen, R. and Clarke, H. (2003) *Parenting and disability: Disabled parents' experiences of raising children*, Bristol: The Policy Press.

O'Malley, P. (2004) *Risk, uncertainty and government*, London: Glasshouse Press.

Ong, A. (2006) *Neoliberalism as exception: Mutations in citizenship and sovereignty*, Durham, NC: Duke University Press.

Ong, A. and Collier, S.J. (2005) *Global assemblages*, Oxford: Blackwell.

Parr, S. and Nixon, J. (2008) 'Rationalising family intervention projects', in P. Squires (ed) *ASBO nation: The criminalisation of nuisance*, Bristol: The Policy Press, pp 161–78.

Peckham, S. (2000) 'Primary care groups: a new opportunity for collaboration and participation?', *Research Policy and Planning*, vol 18, www.elsc.org.uk/bases_floor/rpp/articles/0068563.htm

Phillips, D. (2006) 'Parallel lives? Challenging discourses of British Muslim self-segregation', *Environment and Planning D: Society and Space*, vol 24, no 1, pp 24–40.

Pickford, J. (ed) (2000) *Youth justice: Theory and practice*. London: Cavendish.

Popova, A. and Daniels, H. (2004) 'Employing the concept of the object in the discussion of the links between school pedagogies and individual working lives in pre- and post-Soviet Russia', *Educational Review*, vol 56, no 2, pp 193-205.

Pressman, J. and Wildavsky, A. (1973) *Implementation*, Berkeley: University of California Press.

Prince, M. (2001) 'How social is social policy? Fiscal and market discourse in North American welfare states', *Social Policy and Administration*, vol 35, no 1, pp 2–13.

Prior, D. (2007) *Continuities and discontinuities in governing anti-social behaviour*, Birmingham: University of Birmingham.

Prior, D. (2009) 'The "problem" of anti-social behaviour and the policy knowledge base: analysing the power/knowledge relationship', *Critical Social Policy*, vol 29, no 1, pp 5–23.

Prior, D., Farrow, K. and Paris, A. (2006a) 'Beyond ASBOs? Evaluating the outcomes of anti-social behaviour initiatives – early findings from a case study in one English city', *Local Government Studies*, vol 32, no 1, pp 3–17.

Prior, D., Farrow, K., Spalek, B. and Barnes, M. (2006b) 'Anti-social behaviour and civil renewal', in T. Brennan, P. John and G. Stoker (eds) *Re-energising citizenship: Strategies for civil renewal*, London: Palgrave Macmillan, pp 91-111.

Raco, M. (2003) 'Remaking place and securitising space: urban regeneration and the strategies, tactics and practices of policing in the UK', *Urban Studies*, vol 40, no 9, pp 1869–87.

Respect Task Force (2006) *Respect action plan*, London: Respect Task Force.

Rhodes, R.A.W. (ed) (2000) *Transforming British government, Vol 1: Changing institutions*, Basingstoke: Macmillan.

Roche, M. (1992) *Rethinking citizenship: Welfare, ideology and change in modern society*, Cambridge: Polity Press.

Rodgers, D. (2007) 'Subverting the spaces of invitation? Local politics and participatory budgeting in post crisis Buenos Aires', in A. Cornwall and V.S. Coelho (eds) *Spaces for change? The politics of participation in new democratic arenas*, London: Zed Books, pp 180-201.

Roggeband, C. and Verloo, M. (2007) 'Dutch women are liberated, migrant women are a problem: the evolution of policy frames on gender and migration in the Netherlands, 1995–2005', *Social Policy and Administration*, vol 41, no 3, pp 271–88.

Rose, N. (1996) 'The death of the social? Refiguring the territory of government', *Economy and Society*, vol 25, no 3, pp 327–56.

Rose, N. (1998) *Inventing ourselves: Psychology, power and personhood*, Cambridge: Cambridge University Press.

Rose, N. (1999) *Powers of freedom*, Cambridge: Cambridge University Press.

Ryburn, M. and Atherton, C. (1996) 'Family group conferences: partnership in practice,' *Adoption & Fostering*, vol 20, no 1, pp 16–23.

Sadler, J. (2008) 'Implementing the Youth "anti-social behaviour" agenda: policing the Ashton estate', *Youth Justice*, vol 8, no 1, pp 57–73.

Schram, S.F., Fording, R.C. and Soss, J. (2008) 'Neo-liberal poverty governance: race, place and the punitive turn in US welfare policy', *Cambridge Journal of Regions, Economy and Society*, vol 1, no 1, pp 17–36.

Seidman, S. (1998) *Contested knowledge: Social theory in the postmodern era*, Malden, MA: Blackwell.

SEU (Social Exclusion Unit) (1998) *Bringing Britain together – a strategy for neighbourhood renewal*, London: The Stationery Office.

SEU (2000) *Report of Policy Action Team 8: Anti-social behaviour*, London: Cabinet Office.

SEU Task Force (2007) *Reaching out: Think family*, London: Cabinet Office.

SEU Task Force (2008) *Think family: Improving the life chances of families at risk*, London: Cabinet Office.

Sharma, A. (2008) *Logics of empowerment*, Minneapolis, MN: University of Minnesota Press.

Sheffield Weekly Gazette (2008) 'Goths march for tolerance', *Sheffield Weekly Gazette*, 4 September, p. 10.

Skelcher, C., Mathur, N. and Smith, M. (2005) 'The public governance of collaborative spaces: discourse, design and democracy', *Public Administration*, vol 83, no 3, pp 573–96.

Skills for Health (2003) 'A health sector workforce market assessment 2003', www.skillsforhealth.org.uk/files/323-skills%20for%20health%20.QDX.pdf

Skogan, W.G. (2007) 'Asymmetry in the impact of encounters with police', *Policing and Society*, vol 16, no 2, pp 99–126.

Smith, I., Lepine, E. and Taylor, M. (eds) (2007) *Disadvantaged by where you live?* Bristol: The Policy Press.

Smith, J. (2008) Speech at the 'Anti-social behaviour: We're not having it' conference, London, 8 May.

Smith, R. (2003) *Youth justice: Ideas, policy, practice*, Cullompton: Willan Publishing.

Snow, D. and Bruford, R. (1992) 'Master frames and cycles of protest', in A. Morris and C. McClurg Mueller (eds) *Frontiers in social movement theory*, New Haven, CT: Yale University Press, pp 133–55.

Sparrow, A. (2008) 'Thugs have taken over the streets, says Cameron', *Guardian*, 18 January.

Squires, J. (2006) 'Good governance and good for business too? Equality and diversity in Britain', in S. Hellsten, A.M. Holli and K. Daskalova (eds) *Women's changing citizenship and political rights*, Basingstoke: Palgrave, pp 199–216.

Squires, P. (2006) 'New Labour and the politics of anti-social behaviour', *Critical Social Policy*, vol 26, no 1, pp 144–68.

Squires, P. and Stephen, D. (2005) *Rougher justice: Anti-social behaviour and young people*, Cullompton: Willan Publishing.

Stenson, K. (2002) 'Community safety in middle England – the local politics of crime control', in G. Hughes and A. Edwards (eds) *Crime control and community: The new politics of public safety*, Cullompton: Willan Publishing.

Stenson, K. (2005) 'Sovereignty, biopolitics and the local government of crime in Britain', *Theoretical Criminology*, vol 9, no 3, pp 265–87.

Sullivan, H. (2002) 'Modernisation, neighbourhood management and social inclusion', *Public Management Review*, vol 4, no 4, pp 505–28.

Sullivan, H. and Howard, J. (2005) *Below the LSP*, Issues paper, National Evaluation of LSPs, London: Office of the Deputy Prime Minister, www.odpm.gov.uk/index.asp?id=1162337

Sullivan, H. and Skelcher, C. (2002) *Working across boundaries: Partnerships in public services*, Basingstoke: Palgrave.

Sullivan, H., Newman, J., Barnes, M. and Knops, A. (2003) 'The role of institutions in facilitating and constraining dialogue in partnerships with communities', in C. Scott and W.E. Thurston (eds) *Collaboration in context*, Calgary: University of Calgary.

Sullivan, H., Root, A., Moran, D. and Smith, M. (2001) *Area committees and neighbourhood management*, London: LGIU.

Sundel, K., Vinnerljung, B. and Ryburn, M. (2001) 'Social workers' attitudes towards family group conferences in Sweden and the UK', *Child and Family Social Work*, vol 6, pp 327–36.

Tarrow, S. (1998) *Power in movement: Social movements and contentious politics*, Cambridge: Cambridge University Press.

Taylor, M. (2003) *Public policy in the community*, Basingstoke: Palgrave.

Thomas, S. and Goldman, M. (2001) *Guide to the national standards for bail supervision and support schemes*, Swansea: Bail Support Policy and Dissemination Unit, Nacro Cymru.

Thorne, J. and Stuart, H. (2008) *Islam on campus: A survey of UK student opinions*, London: Centre for Social Cohesion.

Tolman, C.T. (1999) 'Society versus context in individual development: Does theory make a difference?', in Y. Engestrom, R. Miettinen, and R.-L. Punamäki (eds) *Perspectives on activity theory*, New York: Cambridge University Press, pp 70–86.

Uitermark, J. (2005) "The genesis and evolution of urban policy: a confrontation of regulationist and governmentality approaches", *Political Geography*, vol 24, no 2, pp 137–63.

Vaughan, B. (2000) 'Punishment and conditional citizenship', *Punishment and Society*, vol 2, no 1, pp 23–39.

Virkkunen, J. and Kuutti, K. (2000) 'Understanding organizational learning by focusing on "activity systems"', *Accounting Management and Information Technologies*, vol 10, pp 291–319.

Wagenaar, H. and Cook, S.D.N. (2003) 'Understanding policy practices: action, dialectic and deliberation in policy analysis', in M.A. Hajer and H. Wagenaar (eds) *Deliberative policy analysis: Understanding governance in the network society*, Cambridge: Cambridge University Press: pp 139–71.

Wainwright, H. (2003) *Reclaim the state: Experiments in popular democracy*, London: Verso.

Walkerdine, V., Lucey, H. and Melody, J. (2001) *Growing up girl: Psychosocial explorations of gender and class*, Basingstoke: Palgrave.

Walters, A. and Woodward, R. (2008) 'Punishing "poor parents": "respect", "responsibility" and Parenting Orders in Scotland', *Youth Justice*, vol 7, no 1, pp 5–20.

Ward, L. (1993) 'Race equality and employment in the National Health Service', in W.I.U. Ahmad (ed) *Race and health in contemporary Britain*, Buckingham: Open University Press.

Warmington, P., Daniels, H., Edwards, A., Leadbetter, J., Martin, D., Brown, S. and Middleton, D. (2004) *Interagency collaboration: a review of the literature*, www.education.bham.ac.uk/research/proj/liw/default. htm

Websdale, N. (2001) *Policing the poor*, Boston, MA: Northeastern University Press.

Weigensberg, E.C., Barth, R.P. and Guo, S. (2009) 'Family group decision making: A propensity score analysis to evaluate child and family services at baseline and after 36-months', *Children and Youth Services Review*, vol 3, no 1, pp 383–90.

Welsh, C. (2008) 'The Mosquito: a repellent response', *Youth Justice*, vol 8, no 2, pp 122–33.

Welshman, J. (1999) 'The concept of the unemployable', *Economic History Review*, vol 59, no 3, pp 578–606.

Welshman, J. (2008) 'Recuperation and rehabilitation and the residential option: The Brentwood Centre for Mothers and Children', *Twentieth Century British History*, vol 19, no 4, pp 502–29.

Wengraf, T. (2001) *Qualitative research interviewing*, London: Sage.

Werbner, P. (1997a) 'Essentialising essentialism, essentialising silence: ambivalence and multiplicity in the constructions of racism and ethnicity', in P. Werbner and T. Modood (eds) *Debating cultural hybridity*, London: Zed Books, pp 226–54.

Werbner, P. (1997b) 'Introduction: the dialectics of cultural hybridity', in P. Werbner and T. Modood (eds) *Debating cultural hybridity*, London: Zed Books, pp 1–26.

Werbner, P. (2004) 'Theorising complex diasporas: purity and hybridity in the South Asian public sphere in Britain', *Journal of Ethnic and Migration Studies*, vol 30, pp 895–911.

West, L. (2001) *Doctors on the edge: General practitioners, health and learning in the inner-city*, London: Free Association Press.

Wilcox, R. (ed) (1991) *Family decision making: Family group conferences: practitioners' views*, Lower Hutt, New Zealand: Practitioner Publishing.

Williams, F. (2004) *Rethinking families*, London: Calouste Gulbenkian Foundation.

Wilson, A. (2007) 'The forced marriage debate and the British state', *Race and Class*, vol 49, no 1, pp 25–38.

Wintour, P. (2008) 'Labour: if you want a council house, find a job', *Guardian*, 5 February.

Yanow, D. (2003) 'Accessing local knowledge', in M.A. Hajer and H. Wagenaar (eds) *Deliberative policy analysis: Understanding governance in the network society*, Cambridge: Cambridge University Press: pp 228–46.

YJB (Youth Justice Board) (2001) *National standards for bail supervision and support schemes*, London: Youth Justice Board.

Young, M. (1993) *In the sticks: Cultural identity in a rural police force*, Oxford: Clarendon.

Young, I.M. (2000) *Inclusion and democracy*, Oxfoed: Oxford University Press.

Young, J. (2007) *The vertigo of late modernity*, London: Sage.

Zorbaugh, H.W. (1929) *The Gold Coast and the slum: A sociological study of Chicago's near North Side*, Chicago, IL: Chicago University Press.

Index